The History, Art And Palaeography Of The Manuscript Styled The Utrecht Psalter

Walter Gray De Birch

THE

HISTORY, ART AND PALÆOGRAPHY

OF THE MANUSCRIPT STYLED

THE UTRECHT PSALTER:

BY

WALTER DE GRAY BIRCH, F.R.S.L.,

*Senior Assistant of the Department of Manuscripts in the British Museum, Honorary
Librarian of the Royal Society of Literature, Honorary Secretary of the
British Archæological Association, etc.*

. . . . . "ut, quantum ad cognitionem pertinet rerum, etiam praeteritis saeculis
vixisse videamur."—QUINTILIAN, *Instit. Orator.*, xii. 4.

Multæ terricolis linguæ, cœlestibus una.

LONDON:

SAMUEL BAGSTER AND SONS,

15, PATERNOSTER ROW.

M.DCCC.LXXVI.

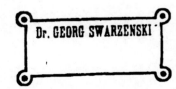

FA 1123.22 Bcopy

TO

THE RECTOR

AND PROFESSORS

OF THE UNIVERSITY OF UTRECHT,

THIS WORK UPON

THE·ANCIENT PSALTER,

PRESERVED IN THEIR LIBRARY,

IS

RESPECTFULLY DEDICATED.

PREFACE.

Λαμπάδια ἔχοντες διαδώσουσιν ἀλλήλοις; *Plat. Polit.* i.

IN putting before the rapidly increasing number of students of the rudiments of palæography this work upon the history and art of the celebrated Manuscript known as THE UTRECHT PSALTER, the author has throughout endeavoured to be plain and concise, as one writing to instruct in a general way the reader who is not learned in the deeper intricacies of the questions implicated, rather than to be hypercritical and captious about the too often conflicting opinions of others far better able to judge than himself upon minute evidence. He is not unaware that he has laid himself open to the criticism of the one school that claims an early date for the Manuscript, or the other that assigns a late date to the Manuscript, or perhaps of both, according as his views agree or disagree with theirs. This is naturally to be expected. No doubt much will be urged that this or that aspect of some part of the argument has been imperfectly treated; the reply is that the questions raised by the Manuscript do not so readily allow of exhaustion or solution within the limits here at command. The literary labours of nearly two years, carried on at every opportunity of leisure, will not have been wasted if they may haply result in bringing about some unity, or at least an important preponderance of skilled opinion, upon the date to be assigned to the writing and pictures of this unique relic of Archaic letters, this golden apple of an exacter archæology which has not always classed palæography as one of her most fruitful branches.

To the Society that has so thoughtfully reproduced the volume in permanent fac-simile the thanks of all literary men of England are due for preserving to their uses at least the faithful shadow of that treasure which it is a regret, and a national misfortune to them, to have lost, whilst to Utrecht and to Holland it is without doubt one of her most valued prizes. Nevertheless it cannot well be said that any one deplores that the Manuscript has fallen ' in pleasant places," where its importance is duly acknowledged, and its preservation carefully studied and maintained.

The thanks, too, of the Author are due to this Society for kindly permitting the use of their negative photograph for the illustration at p. 211, as also to the Trustees of the British Museum, for the liberal permission to reproduce by the autotype process the plate from the celebrated HARLEY PSALTER, given at p. 213; and to the Master and Fellows of Trinity College, Cambridge, for the corresponding illustration derived from the well known

Manuscript entitled the TRIPARTITE PSALTER of EADWINE, which will be found here at p. 214. In consequence of its great dimensions it has been found impossible to reproduce a whole page of the latter on this occasion. A few lines have therefore been omitted from the lower part of the leaf, in order to reduce the plate to a more convenient shape for folding.

The ornamental cover of this volume contains some excellent groups from the UTRECHT PSALTER specially prepared for the engraver by W. R. Cooper, Esq., F.R.A.S., Secretary of the Society of Biblical Archæology; and the Public, as well as the Author, are indebted to him for these details, viz.:— The figure of David seated in a temple, from the first picture in the MS., fully described at p. 193; the Lord in a *vesica*, from the pictures prefixed to Psalms XIII. and XX.; the Sun, Moon, and Stars from Psalms CII. and VIII. respectively; the masonry as found commonly throughout; David from the scene in Psalm L.; and the crown from Psalm XX.

August, 1876.

CONTENTS.

CHAPTER III.

CHAPTER IV.

CHAPTER V.

ILLUSTRATIONS.

ADDENDA AND ERRATA.

Page xv., line 27.   *for* and, *read* of.

Page 75, line 24.   *for* Regulbuim, *read* Regulbium.

Page 203, line 18.   *for* affodit, *read* effodit.

Page 232, line 1.   *for* Syrian, or Anglo-Saxon, *read* or Syrian, but rather Anglo-Saxon.

Page 237, line 29.   *for* carue, *read* carne.

Page 282, line 3.   *for the full point read a comma.*

Page 296, line 8.   *for* S̄P̄S̄S̄C̄S̄PATRE, *read* S̄P̄S̄S̄C̄S̄APATRE.

Page 303, line 3.   *gemyncnesse* (?), but erased as given.   The Brit. Mus. Arundel MS. 60, fol. 130, (a Psalter of equal antiquity) with the Latin *Quicunque* ("Athanasia lex") having a Saxon gloss interlined, reads here *gescindnesse;* but for *gemyncende,* page 299, line 9, the same MS. reads *scindende.*

INTRODUCTION.

By the kind invitation of the Earl of Ashburnham, I have had the opportunity of visiting the Collection of Manuscripts at Ashburnham Place, since the paragraph on pages 121, 122, and note on page 122 were printed; and I am enabled to state that no such Manuscript as that specified by Professor Westwood in this passage is preserved in the library.

siderable time exercised over the minds of masters and disciples, whether of theology, palæography, or of ancient pictorial art, have, as yet, by no means lost their power and influence. The fact of there being an excessively limited number of specimens of man's handiwork upon vellum, that are to be shown as examples of the graphic art deriving their origin during the interval between the fifth and tenth centuries of the Christian era, easily accounts for that transcendent interest springing up around, and as rapidly as it is permanently fostered by, any new acquisition to swell the narrow ranks of those few surviving marvels of an archaic art, which we are now permitted to rejoice over, in that they have escaped the ruthlessness of iconoclasts; the voracious scalpel of palimpsest makers; the greed of monastic mercenaries, who so persistently derived a savage pleasure in mutilating priceless manuscripts for a small gain by the sale of parchment wretchedly reno- vated, or cut up into pieces ; the riotous and wanton destruction of mediæval reformers.

It is true that the existence of this precious volume has never been entirely forgotten since its first rescue from obscurity by Sir Robert Cotton, now upwards of two hundred years ago, and its contents have not been carelessly examined by some of the most renowned controversialists of this intervening period. But it was reserved to a very recent time to witness a far greater agitation respecting the manuscript than had hitherto been set on foot; and it was also reserved, as it were for a prize, to the wondrous improvements which have within the last few years been inaugurated in London, with respect to the art of permanent photographic reproduction, alone to be able, and this for the first time in the history of that powerful scientific agent, to reproduce a perfect fac- simile of the pages of the Psalter.

In the course of this account of the history, art, and palæography of the manuscript commonly called the " Utrecht Psalter," it is intended to treat, in a separate and systematic manner, each of the most prominent points which are embraced by the external and internal aspects of this venerable volume. Thereby an endeavour will have been made to lay before the reader a comprehensive view of the whole subject, the acknowledged utility of which claims, not less than really deserves, the sustained and unflagging attention of all who desire to perfect their knowledge of such ancient productions as is the manuscript which is about to be considered. Before entering upon the minute description of its contents, it will not only be very advantageous to the general reader, whom we here presume to have but a very limited acquaintance with manuscripts of any age, but it will be also useful to some of those whose knowledge of these reliques is somewhat more extended; and it is in no inconsiderable degree necessary towards a correct appreciation of much that is put forward in the following pages, if we glance briefly in review over the leading characteristics exhibited by manuscripts of those centuries of the Christian age to which by various writers, directly or indirectly, the date of the Utrecht Psalter has been assigned. This, although apparently a digression, is really a very indispensable element in the history of the book. For unless the ordinary reader, for whom this account is principally intended, has before him a concise account of the many varieties of writing and artistic productions obtaining in the various schools of learning and refinement during these ages of semi-culture; unless the principal points of divergence and difference between one style of writing and another, between subtle differences affected in con-tiguous kingdoms, between native styles of any one place changing in accordance with the progress of time, and with the power of foreign influences brought to bear upon them, in a manner none the less strongly marked in the final result because that result has been the certain outcome of forces acting insensibly in their operation upon unconscious and unresisting media be demonstrated; unless, too, the correct position of the " Rustic capital," the character in which the Psalter has been conveyed to us in this example in the scale of letter forms, is carefully laid down; and unless the well nigh impossibility of finding any exact counterpart of this book among representative types, and the necessity of comparing it piece by piece with other specimens of early work rather in order to indicate points of dissimilarity than to demonstrate cases of resemblance, is thoroughly grounded in the mind of the reader, it would not be possible for him to acquire so accurate an impression regarding the many important phases which the Utrecht Psalter shows to those who approach its curious pages in a spirit of enquiry after hidden truths of art, history, and theology.

It will also be profitable to the consideration and due appreciation of the peculiar place which this manuscript claims to occupy, as far as regards the pictorial nature of its contents, if some of the principal picture manuscripts which have been attributed to the early periods of graphic art, that is, before the eleventh century, are brought briefly into notice, and their characteristics noted and defined. Of such there are but very few to which it may be useful to allude; for it is, in a great measure, this very scarcity of materials wherewith to compare and contrast the illustrations of the Psalter that has rendered the task so difficult, and the expressed opinion of palæographers so hazardous and conjectural. The more specimens of cognate subjects, whether they partake of the palæographic, the historic, or the artistic point of view, that can be collected together for comparison and side-by-side contemplation, the more easy is the attempt to attribute an era to the manuscript before us, and the more trustworthy is that opinion when it has been thus formed upon the only correct bases for its elucidation.

Another very important and truly massive element in the evidence, is that afforded by the testimony of numerous writers upon the bibliography of palæography, of which so many diverse treatises and extensive compilations exist. The principal works upon this science will be found to have been noticed, and the instructive character of their contents briefly summarised, in that portion of the present work devoted to this particular part of the subject. With the early years of the nineteenth century a brighter prospect dawned upon the science of palæography, of which, indeed, although it had for centuries attracted the attention of the curious, and had justly succeeded in obtaining due weight of importance from the learned, yet the literature which embodied its capabilities and expounded its scope and position among kindred sciences, was not couched in those precise forms of language, nor was treated in that exhaustive and comprehensive manner, which so powerful, and withal so requisite, a branch of human intellectual development demanded, before it could acquire from the world of letters that recognition of, and submission to its canons, founded upon a careful series of deductions obtained from a number of incontrovertible facts.

The evolution of the art of photography enabled those whose literary labours led them among manuscripts, and who studied the forms of writing obtaining in the various epochs of the world, to search out, prepare, multiply, reproduce, and finally collect examples of the choicest and most useful kind towards their object in view, namely, the comparison of styles and dates. And a fatal blow to the art of the copyist, or maker of facsimiles, however deftly he might ply his pen, was delivered by a rapid and unprecedented developing of the method of printing positive pictures by the silver process. These sun-pictures of ancient writings were found, before very long, to be of a greater or less durability, according to the good or indifferent quality of the chemical materials employed in the course of their production, to the dexterity of the manipulation brought to bear upon them during preparatory processes, and to the amount of careful, intelligent labour bestowed upon the whole operation from its beginning to its end. Hence, while there may be said to be practically no limit to the period that a well-prepared silver paper print should retain its pristine beauty and fidelity (and it is indeed a well known fact that many pictures thus prepared are as good at the present time as they were when they were made nearly twenty years ago) ; yet, on the other hand, it is an equally well known fact, and greatly to be deplored, that there are many positive photographic pictures, taken by means of the silver process, that show a deterioration more or less serious; and some, moreover, may be said to have utterly failed, and to have become mere waste paper. This evident want of perfect security and unvarying quality, which was at an early stage of the history of photography felt to be almost inherent to this silver positive process, whether it was owing to the imperfection of the method, or to the variable carefulness of the manipulator, led to a very diffuse number of scientific experiments being made with a view to combining the employment of typographic ink, or some similarly compounded pigment that would not ordinarily be influenced by age or deteriorated by the chemistry of the photographic process, with the accuracy of reproduction alone residing in photography.

The majority of these processes were founded upon the ingenious and well-timed discovery that gelatine could be so treated as to form an impervious and insoluble matrix, or vehicle, that might without difficulty be rendered sensitive to the chemical processes of the photographers, and as easily made insensitive and practicable to the purely mechanical operations of the lithographic printers. This is, in plain and unscientific language, the spirit of all the methods in present operation; and whether the result be invested with this name or that, the principles involved and the methods employed remain the same, although the details be slightly varied, or the special vehicles which are brought into use be alternated with substances giving practically the same result. It is to a process, whereby the peculiar power of gelatine to absorb, and yet not be dissolved, is made to subserve the needs of the photo-lithographic printer, that the autotype system of permanent lithography, practised with such eminently successful results by the Company that holds and works the Patent at the present moment, owes its great and increasingly eminent position in the first rank of unchanging photographic processes. And it is in a great measure due to the practicability of this means, which ranks second only in sharpness and faultless faithfulness to the original, that is, to the well developed and carefully prepared silver positive, that success in the study of palæography has been attained, and that the efforts of those, who had before laboured under the disadvantage of being unable to put before their readers pictures of the actual writing of the manuscripts under their critical examination, are now and for the future in a position of being easily illustrated and graphically delineated without either trouble, failure, or expense.

This autotype process was selected by those to whom it fell to direct the photographic reproduction of the Utrecht Psalter—a work then, and, as far as England is concerned, even now, without a parallel —not only on account of its plainly manifest advantages of cheapness, and its self-evident durability, but in no slight degree because also of the evenness and sameness of tones and qualitative depths obtaining throughout the whole of the impression ; a result difficult, if not wholly impossible of acquisition in any other process whatever. The consequence is that we have to-day a fac-simile of one of the most important and interesting manuscripts known to palæographical and theological enquirers, wherein is combined scrupulous adherence to the prototype with an endurance and cheapness contrasting favourably with the productions of every other competitive process. It was, indeed, fortunate for the Palæographical Society that the manifold disadvantages which the old school of palæography, as represented by those who were of necessity driven to the employment of copies and fac-similes, made by the hand of the artist; such as, for example, Mabillon, Bastard, Wailly, Anderson, Chassant, Walther, Silvestre, the Benedictines who composed the *Nouveau Traité de Diplomatique*, and a large number of other writers, principally French, had for long laboured under, had been removed one by one, and that the single obstacle to success, the deficiency of a mechanical means of making the facsimile, was at length fairly removed from the path of future investigators. It is undoubtedly by reason of this marvellous power of appealing to the eye in that irresistible, because incontrovertible, manner, that the Society is able to say with truth that it has done more towards the dissemination of the true principles of palæography than any one who has preceded its endeavours.

Since the adaptation and employment of the photographic element, we may denote the work done as belonging to the new school ; and this new school not only presents a perfect reproduction of the subject discussed, but aims at a more correct and more critical examination of the manuscripts which it undertakes to illustrate. Without the aid of the autotype process it is probable that the facsimile of the entire Utrecht Psalter would never have been attempted, or if it had been attempted it would have been found to fail in some important element.

There may be mention made here of another photographic process which is most peculiarly fitted, to all appearance, for the correct reproduction of ancient manuscripts, and as largely employed in France, perhaps, as the autotype in England. It is that worked by M. Dujardin of the Rue Vavin, Paris, who has succeeded in perfecting a method of applying photography to a hard metal plate, generally steel, whereof the surface is acted upon by an acid mordant which leaves a matrix of great hardness and equal delicacy, and capable not only of printing with ordinary inks the writing of the manuscript original, but also the imperfections and stains upon the vellum itself. This novel and interesting process, while it rivals the autotype in clearness of outline, outstrips it in the power of producing an unlimited number of impressions, because the metallic plate upon which the facsimile is, so to speak, engraved, can be utilized for all intents and purposes in the same manner as an ordinary engraving in steel or copper plate. In this respect the method of M. Dujardin possesses a very powerful and undoubted advantage over that of the autotypes. But nevertheless it has been considered by those who have given the greatest amount of attention to these subjects, that of individual methods the autotype process stands pre-eminent, while the difficulty which attaches to the fact that the impressions, after three hundred copies or so have been struck off, gradually lose that clear, sharp fineness of outline which is so necessary to a good facsimile, may be avoided by limiting the impressions obtained from one negative photograph to the above-mentioned number, and then preparing a second or a third negative and as many in fact as need requires. On the other hand, in cases where a large and simultaneous number of copies is required, there can be but little doubt that the invention of M. Dujardin claims a careful and valuable position in the scale of reproductive methods applied to the facsimile of manuscripts. So valuable has this invention been found to be, that already some specimens of important palæographic objects have been disseminated by its means throughout the world of literature, and a result has been obtained which was absolutely impossible in the days of the older continental palæographers.

M. Leopold Delisle, the talented Director of the Bibliothèque Nationale, has in this way been enabled to put before us an important and hitherto unpublished fragment of Eugyppius consisting of six folio pages in facsimile made by this process which he has selected as the best available for his purpose which is found in active operation in France at the present time. So pertinent is the statement made by M. Delisle with regard to these operations that no apology is required for a short extract from his *Notice sur un Manuscrit Mérovingien contenant des Fragments d'Eugyppius appartenant a M. Jules Desnoyers*, published at Paris during the present year :—

"Le progrès des études paléographiques dépend

en grand partie de l'abondance et de la perfection des fac-simile que les professeurs peuvent faire passer sous les yeux de leurs élèves ou qui peuvent être joints aux ouvrages didactiques, aux mémoires d'erudition, aux editions d'anciens textes, aux catalogues des collections de chartes ou de manuscrits.

"Pendant longtemps il fallut se contenter d'imitations plus ou moins fidèles, obtenues soit par le dessin, soit par le calque, et dont la gravure ou la lithographie permettait de multiplier les exemplaires. Les fac-simile ainsi obtenus au XVIIᵉ et au XVIIIᵉ siècle laissaient beaucoup à désirer. Les planches qui ornent le *De re diplomatica* de Mabillon, la *Palaeographia graeca* de Montfaucon, le *Nouveau Traité de Diplomatique* de Tassin et de Toustain donnent une idée tres-insufficiente des originaux.

"Les artistes du XIXᵉ siècle ont fait oublier tout ce que leurs devanciers avaient fait dans ce genre ; leur plume ou leur burin a exécuté de veritables chefs-d'œuvre, et les planches que Jacobs a gravées pour les *Eléments de Palégraphie* de M. de Wailly, celles de la *Paléographie universelle* de Silvestre, et celles du grand ouvrage de M. de Bastard méritent une grand confiance et peuvent servir de base à des études critiques et approfondies. Les lithographies qui ont été tirées dépuis 1835 jusqu'en 1874 pour l'enseignement de l'Ecole des Chartes, et qui portent sur près de six cents monuments, ont aussi rendu de grands services ; elles forment un cours à peu près complet de paléographie, et principal reproche qu'on doive leur adresser c'est d'avoir été tirées a si petit nombre qu'il est à peu près impossible de s'en procurer des collections.

"Les fac-simile produits par la gravure ou la lithographie présentent cependant des inconvénients de plus d'un genre. Il est impossible de les amener à un degrè convenable d'exactitude sans un sûreté de coup d'œil et un habileté de main qu'il est donné à peu d'artistes d'acquérir. C'est un travail long, ingrat, coûteux, et qui doit être dirigé, surveillé et corrigé avec la plus minutieuse attention. Souvent le dessinateur est à son insu conduit à deviner ou à interpreter un peu arbitrairement certains détails des monuments originaux, et beaucoup de fac-simile trahissent en plus d'un point les préoccupations du savant qui les a fait exécuter.

"La photographie devait amener une révolution complète dans ce genre de travail, et le recueil publié à Vienne par M. Sickel, sous le titre de *Monumenta Graphica medii aevi*, peut être cité comme une des ouvrages de paléographie auxquels l'art du photographe a été appliqué avec le plus de succès. Il restait cependant un obstacle à surmonter. Les anciens systèmes de reproduction ne pouvaient pas être abandonnés tant que la solidité et la durée des études photographiques n'etaient pas garantiès d'une maniere absolue, tant que les épreuves ne pouvaient pas être imprimées avec une encre grasse analogue à celle dont on se sert pour la typographie, la lithographie, ou la taille-douce. Ce difficile et important problème est aujourd'hui résolu, et differents procédés permettent de transformer un cliché photographique en une planche dont les imprimeurs ordinaires peuvent tirer des épreuves inalterables. Par la, une voie nouvelle s'ouvre aux études paléographiques.

" Desormais, les manuscrits les plus importants pourront être reproduits avec une irréprochable exactitude, depuis la première jusqu'à la dernière page, et un jour viendra, où toutes les grandes bibliothèques auront l'équivalent de quelques-uns de ces livres antiques qui font la gloire des bibliothèques de Rome, de Florence, de Milan, de Vienne, de Paris, et de Londres. L'example est déjà donné. *Le psautier de l'universite d'Utrecht vient d'être, au Musée britannique, l'objet d'une publication peu couteuse, dans laquelle on peut étudier avec une entière confiance l'un des plus curieux monuments de la calligraphie et du dessin au VIIIe ou au IXe siècle.*"

It is unnecessary here to pursue the subject of manuscript reproduction any further, limiting here, too, the remarks upon this point of consideration, and candidly stating that no other known processes combining fidelity to original types, with the attributes of guaranteed durability, fairly easy multiplicability, and moderate expense, can be for a single instant compared with the silver negative, the autotype of Spencer, Sawyer, and Company, and the Dujardin facsimile.

Yet, while there are points more than one wherein each one of this triad indicates weakness and want of perfection :—the silver, for example, in its variability, its want of uniformity, its occasional mistiness and indistinctness, and its too powerful rendering of blemishes, stains and shadows on the vellum ;—the autotype in its occasionally imperfect scale, its frequent sponginess, its extreme flatness and want of vitality, its limited power of reduplication ; that of M. Dujardin in its hardness and in its manifest want of power in the half tones and imperfectly graduated depths :—nevertheless these, which are, after all that can be said, comparatively trifling defects, are not by any means insuperable ; and the rapid progress of enterprise and invention must, before much time can elapse, devise such improvements that will have the effect of bringing each of these three principal methods more closely into equality of competition, as the foremost in the roll of processes to be employed in this particular and most difficult demand made upon the skill and science of the palæographer.

Without these, or kindred powers, the present state of palæographic science had been susceptible of but little improvement. For while the teaching of the Benedictines in their colossal work, the *Nouveau Traité*, the propositions of Bastard, Mabillon, Montfaucon, Wailly, Silvestre, and others, are for the most part perfectly sound and to be relied upon with that implicit faith that is justly due to those who have bestowed, as these illustrious masters have done, no small portion of their life and labour upon their works, yet these great palæographers laboured under an unfortunate inability to set before their pupils, in practical illustration and profound theories, faithful representations of materials most indispensable for the right appreciation of the matters under their consideration. They were, in point of fact, under the stern necessity of having to be content with the best productions of the manual skill of artists who, although they for the most part produced excellent facsimiles, yet they not unfrequently failed to catch the spirit of the original, and thus produced not only an unfaithful, but, which was worse still, a deceptive picture.

It was not until the summer of 1873 that the formation and rapid encadrement of the Palæographical Society of London, due in the first place to the energy and scholarship of Mr. Edward A. Bond, keeper of the Department of Manuscripts in the British Museum, and to the most cordial co-operation of other gentlemen employed in the same department combined with the support of several other influential palæographers in England, wrested from France the position that nation had hitherto occupied as the foremost exponents of this enlightened science. And the seat of palæography, in its most advanced form, passed from Paris, where the labours and assiduity of Mabillon, Wailly, and others already mentioned by name had located it, to the English capital, where the serial publications of the Palæographical Society justly, at least for the present, claim an uncontested chief position. It is, nevertheless, to be sincerely desired, that, just as in France, the science first obtained that credit, position, and indagation, which laid the foundation of its critical precision and value to-day, as a new branch of human knowledge, so, also, in France before long we may see successful efforts brought to bear upon the establishment of some machinery which shall result in producing, fostering, and extending the operations so splendidly achieved by the Palæographic Society in England.

The only possible way of advancing the science[1] is that propounded and followed by this Society, which puts before the eye, first a perfect and beautifully executed facsimile of the archetypal manuscript page; secondly, a correctly printed copy of the contents of the leaf reproduced; and finally, a short but concise and lucid statement of the main facts of the dates, history and surroundings, written from an inspection of the entire volume of which the given specimen has been selected with discrimination as a fair representative of the style occurring throughout. The Utrecht Psalter, executed throughout by the autotype process, is the first entire Manuscript which has been reproduced and issued to the circle of palæographic students through the agency of this Society. And in this case the description and typographic duplicate have not yet been published, if, indeed, it is contemplated by the Society to prepare and issue such a work. Hence, while of the other issues of the Society, information of the most useful character is to be found side by side with the facsimiles, in this case we are left, in a certain measure, to form our own conclusions, and to exercise our own individual judgments upon the reproduced Manuscript. Not that there exists no printed record

---

[1] "L'un des meilleures moyens de développer et de faciliter l'étude de la paléographie consisterait à publier d'excellents facsimile photographiques, d'après lesquels l'œil se familiariserait avec les écritures de chaque pays et de chaque époche, à choisir des types authentiques auxquels, pourraient être ramenés les exemples qu'on rencontre le plus souvent, à joindre aux facsimile une copie en caractères courants qui servirait aux exercices de déchiffrement, et des commentaires dans lesquels on indiquerait la nature du texte, la date, et le lieu de la transcription et les particularités dont il faut tenir compte pour bien connaître les usages suivis par les scribes depuis l'antiquité jusqu' à l'invention de l'imprimerie. Pour donner un exemple de ce qui pourrait être tenté dans ce genre j'ai pris un volume dont il n'a, je pense, été question dans aucun traité de paléographie . . . ." *M. Leopold Delisle, l.c.*

of the opinion of several of the most eminent palæographers respecting the Manuscript, because, as will be presently demonstrated, the opinions of several may with profit be collected, examined and collated, but these opinions are to be sought in quarters entirely distinct from the ordinary channels of such information, and in almost every case they have been, perhaps unnecessarily, surrounded with, or at least in some way commingled with theological arguments, dissertations, or pretensions revolving around the consideration of the Athanasian creed.

Now it is very necessary to say here, although the exact position will be more thoroughly defined hereafter, in the chapter dedicated to the special features of the case, that this theological element is, must be, and cannot but ever remain, entirely distinct and subordinate in interest to the palæographical interest, in the matter of the Utrecht Psalter. The two aspects, the divine and the profane, which this Manuscript presents to view, not only do not need any commixture of any kind or sort, but they actually suffer by the absurd attempts made by so many individuals to mingle the two streams of evolution, which really diverge from each other the further and more persistently they are followed. The history of this ancient literary relic, its external evidence, its wondrous art, its palæographical merits and claims, are alone the bases on which to fix ideas and lucubrations respecting its age, its probable date, whether of transcription or illustration, its object, and its ostensible use. When these questions have been worked out, solved in a manner more or less satisfactory in proportion as tangible materials exist ready to our hands for their resolution, the theological question at stake can then, and then only, be approached in a manner sufficiently clear and unprejudiced to warrant our hopes of arriving at a correct opinion regarding these enquiries also. In other words, the question demanded of palæography is this :—What is the date of the writing of the Utrecht Psalter? Of the theologian :—Is the text of the Athanasian Creed found in this Manuscript the earliest known?

To some extent, it is true, the ideas contained in these two questions are identical. But the reply to the second cannot be framed with regard to any useful issue until the answer to the first has been thoroughly discussed, examined, and laid down. Strange to say, this remarkable Manuscript has been made the subject of many treatises, all partaking of a controversial and quasi-theological nature. No printed accounts of the book are yet in existence which leave entirely out of their consideration the theological aspect of the matter; unless, indeed, we except the reports published in a fasciculus with an introduction by the Very Reverend the Dean of Westminster. And these, from the form of the introductory matter by which they have been, so to speak, strung together, and from the fact that their publication is due to a gentleman who has a strong theological bias in the affair, must be considered in some way connected with a theological view.

Separate chapters have been devoted to the history

of the externals of the work, that is, its antiquarian
nature, looking at it as an object, and apart from
the writings 'and drawings; to the tracings of
the successive owners of the volume; its adventures;
its present condition.   As the consideration of the
bibliography of the science of palæography will not
have proved altogether unprofitable to our average
enquirers, so too the bibliography of the Utrecht
Psalter itself—a mass of literature of no small
proportions—has been most carefully sifted, and the
principal statements examined and compared as well
as may be within the limited amount of space here
available.   In this, which is, indeed, one of the most
interesting branches of the entire subject, a very great
quantity of difference of opinion has, unfortunately,
been placed upon record, and an attempt has been
made, in the chapter assigned to this branch, to
balance if not harmonize the expressions employed
by the several writers.   The names of Waterland,
Westreenen van Tiellandt, Westwood, Hardy,
Bond, Swainson, Delisle, and others may be here
mentioned as the principal writers, or reporters
upon the Manuscript.   Some account also will be
found to have been given of an interesting volume of
tracings executed in or about the year 1858, which
passed into the Department of Manuscripts in the
British Museum and is now numbered "Additional
Manuscript 26,104."   To the most invaluable Manuscript, "Harley, 603," in the same library, apparently
a copy of the Utrecht Psalter prepared at a period
considerably later, a very great amount of interest
and speculation is attached ; and the present volume

would have been justly pronounced incomplete without some account of this important link in the mysterious chain which unites our thoughts and researches of to-day with the venerable Psalter which reaches far back towards the commencement of the Christian era.

To the artist, and to the draughtsman, the lengthy notices of the art of the illustrations will offer many attractions to be found nowhere else but here, and an invaluable lesson may be learned by a studious perusal of these numerous specimens of the skill of several very ancient master-members of the divine craft of drawing. Many of these pictures, of uniquely beautiful merit, have been minutely described in the following pages, and the facsimiles which accompany the descriptions will enable the intelligent reader to acquire faithful ideas concerning the others, and to perceive, and give due credit to the extreme skilfulness of the original designer of these pictorial allegories, for his translation of the tropes and metaphors of the Hebrew poet's diction into harmoniously woven ideographs of weirdly fascinating charm, wrought in a style, which for conception, detail, perspective, and general application of means to an end, stand alone, inimitable, unrivalled, and unimpeached.

In a similar manner, to the palæographer, whose business lies chiefly in the comparison and collation of letters, their forms, their slopes, their character, their *ensemble*, the art of the writing is perhaps more important than that of the drawings: for, while the latter are more enticing, and appeal more directly to the eye, the former may be compared with at least a few correlative specimens, whereas there is nothing, or hardly any thing, with which for their affinity's sake the illustrations may be contrasted. As this art is an element of the greatest weight in the answer to be given to the question demanded of the palæographer, it has been examined, in the chapter apportioned to its contemplation, with that care and consideration which a long period devoted to the study of mediæval writing can alone bring to bear upon it: and the style of the text, the "Rustic Capital," has been traced from its origin to the gradual decay of its employment among the scribes of the Western Empire, when it gave way before the irresistible progress of more utilitarian forms of letters. Some especially conflicting points, exhibited either by the manuscript itself, or contained in the treatises of those authors who have written upon it, have been selected and discussed'; but it is hoped that the remarks offered under this head will not be taken in other than a friendly spirit of impartial investigation rather than of adverse criticism, because it is believed that more satisfactory progress towards a correct elucidation of the hidden mysteries of the Utrecht Psalter can be made by deliberate investigation, than by employment of sweeping assertions and imperfect generalization from facts of unusual occurrence or extreme rarity.

The text of the creed, called that of St. Athanasius, has been given from this Manuscript, for the first time. And side by side with it will be found collations from other manuscript versions of its text, the student being thereby enabled to perceive the differences of the various editions of this ancient symbol of the Christian Faith. The position of the theologians, who reject as spurious, or accept this as a genuine composition sanctioned by the early Fathers, retained and accepted by the Church, and imperatively demanded of every member of the church of Christ from the day of its alleged origin until the present time, has been indicated, and the aspect of the two sides noted. The cycle of literature appertaining to this matter is as enormous as that called into existence by the palæography of the Psalter itself. Some account will be found of the principal works in connection with this theological controversy, but inasmuch as this very controversy has been shown to be subordinate to purely scientific considerations, so a less amount of space has been devoted to it.

- An attempt has been made to discover the probable date of the Manuscript, to mark the place of its origin, to point out the time of the execution of the pictures, the object, actual use, and destination of the contents; and a summary of general conclusions, with a notice of the aspect of future additional resolutions likely to be arrived at, concludes the present work, which has been, it may be said with truth, one of great and increasing toil, not however entirely destitute of that reward which is reaped in the shape of advantages gained from the assiduous examination of so many points of interest seldom brought together in and about a single manuscript.

This examination has been conducted throughout

in an independent, impartial, and purely literary manner, as most rightly befits the enquiry; and it is in this serene spirit of impartiality, avoiding all captious or devious feelings, that an approach can alone, with fair expectation of success, be made towards the solution of a question, such as the one before us claims to be considered—a question, be it remembered which is involved in all the obscurity which must of necessity attend and surround that wondrous work of ancient art, the Utrecht Psalter; over which we may here at least, on the threshhold of our description, take for granted that more than a thousand years have now rolled.

The true solution, after all that can be advanced, may only be reached by removing one by one the many obstacles which stand in the path of our way towards obtaining a full and fair prospect of the main points, and of these some will be presently shown to be still *sub judice*, and indeed likely for long time to remain unsolved, because the subordinate issues, and parallel considerations are in many cases impossible of satisfactory determination by reason of the insufficiency of positive and conclusive evidence bearing upon them in a direct manner.

CHAPTER I.

IN this opening chapter it is intended to present
to the reader a brief account of the general
principles of palæography, that is, the science and
art of ancient writing, from the earliest century to
the close of the tenth century of the Christian era,
but chiefly of course with regard to the styles of
writing found in the Utrecht Psalter; some notice
of the pictures found in early manuscripts ranging
over the same space of time; and a summary of the
principal works which, taken together, make up the
bibliography of palæography. Although it has been
by some considered and expressly stated that a
marked Oriental influence is plainly exhibited by
some of the drawings of this book, (and this especial
aspect will be considered separately in another
place) it never has been suggested that the writing of
the Manuscript is in any kind of manner connected
with, or to be explained by Oriental influences, or
that it is the work of a scribe of some Oriental nation

copying a language, and forms of letters which he did not understand ; and yet there is no doubt that the individuals who transcribed the Manuscript, or at least some of them, were unacquainted with the Latin language. Hence, however, there really exists no necessity for giving here any special account of palæography other than European, that is of Western, employment.

This great main stem of the science of palæography divided itself, almost at the very outset into two lesser branches ; one small, confined, of restricted influence, and comparatively unnecessary to be taken here into any but a very transient consideration ; the other, one which will demand our careful examination, is large, extensively ramified throughout nearly the whole of the most enlightened area of Europe, and possessed of the most varied forms, styles, influences, and conventionalities. Of these the first mentioned is the Greek writing and alphabet. This alphabet although in some respects resembling the Latin alphabet to which it was closely allied, became subject to varying effects of time, race, and circumstances, at an early period. The Greek palæography, as expounded by D. Bernard de Montfaucon in his *Palaeographia Graeca, sive de Ortu et Progressu Literarum Graecarum, et de variis omnium saeculorum Scriptionis Graecae generibus, etc.,* Parisiis, 1708,—a work which is even now without a rival, however many its shortcomings may be,—is of a very important and interesting character, and according to this author the art of writing in Greek characters, and the study of the Greek language generally, was established in many parts of Italy as well as in its more natural homes of Turkey and Greece, and this at a very early period of the middle ages. Montfaucon mentions Sicily, Calabria, Euboea, Crete, and many other places, where colonies of Grecian *literati* established schools of writing, and he indicates many manuscripts which were prepared and written in these localities. The same author also points out an important series of early dated manuscripts which must be carefully examined and the differences of their letter forms noted by the student of Greek palæography.

The Greek alphabet was in part applied to, and furnished several letters to the Russian and other kindred tongues of Eastern Europe and Western Asia; and in the fourteenth century, throughout the major portion of Italy, the study of the Greek language was kept up, and in the fifteenth greatly promoted and extended. The fall of Constantinople had the effect of driving to Italy many Greeks of conspicuous erudition, so that that century may be considered to have been the most flourishing period of Greek literary culture in places other than its native home. Of the origin of the Greek letters from those in use among the Phœnicians of Asia Minor we have little to consider here. The forms of the letters gradually acquired those shapes in which we now possess them, and these forms underwent gradual changes from the oldest capitals to cursives and minuscules, the due effect of various surrounding influences and mutations of feeling inherent in every living speech. These changing types have been well criticised and extensively examined by those who have written upon the subject of Greek handwriting, of Greek palæography and literature. The student who would desire to examine with advantage the various styles of letter forms employed by this erudite nation, cannot do better than peruse Montfaucon's great work, the title of which has been mentioned above; and the following works which specially treat of this subject :—W. Wattenbach, *Anleitung zur Griechischen und Lateinischen Palæographie*, quarto, Leipzig, 1872— A. Kirchhoff, *Studien zur Geschichte des Griechischen Alphabets*, quarto, Berlin, 1863—J. B. Gail, in *Le Philologue*, Tome xviii. Paris, 1825, a collection of several hundred specimens of Greek handwritings of all ages and styles; Sabas, Episcopus Mojaisky, *Specimina Palaeographica Codicum Graecorum et Slavonicorum*, quarto, Moskwa, 1863; *Facsimiles of Greek Papyri*, published in Paris 1865, large folio; the Facsimile of *Philodemi Epicurei de Ira Liber*, edited by Theodorus Gomperz from a papyrus found at Herculaneum, octavo, Lepsiæ, 1864; Photographic Facsimiles of the Remains of the Epistles of Clement of Rome, made from the unique copy preserved in the *Codex Alexandrinus*, folio, London, 1856. More general information may be obtained from works which belong to the art of palæography, and of which some account will be given further on.

A variety of instructive specimens of Greek writings will also be found in M. J. B. Silvestre's great work[1] entitled, *Universal Palæography; or Facsimiles of Writings of all Nations and Periods, copied from the*

---

[1] This work cost nearly £20,000 in production, and is now very rare.

most celebrated and authentic Manuscripts in the Libraries and Archives of France, Italy, Germany, and England, which was translated and edited, with corrections and notes, by the learned Sir Frederic Madden, in 1850. Upwards of forty plates of Greek writings, exquisitely prepared by hand and coloured to represent facsimile, as perfect in their way as can possibly be, are contained in this work; the principal of these indicate to us uncial writing of the third century before Christ, down to the second, fourth, sixth, seventh, eighth, and tenth centuries after Christ; small capital writing of the first century before Christ; cursive hands of the second, third, seventh, and later centuries of the Christian era; sloping uncial, a very peculiar hand, of the eighth and ninth centuries; mixed uncial of the ninth century; and minuscule of the tenth. Of these, the cursive Greek is in fact the ordinary writing found in common use among the people, and is so constructed by means of conjoined letters, ligatures, and arbitrary signs as to be entirely unlike the set and formal book-hand. This, and in fact all forms of Greek writing practically followed the same changes as did the European or Latin handwriting; and it is unnecessary to the consideration of the Utrecht Psalter to pursue our investigations into this branch of palæography any further, except perhaps to mention that out of the Greek alphabet (which was itself a branch of the Phœnician, and therefore to a great extent linked with Oriental forms), there arose three great families: (1) the Coptic, which has few important changes to shew, and preserves its shapes which are found in the oldest manuscripts far down into the middle ages; (2) the Sclavonic, the parent of the Cyrillian, whence are derived the Russian, the Servian, the Moldavian and Bulgarian forms; parent also of the Hierony-miant, whence are deduced the two forms of the Glagolitic; (3) the Mæsogothic.

The origin, however, of the Latin alphabet is to be traced to the Pelasgic, a younger offshoot of the Phœnician than is the Greek, and closely allied in its affinities to the Etruscan, Volscian, Oscan, Samnite, and other alphabets of the Italian peninsula, which forms indeed it gradually overcame and superseded. The Latin alphabet, with irresistible force of inherent utility and easy adaptability to Western speech, was, in progress of time, adopted by every country as it came in turn under the civilizing influence of Roman occupation; and Italian, French, Spanish, Portu-guese, Anglo-Saxon, English, Irish, German, Icelandic, Runic, in fact every enlightened language of the Empire, introduced the use of this alphabet into their writing; and each rendered the subsequent adoption of the letters by their neighbours more imperative and more easy of performance.

But with this adoption, the handwriting which obtains in mediæval Manuscripts has become the subject of so great a variety of changes, that it will be necessary to describe some of the principal varia-tions. There are (and it should be carefully borne in mind), two distinctly different forms: the *cursive*, a flowing, rapid, written character, formed in loose, straggling shapes such as best befit the rapid " pen of a ready writer," and found very extensively in *graffiti* or wall scribblings, epistolary texts, domestic documents, charters or deeds between two private parties principally partaking of some form of land-conveyance, and matters not intended to be of a literary endurance; the other style of writing, and the one which our purpose demands that we should consider very carefully, and treat of very minutely, is the formal, set, and fixed *book-hand*, the work of the calligrapher, καλλιγράφος, a fine hand-writer, as opposed to that of the ταχυγράφος, a tachygrapher or rapid writer.

The oldest forms of writing,—diverting our attention from the ideographic, or pictorial, systems which undoubtedly existed in a more or less complete manner from the very earliest appearance of man upon the earth,—by means of a phonetic alphabet are of two kinds termed *capital* and *cursive*. We may, without encroaching on too much space, or endangering the continuity of our ideas, take a hasty glance at the history of the cursive hand, before we concentrate our thoughts upon the book hand. There can be no doubt but that a kind of rapid writing was necessarily employed by the Romans during the empire, although it has been the subject of controversy in present times whether the citizens of the Roman state made any extensive use of this kind of writing. At any rate it is very difficult to imagine that the numerous kinds of mutual exchange and intercourse, the familiarity, and rapid intelligence, the extensive operations of a mercantile and financial character, the constant needs of a great mass of population grouped together in the restricted space

we know Rome to have been, could have existed
without some such medium as is plainly afforded by
the cursive handwriting, which we may therefore
without much doubt believe to have been invented,
or at least improved, and perfected, by the tachy-
graphers of Rome, to save themselves the time,
trouble, and need of dividing the letter of each word
in a conventional way which admitted of no abbreviation or modification. Passages may indeed be
gleaned from Eusebius, Quintilian, and many other
classical authors from which we may infer the
existence of this cursive style throughout the Roman
empire. Notice may be here made of a very valuable
and important manuscript at Milan; it is written on
Egyptian papyrus, and the text contains the
translation in Latin, by Rufinus, of the then most
popular works of the historian Josephus. This
manuscript is referred by the agreement of the best
authorities to the later half of the fourth century,
A.D. 350-400, and to the reign of the emperor
Theodosius. It is written in a cursive hand, with
conjoined letters, and presents many formidable
difficulties even to those most skilled in deciphering
such ancient scripts. It has been argued, and with
apparent good reason, that because very few, or no
other examples of this cursive Roman hand occur
before the fifth or sixth century (when the book hand
forms were in full employment) it may well be
believed that this form of writing was not in use for
manuscripts or literary texts, but only for documents
of an ephemeral nature which have therefore had
infinitely less opportunity or necessity of preservation

than writings of an enduring interest. At the same time it should not be forgotten, that the dearth and scarcity of the vehicles of writing, namely, papyrus and parchment, was at its height about the seventh century, and transient documents in cursive hand would be selected naturally by the scribes to be erased in preference to Manuscripts in book hand. Hence we must not forget that what remains to us to day of this class of writing cannot but be out of all proportion small in comparison with the extensive character of its employment.

The tablets of wax, discovered in the year 1790 in one of the gold mines of Hungary, and inscribed with a Latin Act written in a kind of cursive minuscule character, for some time took the world of palæographers by surprise, and the first and oldest place was assigned to these objects. But it was not until after the year 1840 when they were published at Leipsic by their possessor, M. Massmann, that they were discovered to be forgeries. We may therefore dismiss from our minds any further consideration of these, other than perhaps some gratification at the detection of the fraud sought to be palmed off upon the historian and palæographer.

A fine (and without doubt authentic) specimen of cursive Latin writing is to our hands in the Testamentary Charter of Ravenna, preserved in the Bibliothèque Nationale, Paris. This has formed the subject of a plate in Silvestre's Palæography, and from an inspection of this it is clear that there are in it but few points of resemblance with another specimen, namely that of an imperial rescript, which has been assigned to the third or fourth centuries of our era, inasmuch as four only of the letters are exactly alike, and the remaining letters of the alphabet totally unlike. How far these changes are the result of different dates alone, or of locality and national influence, must be left to the general consideration of the reader; but we may take it as a general rule, that changes which are the outcome of lapse of time only, and not the result of external modifications, are very slowly manifested in writings. Whereas, on the other hand, changes which are undoubtedly due to the influence of locality acted upon by external political pressures, to varying forms of thought, to courses of mental activity suddenly diverted, retarded, arrested, remodelled, are rapid, well marked, and as clearly different as are the causes which may have operated to bring about those very results.

Another very interesting example of the cursive handwriting of the Empire in the sixth century is afforded by a papyrus, formerly also from Ravenna, and now in the British Museum. Parts of this have been facsimiled by the Palæographic Society on two occasions (Plates 2, and 28). Of this we are told, that the letter *a* is very similar to *u*, but the former is joined to the following letter while the latter is unconnected; *u* is, however, frequently linked with the preceding letter, in which case it takes a' more cursive form; it is also indicated by a flourish above the line: *a* is sometimes written above the line in combination with another letter: *d* and *q* are open when linked with the preceding letter; *i* is most frequently combined, and falls below the line; *t* is capable of combination with almost any letter. The actual date of this writing has been fortunately recorded, A.D. 572, in the seventh year of the Emperor Justinus.

Another most useful comparative specimen of cursive writing is that mentioned and figured by Silvestre (Plate clxiv.), as cursive Romano-Gallican; it is a fragment of the Homilies of St. Avitus, written upon papyrus, and now deposited in the Bibliothèque Nationale, Paris. It is ascribed to the early part of the sixth century, and in the course of its description we may gather the following valuable information respecting the dissemination of the Roman forms of letters throughout subjugated districts :—" Without stopping to investigate what system of writing was in use among the Gauls before the Roman Invasion, we must take for granted the introduction of Latin writing throughout all the Gaulish provinces which successively succumbed to the invaders; and that this kind of writing became more and more general in proportion as the authority of the conquerors became confirmed, and their ideas and language were adopted by the conquered; in proportion, in short, as the Gauls became more and more Romanised." Hence it was necessary that these conquered nations, Gauls and others, should study and make use of the language and the writing of the Romans, their conquerors, and the same writing was used in the mother city of Rome, and in the most outlying province under her sway. Yet there are subtle differences which can be easily detected on close and careful examination between examples, few and rare as they are, of the colonial and the native style.

But it is unnecessary to pursue this subject further, and we may pass on to the consideration of the uncial character in which portions of the Utrecht Psalter, namely, the headings and commencing lines of the Psalter itself, and the text of the fragments of the gospels which succeed the Psalms in the volume, have been written. One of the earliest known specimens of Roman uncial character is that of the *Respublica* of M. T. Cicero, a palimpsest manuscript in the Vatican library, to which the extreme antiquity of the third century at least must be universally conceded. Of this writing the words are not divided, the letters are not truncated, and their summits are short, and as it were, circumflexed. The transverse or horizontal strokes are, like the heads and tails of letters out of line, short and cut off with an oblique form. The employment of this kind of writing for several centuries after the date already mentioned, may occasion some difficulty in arriving at the precise determination of the age of this manuscript; but Silvestre ascribes it to the third, and Cardinal Mai, he tells us, does not hesitate to refer it to the second or third century of our era.

Of the fifth century, we may examine, for Roman uncial writing, Silvestre's facsimile from the works of St. Cyprian in the Bibliothèque Nationale, Paris,[1]

---

[1] *Supp. Latin*, No. 712. Formerly in the Library of St. Germain des Près.

the date of which that author and his learned translator attribute to the fifth century, Montfaucon to the seventh, but the Benedictine authors of the *Nouveau Traité de Diplomatique* to the fourth or fifth, since it exhibits all the characteristics of that period. " The vellum is extremely thin and white," according to these authorities last adduced, " each line is written on a horizontal stroke which is only drawn to the width of the page and does not extend entirely across the leaf. . . . The words are not at all divided. . . . *Dominus* is generally abbreviated DMS., which is a mark of the highest antiquity." Concerning this particular abbreviation we shall have occasion to speak more at length in the description of the writing of the Utrecht Psalter itself. " The Y is without dots, and the F has only two thin horizontal strokes. . . . There are no stops except such as have been subsequently introduced. Scarcely any orthographical errors occur, nor abbreviations, except in a few of the final words. The name *Christi* is written in Greek letters **XPI**."[1] These minute details are to be taken as so many " special palæographical precepts," and are sufficient to indicate the soundness of the opinion of the Benedictines respecting the age of the Manuscript, as well as to guide the examination of other contemporary Manuscripts, and the several peculiarities will bear remarkably upon the Utrecht Psalter when the uncial part of the text is examined. Of this Manuscript the writing is Roman uncial, " elegant, full, moderately tall, continuous,

---

[1] *Nouveau Traité,* Tom. III., p. 55, note 1.

semi-angular, with very fine hair strokes, the letters being round and half-detached. M at the end of a line is indicated by a stroke with a hook at each end, or in the shape of an ∽. B. at the end of a line, is written for BUS. Some of the letters . . . are conjoined at the end of a line. A E are almost always detached. N, at the beginning of the page, is larger than the rest, which is another critical mark of the great antiquity of the Manuscript. Of the succeeding century a very fine specimen of Roman capital writing is given by Silvestre from the fragments of the Virgil in the library of the Vatican, now about twelve in number, but formerly part of a volume of several hundred leaves. These have been considered the finest, most elegant, and largest Roman writing known, and all writers admit that it indicates all the characteristics of very great age. The facsimile given by Silvestre is from the *Georgics*, and the writing is in large Roman capital letters, neat and broad, the summit and bases simply formed, the cross strokes not truncated, the A without a middle stroke, smaller letters sometimes used at the ends of lines, very few abbreviations, and those of the simplest character, such as B. with a short stroke for BUS, Q. for QUE. The words are run together. Professor Wattenbach, of Berlin, and Dr. Zangemeister, of Heidelberg, are now publishing specimens of this Roman capital hand in a series of photographic facsimile plates from early Latin MSS., entitled *Exempla Codicum Latinorum*. The principal Manuscripts suited to their work are the papyri of Herculaneum, the codices of Juvenal,

Plautus, Virgil, and other texts of classical
authors deposited in the Vatican and similar
libraries.

Silvestre gives an excellently chosen example of
Roman capital writing of the commencement of the
ninth century from the Latin gospels of St. Medard
of Soissons; this Manuscript is written with liquid
gold, and contains specimens, not only of capital
writing, but also of the fine Gallican majuscule and
uncial characters. Some of the capitals are tall and
elegantly formed, but unequal in size, some of the
strokes terminating in short curved ornaments. The
volume, which is considered to be one of the most
valuable extant, is of remarkably large size, written
on extremely fine vellum, and celebrated for the
perfection of its writing and the beauty and variety
of the ornamentation which has been lavished upon
it. Tradition affirms that the Emperor Louis Le
Débonnaire (A.D. 814-840) presented the book to the
church of St. Medard, but Bastard and other
palæographers ascribe the date of this volume rather
to the eighth century; and this view is, according
to Madden, very reasonably entertained, seeing that
the volume presents many similar points of comparison with the golden evangeliary of Charlemagne,
written in the year 780, and now in the Bibliothèque
particulière at the Louvre, with the golden gospels
given in the year 793 by the same monarch to St.
Angilbert, and now in the Abbeville library, and with
the golden gospels in the Harley collection in the
British Museum, No. 2788. This latter Manuscript
is almost a duplicate copy of the St. Medard gospels.

The illustrations of this are in the Byzantine style of art.

Many other fine examples of Roman capital and uncial writing, in Manuscripts executed without doubt during the period under review, might easily be mentioned, but it is now necessary to consider that particular subdivision of the simple capital which has been termed the *Rustic Capital*, or *Rustic Roman*: and as our Utrecht Psalter is written in this very hand it will be necessary to examine this branch of the handwriting with great consideration. One of the earliest, if not the very earliest Manuscript written in this hand, is the square Virgil in the Vatican library, No. 3225, and one of three Manuscripts of this celebrated poet, which have long attracted the admiration of all lovers of ancient art, as well as the veneration of all scholars for the purity of the text they exhibit. This No. 3225 is considered the oldest of the three : it is of a square quarto size, such as is usually found in very old Manuscripts, and in this point it may be compared with the Utrecht Manuscript. It is written upon vellum, and the text is adorned with many paintings, the subjects referring to the incidents of the contexts. The style of execution, as demonstrated by the few surviving portions of the volume, demands careful examination. From the very earliest time that the study of palæography formed one of the subjects of literary enquiry this Manuscript has acquired a very great interest in the eyes of the scientific. In 1686 Emmanuel à Schelestrate, prefect of the Vatican, J. P. Bellorio, and the renowned Mabillon examined it very carefully, and united in drawing up a written account of the results of their joint investigation. The examiners considered that while the styles of the illustrations were those which would have obtained in the age of Constantine, such as temples, victories buildings, galleys with double banks of oars, Phrygian costumes and armour, yet that all these details had been executed in a manner far superior, in point of design, to the work which that declining age was capable of producing, and hence they came to the conclusion that the work must be attributed a period anterior to Constantine, and the rather referred to the time of Septimus Severus (A.D. 193-211). They observed, too, nothing which is not agreeable to the older period of the Roman empire.[1] Silvestre[2] says of this Manuscript : " The peculiar forms of some of its letters have afforded grounds for determining its real age, and those who regard it as of the age of Septimus Severus, (the beginning of the third century), refer to the G, the half-circle of which is generally terminated by a small comma-like stroke;—the same form being found on a sun-dial which is assigned to that period. It will be seen that the Manuscript is written in majuscule Roman capitals, of an elegant but somewhat careless form; the bases and tops short, the latter horizontal, and the bases circumflexed." At this part of the detailed description Madden takes occasion to observe that " It may be remarked that this

[1] Cf. *Nouveau Traité*, III., 57 *n.*; *Catalogue of the Lansdowne MSS. in the British Museum*, Vol. II., p. 198, col. 1; and Hardy, *The Athanasian Creed*, etc., p. 25.

[2] Vol. I., p. 265-267.

minuteness of observation on the forms of the letters is not always borne out by the text, nor easy to be literally rendered. The tops of many of the letters are precisely of the same form as the bases, and it is not a correct distinction to state that the former are horizontal, and the latter *en forme d'osselet* (~) or circumflexed." The original description proceeds thus: "The cross strokes are still shorter, but horizontal, the words are not divided, and the phrases punctuated; the point on the top of the line indicating a full stop, and when placed in the middle or at the bottom, being equivalent to a comma or semicolon. The second stroke of the U is prolonged below the line, which is peculiar to this kind of writing. Schelestrate says, that the U in this Manuscript is round, whilst Mabillon calls it square; but the fact is, that the two strokes of the letter are united on the level of the line by the rounded up-stroke from the bottom of the first limb, and as this stroke was executed with more or less care, the letter appears square when negligently written, although in reality rounded when regular. The letter A is destitute of the cross-stroke; its first limb is perpendicular, and the second strong and oblique, and extends beyond the point of formation at the top. The F is taller than the other letters, its top stroke sometimes horizontal, its cross stroke very short, and the base curved; the P is not perfectly closed; the top of the T is very short, scarcely exceeding its base, both being curved; the L has its perpendicular stroke above the line, and dilated gradually to the top, which is bent to the left and obliquely formed; the two half circles of the O are united at a point on the left of the central line. The general character of the writing is massy, close, and square in all the rectangular letters." Such is a very excellent account of this wondrous Manuscript, and readers who wish to see some of the spirit of the drawings which it contains, may, with profit, consult the original coloured drawings of the miniatures, which were made for the Cardinal de' Massimi in 1642, and after passing into the collections of Bartoli, Mead, and Askew, found a final resting place among the Lansdowne Manuscripts in the British Museum, No. 834.

Of this Manuscript, the following extracts are taken from the description in the Catalogue prepared in 1819 by Sir Henry Ellis, keeper of the Department of Manuscripts in the British Museum, for the Commissioners of Public Records, and may be considered to represent the opinion of that learned antiquary: "A facsimile copy of the celebrated Virgil preserved in the Vatican library, made by Pietro Santi Bartoli, and accompanied with fifty drawings in gold and colours, besides the very elegant frontispiece which has the following inscription:—*Camillus Maximus imagines ex P. Virgilii Maronis veteri codice qui in bibliothæca Vaticana servatur Urbani VIII. Pont. Maximi concessu pingi curavit, MDCXLII.* Of the age of the original Manuscript it would be impossible to speak with certainty, and various have been the opinions of learned men on the subject. It has been carried as far back as the reign of Septimius Severus; but certainly without the least authority, and with every probability of erroneous conception. They seem to be nearer the truth who ascribe it to the time of Constantine the Great, especially if there be, as is asserted by the Abbé Winckelman, a nearly contemporary memorandum in the MS. itself to that effect, which, if genuine, will do away with the opinion of those who, by collation with the Florentine Virgil, contend that it is not earlier than the fifth century. Another set of critics admit the Manuscript to be of the time of Constantine, but consider the paintings as copied from originals of a much earlier period. This opinion seems to have been founded merely on the style of Bartoli's copies; and it is to be remembered that this ingenious artist has been accused of a systematical intention of making several meaner specimens of art appear as the production of a better age than they really belong to. It is certain, however, that none can have the fair means of judging without a comparison of the copies with the paintings in the Manuscript. There have been several publications of it accompanied with Bartoli's engravings. The Vatican Manuscript in question (for there are others in that library with which it has been confounded) is written on parchment, but is said to be sadly mutilated and to contain only fragments of the Bucolics, the Georgics and the Æneid." . . . . "Cardinal Camillo Massimi, who died in 1677, had himself begun the publication of these drawings, but did not live to complete it. He was a passionate lover of the arts, and had been taught to draw by the celebrated

Nicolas Poussin. Being a great admirer of the paintings left by the ancients, he had employed Bartoli to make copies of all that were then remaining at Rome; and this collection was purchased in 1738 for £200 by Dr. Mead." . . . . "The present Manuscript, which undoubtedly formed a part of the above collection was sold among the Doctor's books, and purchased by Dr. Askew for five guineas, at whose auction it was again bought by the Marquis of Lansdowne for twenty guineas."

It is difficult, without a collation of the original with this copy, which has been executed throughout in a very careful and elaborate manner, to say how far it deserves to be called a faithful facsimile; but the paintings of the copy appear perhaps too highly coloured, too artificial and picturesque, for the period to which the original has been fairly assigned, and the artist has certainly allowed his own style, and the prevailing style of his period, to influence the feeling of the illustrations. The writing is undoubtedly some of the oldest *Rustic* character now in existence, and of an age when the distinctions between the capital and the Rustic had not become so clearly defined and so manifestly divergent, as we may observe them in later examples.

Another very beautiful example of this peculiar character is well exhibited by another classical Manuscript in the same library. It is the well known copy of the Comedies of P. Terentius Afer, (Vatican MS., No. 3226). This ancient book, which has received the distinctive appellation of the *Vatican*

Terence, has long been a prominent theme of admiration with all the principal writers, on palæographic subjects. The great popularity of the works of the comedian Terence sufficiently accounts for the expectation we should naturally have, that some example of them, executed at a very remote period, such as this Manuscript is, should exist, and it is most probable that this particular volume was executed in the fourth century, and for a Roman library or for a wealthy and intellectual citizen of that empire. A contemplation of this very elegantly written Manuscript shows that the general form of the letters, resembling very closely the Roman capitals in many respects, yet is of that irregular nature which developed into the well-defined Rustic of succeeding centuries, when the broken, acute, and irregular strokes, here seen in their earliest forms, became thoroughly developed and more distinctively applied.

For Roman Rustic writing of the succeeding century, we may examine a very typical example in the well known Manuscript of Virgil's works, which is preserved in the Laurentian library at Florence. This Manuscript has created a great amount of criticism among the principal palæographers, and its exact position with regard to other specimens of Rustic writing has frequently been contested. Silvestre, in his great work on palæography, gives a circumstantial account of its history from its acquisition by Cardinal Ridolfo Carpi, who died in 1549, to its admission into its present resting-place; and proceeds to describe the peculiarities exhibited by its writing in the following words:—" It is a moderately-sized quarto volume, of a square form, written on vellum, in perfect preservation, and consists of four hundred and forty leaves written on both sides, in capital Roman letters, elegant and massive, with the bases, cross, and top strokes Rustic and short; a few of the down strokes reaching below the line, and some of the letters taller than the rest, with the words not separated from each other. The first three lines of each book are written in vermillion. The abbreviation B. signifying *bus*, and Q. *que*. The scholars of Italy have regarded this Manuscript as earlier than the fourth century, but this opinion is not followed by those of other countries." Luke Holstein[1] referred it to the end of the fourth century, about the time of the Emperors Valens and Theodosius; at all events, it is certain that the Manuscript was in existence at the close of the fifth century, since it bears an inscription at the end of the Bucolics respecting its correction by the hands of Turcius Rufus Apronianus Asterius, a literary citizen of Rome, who enjoyed the dignity of Consul in the year 494. It is on these grounds that this volume has been more generally referred to the fifth century, and in this latter view Silvestre and Sir Frederic Madden appear to concur. The librarian Bandini, in his *Catalogus Codicum Latinorum Bibliothecae Mediceae Laurentianae*, tom. ii. coll. 281-299, gives an exhaustive account, historical and descriptive, of this

---

[1] "Virgilius majusculis litteris scriptus in quadrato, omnium Codicum hujus Bibliothecae est antiquissimus, *mille ducentorum circiter annorum*, nam circa Valentis aut Theodosii tempora scriptum existimo. (*Bandini*, II., 293.)

ancient Manuscript, and in the opening sentences says of it :—" Inter Virgilianos Codices manu exaratos, qui plurimi in hac servantur Bibliotheca, unus hic, quo de agimus, longe ceteris praestat, sive characteris antiquitatem, sive elegantiam spectes, adeo ut jure optimo Nicolaus Heinsius, Musarum deliciae ac Parnassi decus, in Praefatione suae omnium emendatissimae Virgilianae editionis, eumdem Codicem dixerit *unum instar omnium, qui parem vetustate nullum per Europam universam habeat.*" In another passage, he says, concerning the date :— " Ceterum annus, quo idem codex exaratus fuit, in obscuro latet, et satis credibile videtur antiqua manu fuisse scriptum." The same author, after reviewing the various criticisms which have been promulgated respecting the age of the writing, sums up the description of the volume as " Codex membranaceus MS. in 4 min. Sæc. V. vere insignis optime servatus et initio mutilus." This Manuscript has been printed in facsimile letters by P. F. Foggini, Prefect of the Vatican, in 1741.

Another very useful example of Rustic writing of this century is that which is afforded us in the Vatican Manuscript No. 3867, a Virgil, ornamented with miniatures. This too is one of those relics of bygone ages which excite admiration and astonishment at the beauty of the design and the excellence of the execution, and at the same time stir up within us the regret that so very limited a number of such specimens exist, saved by we know not what fortunate accident, out of the general and almost universal destruction which the barbarity of the early middle ages, when all learning and art were thrust down by the rude shocks of conflicting greed for power and love of wholesale conquest, brought to bear upon the priceless productions of ages anterior to their own. Of the origin of this Manuscript little is known beyond the fact of a discovery by Montfaucon that it formerly belonged to the monastery of St. Denis, in France, as early as the thirteenth century, before it was deposited in the library where it is now preserved. A facsimile of a few words of this volume will be found in Mabillon *De Re Diplomatica* (pp. 352, 353), and in the *Nouveau Traité*, III., 61, 62 ; while in Silvestre (Plate CII.) a complete page of the work is given for the first time. This leaf shows a miniature of " three shepherds, engaged in discourse, surrounded by their flocks;" their names appear " on the top line of the text, taken from the third Eclogue of the poet of Mantua. This top line, as well as the names of the speakers introduced into the text, is written in red, the use of which is an acknowledged mark of antiquity. The letters are of the same form and size throughout the Manuscript ; they are of the kind termed Roman Rustic, or negligent capitals, and of a rectangular form, as distinguished from the round uncial letters. They are taller than broad ; rather narrow, but elegant, with the bases, crossstrokes, and summits circumflexed. The V is rather rounded at bottom ; the horizontal strokes of the E are very short ; A is without the middle stroke, and the thick stroke is elevated above its junction ; the T without a clearly defined top-stroke ; P with a very small and rather open bow; L without a cross-stroke at the top; F and B with strokes exceeding the ordinary height of the lines; the vowels OE and AE always separated; Y *not dotted;* the tails of L and Q prolonged beneath the lines; and at the ends of lines the letters of a smaller size. The words are not separated *and the punctuation which occurs after each word (often faulty by confounding the syllables) has been added by a later and unskilful hand;* entire pages being found without any stops." Mabillon and Montfaucon considered this Manuscript one of the very oldest date; Bottari, the Vatican librarian, was inclined to date it before the fourth century, but the Benedictine authors of the *Nouveau Traité* were unwilling to accord that antiquity to it; Silvestre states that it does not appear to be later than the fifth century, and gives it as his opinion that the paintings evidently belong to the period of decline of art; while, on the other hand, Seroux d'Agincourt in his *Histoire de l'Art*, (II. 74, III. 69) would place the miniatures as low as the twelfth or thirteenth century!

Another very instructive example of Roman Rustic handwriting is that found in the fragments of Sallust's *Roman History*, preserved in that world-renowned repository of classical Manuscripts, the Library of the Vatican. These fragments consist, unfortunately, of but four leaves of vellum, containing in all eight imperfect pages of the historical text. The history of these Manuscript fragments is, that the first discovery of them is attributed to Andreas Schott, a learned native of Antwerp who flourished in the sixteenth century. He sent them to the illustrious editor of classical texts, Justus Lipsius, and from this latter they were in turn acquired by Pierre Daniel. At this stage of their history they were for a time lost to reputation, and we do not find them noticed again, until after a lapse of two hundred years, when they were acquired in France by Christina, Queen of Sweden, who presented them to the Vatican Library, and there they are now carefully preserved. These fragments were edited by Cardinal Angelo Mai, the celebrated discoverer of so many Palimpsests, in his work entitled "*Classicorum auctorum e Vaticanis codicibus editorum tomus I, curante Angelo Mai,*" published at Rome in 1828. Silvestre, as well as the learned author of the above work, reproduces a facsimile of the writing, from which it may be gathered that the hand is the "*Rustic Roman Capital,* rather tall, with short heads and bases, thick and circumflexed, and with short cross strokes; some of the tall letters reaching above the line; the words continuous, without either punctuation or abbreviations, and with a few of the letters slightly inclining to the uncial form." This Manuscript is written in the form of two columns to the page, and Silvestre concludes his interesting account of these literary remains by stating that they were "unquestionably written in the fourth or fifth century."

Another invaluable specimen of the beautiful Rustic Roman Capital may be examined in the Manuscript No. 8084 in the Bibliothèque Nationale, a copy of the poems of Aurelius Prudentius

5*

Clemens, a native of Saragossa (born A.D. 348);
an imperial soldier, and, in later life, a Christian
poet, whose poems, while they are generally ranked
with the concluding pieces on the list of Classical
authors, yet bear no insignificant resemblance to the
rhyming monastic versification of centuries later
than the fourth. These poems appear, from their
very nature, to have been always in great request
and esteem, and it is very probable that numerous
examples of them were in circulation among the
Christian subjects of the Empire. A page of this
Manuscript has been given in facsimile by Silvestre,
and this author attributes its date to the sixth
century, although Mabillon without hesitation considered that it should rather be referred to the
fourth century, and thereby would appear to make it
contemporary with the writer himself. This latter
author is followed by Natalis de Wailly, in his
Éléments de Paléographie (v. II., pl. II.) who gives
four lines in facsimile, and assigns the Manuscript to
the fourth century.

There are several points of very great interest
in this venerable Manuscript, which has been truly
described as one of the most ancient as well as
most " elegant productions of the graphic art in
Western Europe." One especially interesting point
is, that it is, by universal consent, attributed to
the same period in which a powerful section of
critics has placed the Utrecht Psalter itself. It is
written upon vellum of unequal quality, but the
vellum has been carefully selected for perfectness
and finish. In its present condition it is represented

by a collection of 158 leaves arranged in *quaternions*, or gatherings of four leaves each, which are respectively numbered with Roman numerals, preceded by the letter Q. for *quaternio*, placed at the foot of the page. This peculiar manner of direction to the binder is by no means confined to this Manuscript, and is found in those to which the most extreme antiquity can be assigned. There are indications that the writing is the work of a learned scribe and not a mere calligrapher, and the corrections which exist are such as we should naturally expect in a Manuscript of this nature. Sir Frederic Madden thus describes the nature of the letters. "The letters are tall and elegant, with words continuous; with thick oblique strokes and slender vertical strokes; the letters upright; the F and L rising above the line; the A without a cross stroke; the middle bar of the E extending on each side of the perpendicular stroke; the H nearly resembling K (a form which occurs in the codices of Terence and Sallust in the Vatican Library); and the U and V triangular. Some of the letters are conjoined in the body of the text but more commonly at the end of lines. The chief character of the writing consists in having the bases and cross-strokes circumflexed."

Of this most beautiful specimen of bold and firm Rustic character, the Palæographical Society has given two very excellent full-page facsimiles in permanent autotype photography; and this style of reproduction may be compared with that method employed by Silvestre, with much advantage and interest; inasmuch as a comparison of these two principal forms of facsimile,—viz., the sun- or nature-picture, which perpetuates on its face even every tiny speck or hair mark which obtains over the whole surface of the vellum, and the hand-made engraving or artificial lithograph, which studiously avoids all unnecessary blemishes, and so throws up the characteristics of the letters into stronger relief,—clearly indicates the amazing superiority of the first-named chemical process. The Manuscript, whence these two pages of these early Christian poems of Prudentius have been derived, is described by the Palæographical Society as of the beginning of the sixth century, written on very thin vellum, 155[1] leaves, measuring 11⅞ inches by 11 inches, and with a complement of twenty lines, sometimes nineteen, to a page. The occurrence at folio 45 of a half-erased note in semi-uncial characters, which has been deciphered thus, ". . . . . . *tius Agorius Basilius*," written in the same handwriting as are the marginal notes explanatory of the various metres of the poems, has led to the identification of the anno-tator, as *Vettius Agorius Basilius*, more commonly known under the name of *Mavortius*,[2] Consul of the West in the year 527. The gatherings are nearly always of eight leaves, signed on the *verso* of the last leaf; the numeration begins afresh after the quire signed x. The ruling is on one side of the leaf and has been made with a dry point; this lining often

[1] Silvestre says 158, *see page* 29.

[2] Professor Ramsay states (Smith's *Dict.* of G. and R. Biogr.) that according to Bentley, this writer arranged the works of Horace in their present form; and that he is supposed, by a recent critic, whose reasonings will not bear close investigation, to have interpolated a number of spurious pieces.

extends beyond the vertical bounding lines. The writing, which is in *Rustic capitals*, is without separation of words, and placed between lines. The first three or four lines of some of the pieces are written in red ink, and there are running titles in smaller characters in different portions of the Manuscript.

The two plates represent, according to the Editors of the Palæographical Society's Publication, specimens of writing by two different hands. Contractions are sparingly employed, and confined to the sacred names; the constantly recurring Q. for QVE, and B. for BVS, which have been already referred to in descriptions of older Manuscripts; and a final M occasionally eliminated, a horizontal stroke, hooked at the ends, being placed after the word, in a line with the letters and in place of the M for which it is substituted. *There are no accents, and there is no original punctuation, but some full points have been inserted at later dates.* The forms of the letters demand careful examination. A has no cross-bar and the thick right hand line always passes beyond the thin stem of the left hand. The upper loops of B, P, and R, are smaller in proportion to other shapes. C and D are firm and stable, but not very full or rounded in their curves. The three cross-strokes of E are short, slightly curved, and placed in such a position with regard to the vertical stroke that they project equally on either side, like the arms of the ancient Greek ξ (ℨ) as given in Jelf's Grammar, from Sacellaropoulu and Böckh. The cross stroke of F is formed on the same plan, the summit of this letter forming a bold flourish, "sometimes broken at the beginning by lightness of hand." This letter is carried far above the line of the others, probably to distinguish it from the E which in other respects it is very like. The final stroke of the G is short, thick, and up-turned, sometimes disconnected from the other part of the letter. H in this Manuscript is of a very remarkable shape, like a modern K, and L like F rises above the line. " O is sometimes reduced in size when following C ; the bow of P is open ; the lower stroke of S is horizontal ; Y *is not dotted*, and sometimes rises above the line. Combinations occur of ND, NS, NT, OS, UM, UNT, UR, US, UT. Initials of paragraphs are of the same character and size as the letters of the text." As regards correction, marks to indicate erasures are dots placed above the letters, or sometimes beneath them. " Words are also scored through with the pen. Alterations are interlined. There are a few corrections and marginal marks of later date. Notes of the metres of the different pieces, etc., are written in the margins in a small half cursive hand of mixed uncials and minuscules of contemporaneous date." No ornamentation has been employed throughout the Manuscript.

Sir Thomas Hardy (in his *First Report* on the Athanasian Creed, at page 23, and in his *Further Report*, at page 37, both of which Treatises will be carefully examined presently,) speaks of the writing of this Paris Manuscript, which he admits to be of the sixth century, as so wholly resembling that of the

Utrecht Psalter that it is difficult to believe that the
two Manuscripts were not written by the same
scribe. This statement must, however, be accepted
with great reservation, for apart from the general
Rustic appearance of the letters of either Manuscript,
their individual characteristics are diametrically
opposed to each other : for in the forms of this Paris
MS. 8084, there is a boldness, firmness, breadth and
grandeur entirely wanting in those of the Utrecht
Manuscript which slope and occasionally totter,
while they are smaller and certainly less dashingly
penned than their brilliant predecessors in the poems
of Prudentius in this French codex. Sir Thomas,
nevertheless, argues, from an inspection of the first
three out of a passage of six lines *commencing a hymn*,
taken from this Paris Manuscript, given ' in the
Nouveau Traité de Diplomatique, and not from an
actual inspection of the book itself, nor from a
photographic copy, that the words of the hymns are
run together but divided by virgules according to
the metrical scansion of the lines ; and he quotes a
passage so punctuated or scanned commencing
thus :—

DAPU,ERPLEC,TRUMCHO,RAEIS,UTCA, NAMFI,DELIBUS

This three-line example, which has evidently
been so scanned to indicate the metre of the whole
hymn, and another specimen taken equally from
the French work already referred to, are selected
in support of the statement : " not only that

' Plate 35, Tom. B, p. 50.

Manuscripts of the sixth and seventh century contained punctuation, but that it was liberally used at this early date." At the same time the learned Reporter selects a third example from a sixth century Rustic Manuscript (Vatican, Palatin. 1631) where no such marks of scansion are employed, "for the purpose of showing that punctuation is no criterion of the age of a Manuscript." Now, it is only necessary to say here, that the comma-like marks of scansion in the line quoted above cannot be regarded in the light of *punctuation*, in the ordinary acceptance of the term; and as the two photographic facsimiles of this Prudentius, from which the Benedictine authors of the *Nouveau Traité* profess to have copied them, fail to exhibit any such cæsural or tonic marks, which have been called *punctuation*, we are compelled to believe either that these marks have been inserted into occasional parts of the Manuscript at uncertain periods, and for purposes of indicating the quantities of the feet, and for instruction in reading, or that the virgulated specimen has been by some means erroneously ascribed to the Paris Prudentius instead of being attributed to another unidentified Manuscript of similar age, character, and contents, which may indeed exhibit these virgules as they are represented in the facsimiles. This latter case would indeed appear to be more likely than the former, and to acquire greater probability from the fact that the facsimile given in the above French work does resemble the writing of the Utrecht Psalter more closely than that of the Prudentius of which we have two pages before us by the operations of the Palæographic Society. It is unnecessary to digress further in this place respecting the punctuation of Manuscripts, as the subject will be considered hereafter in connection with the stops found in the text of the Utrecht Manuscript.

Other fine specimens of Rustic Roman writing of the sixth century might be here mentioned and described at length, but we must be content to merely indicate their existence by referring the reader generally to the works of Silvestre and Mabillon, the *Nouveau Traité*, and such other books which treat upon this branch of palæography, the full titles of which will be found further on in this present chapter.

The *Amiatine Bible* has been selected by Bandini as a vehicle for a very interesting and learned dissertation inserted into the *Bibliotheca Leopoldino-Laurentiana*,' wherein he expresses his opinion that this Manuscript, which derives its appellation from the fact that it formerly belonged to the Cistercian monastery of St. Saviour on Monte Amiati, near Chiusi in Tuscany, is of the sixth century. But Silvestre places it in the succeeding century, and so would demolish an interesting theory, implicitly believed in the eleventh century, that it was entirely written by the hand of the sainted Pope Gregory the Great (who died in A.D. 604), because it contains a note relating to *Servandus* who died in the year 543. This Manuscript contains the Old and New Testaments, according to the Vulgate Version, and is very finely written upon choice vellum. The first of

' Tom. i., cols. 701-732.

the two facsimiles given by Silvestre shows writing of
" tall, irregular, inelegant Rustic Roman capitals
with the words divided, mingled with some uncials
truncated at the base, and the summits simple or
bent; the V, U, and N, with strokes below the line;
the cross strokes of the E not truncated; the A
generally without the bar, and the thick stroke
topping over the thinner; most of the angles of the
letters being turned upwards into a kind of hook.
Such a writing may be of all ages, either original or
by imitation; but from the union of its various
characters the volume may be referred to the
seventh century."

The Bibliothèque Nationale, at Paris, offers us,
through the medium of the author and translator
whom we have already quoted on several occasions,
a valuable example of Rustic Roman capitals mixed
with Gallican uncials of about the sixth or seventh century (No. 669, *Suppl. Lat.*) in the *Epigrams of Prosper
of Aquitaine*, a disciple of St. Augustine, and a famous
doctor of the church, who died in the middle of the
fifth century. The present volume of his works is
esteemed to be one of the most precious treasures
among the Manuscripts in the Bibliothèque Nationale, and this on account of its great antiquity
and unrivalled calligraphy. Silvestre details the
history of the book at length, wherein it appears to
have formerly belonged to the Benedictine Abbey of
Fleury, or St. Benoit-sur-Loire, and to the Library
of Sedan. From the facsimile we may observe that
the heading and rubrics are written in " rather
elegant massive Roman capitals of the Rustic form,

with short oblique summits and bases, and with a few of the top strokes long and curved. Such is also the character, of the writing of the rubricated titles after the text of the preface." But the preface itself, as well as two epigrams given in the plate (CXIII.) are, on the contrary, " in elegant Gallican uncial writing, with full strokes and continuous, the letters wide apart, the tails obliquely cut off, and, at the ends of the lines, the letters smaller and conjoined." It is worthy of remark in this Manuscript that the letters N T are conjoined, a practice originating at a very early period and occurring constantly in almost every kind of writing down to the twelfth and even later centuries. The beautiful execution exhibited by the Manuscript, which has been copied on the finest white vellum, is also a subject of proper admiration, and the date may be placed to the sixth, or at the latest the seventh century.

Although it would be indeed difficult to point out any Manuscript written in Rustic characters throughout the whole of its contents, to which any date more nearly approaching our own times than the seventh century could or has been rationally assigned, yet the partial use of the Rustic Roman capital lingered for many ages among the scribes and illuminators of the next three or four centuries, and we may at pleasure select from our own National Library in the British Museum, or from the plates of the principal works on palæography, any number of Manuscripts written in majuscule or minuscule character, adorned with headings, rubrics, titles, and initial letters derived from Rustic prototypes. It will, however, be unnecessary to prosecute our researches any further into this subject, and the consideration of the Rustic letter may be brought to a close with the examination of a facsimile from a Manuscript in the Library of Corpus Christi College, Cambridge (No. 286) which, through the assistance of the Palæographical Society, is fortunately accessible to the body of students of the ancient art of writing, and of which a full-page illustration will be found in Part IV. pl. 44 of the publication of that Society.' This specimen of Rustic letter consists of the single hexameter line

+IURASACERDOTII·LUCAS·TENET·ORA·
IUBENCI

which has been carefully inscribed along the architrave of an architectural erection placed around the seated figure of St. Luke the Apostle and Evangelist. The sentence evidently is epigrammatic, and contains an allusion in its first part to the priestly nature of the twelve disciples, and in its latter portion to the symbolical representation of the winged calf, the emblem of St. Luke in the Revelation (iv. 7), the *ora juvenci* referring to the depiction of a winged calf, half length, holding a book, and placed upon the architrave and beneath a semicircular arch overhead. This specimen of Rustic, of the seventh century, indicates that the character was still in possession of all the beauty and

' Compare the same picture, coloured, in Westwood's *Palæographia Sacra*, where the emendation of *Jure sacerdotis* is proposed.

individuality, but beginning to lack the regularity, firmness, and strength, that some of the last whole-text specimens of the Rustic Roman character possess. The letters, though perhaps rather circumscribed in size, are, for the most part, of excellent shape ; the A open without a bar ; the upper loop of the B considerably smaller than the lower loop ; C and D fully rounded ; the bars of the E more pronounced and not carried out so far on the left side as on the right ; L is carried above the line; the O possesses two forms, a very round one in the second word, a more purely Rustic shaping in the fifth ; T also has two forms, for in the word SACERDOTII and the first T of TENET this letter has its trunk carried far up above the line, but the second *t* in the latter word is smaller and of a similar size to the context. The miniatures which accompany this figure have descriptive marginal sentences written in small uncial characters.

This part of the subject may now well be dismissed with a tabular synopsis of the principal styles of writing used in the Western Empire up to the tenth century, for there never has been any serious endeavour to place the date of the Utrecht Psalter later than that epoch. In the following table references will be found to typical and world-renowned Manuscripts, of which the originals are preserved in the British Museum and other European Libraries, and of which facsimiles are for the most part given in the leading works on Palæography. The italic columns indicate the century to which, by preponderance of critical opinion, the respective

codices have been assigned, the subdivisions containing the columns show the styles of handwriting
in their order of antiquity, viz., Cursive, Capital,
Rustic Capital, Uncial, and mixed styles, and the
general arrangement of the table easily explains
itself without further comment:—

*Tabular Arrangement of Typical Latin Manuscripts and
Handwritings, to the Tenth Century.*

(*a.*) CURSIVE CHARACTERS.

Earliest.

    Graffiti of Italian cities.

2nd century after Christ.

    Forged wax tablets, *see page* 9 *supra.*

3rd cent.

    Latin Papyrus, *v. Le Moyen Age et la Renaissance,* tom. 2,
        Manuscrits, pl. 12.

    (Letronne, pl. 47 ?)

3rd or 4th cent.

    Papyrus of Ravenna at Paris, *see page* 9; Silvestre, pl.
        xcviii.

5th cent.

    G. Marini, *I Papiri Diplomatici,* No. 73, *circ.* A.D. 444.

    ibid., No. 82, A.D. 489.

    ibid., No. 84, A.D. 491.

6th cent.

    Marini, Nos. 85, 116, 86, 74, 99, 87, 75, 131, 138, 121,
        dated A.D. 523, 541, 553, etc.

    J. A. Letronne, *Diplomata et Chartæ Merovingicæ Ætatis,*
        pl. 1-2, dated 558, 566.

    Papyrus of Ravenna in British Museum, A.D. 572, *see p.* 10.

    Homilies of St. Avitus, *Le Moyen Age,* pl. 16. Silvestre,
        clxiv. *see p.* 11. (Cursive Romano-Gallican).

    Parisian Ravenna-Testament, Silv. cxxxiii.

6th or 7th cent.

    Marini, Nos. 90, 92.

7th cent.

ibid., No. 95, A.D. 639.

Letronne, *passim.*

Silv. pl. clxv., clxvi.

7th or 8th cent.

Ambrosian Josephus, Palæographical Society, pl. 59.

(*a.** Cursive Lombardic.

8th cent.

See Champollion-Figeac, *Chartes et Manuscrits sur Papyrus.*

Silv., pl. cxxxvii.

Silv. clxvii., clxviii. (Diplomatic Merovingian).

Letronne, *passim.*

9th cent.

Marini, No. 126 :—Champollion-Figeac, pl. 10, A.D. 877 :—
Letronne :—Silv. cxxxviii., cxxxix.

Silv. clxxii., clxxiii. (Carlovingian Diplomatic).

Letronne, pl. 48 (Merovingian).

10th cent.

See Champollion-Figeac.

Silv. clxxiv., clxxv.

(*b.*) Capital Characters Throughout.

6th cent.

Vatican Virgil, No. 3256, *see* p. 14.

(*c.*) Rustic Characters Throughout.

3rd or 4th cent.

Vatican Virgil, No. 3225, *see* p. 16.

Vatican Terence, No. 3226, p. 21.

4th or 5th cent.

Vatican Sallust, p. 26.

5th cent.

Florentine Virgil, p. 22.

Vatican Virgil, No. 3867, p. 24.

6th cent.

Parisian Prudentius, No. 8084, p. 27.

(*d.*) Uncial Characters Throughout.

3rd cent.

Vatican Palimpsest Cicero, No. 5757 ; Silv. pl. xcvii.

5th or 6th cent.

    Parisian Cyprian, *see* p. 12.

    Gospel of St. Luke at Milan ; Pal. Soc., Pl. 54.

6th cent.

    Vienna Livy, No. 15 ; Silv. cviii.

    Parisian Livy, No. 5730 ; Pal. Soc., Pl. 31, 32.

    Parisian Code of Theodosius ; Silv. cix.

    Psalter of St. Germain, at Paris ; Silv. cx. (*Gallican*).

6th or 7th cent.

    Gospels in B. M., Harley 1775 ; Pal. Soc. pl. 16 (but *Capital Colophons.*)

7th cent.

    Pandects of Justinian, at Florence ; Silv. cxv.

    Stoneyhurst Gospel of St. John ; Pal. Soc., pl. 17.

    Corp. Chr. Cambridge Gospels, No. 286 ; Pal. Soc. pl. 33, 34. (*Rustic heading.*)

    Book of Kells, Pal. Soc., Pl. 55, 56, 57, 58.

7th or 8th cent.

    Palimpsest Arian Fragments, etc., in Vatican, Silv. cxvi.

8th cent.

    Gospels in B. M., Additional 5463.

    Munich Theodosian Code, Silv. cxii. (*Gallican*).

    Gregory of Tours, at Paris, Silv. cxix.

(*c.*) CAPITAL AND UNCIAL CHARACTERS MIXED ; OR CAPITAL HEADINGS TO UNCIAL TEXTS.

6th cent.

    Lindisfarne Gospels, B. M., Cotton, Nero D. IV. *See* Pal. Soc. pl. 3-6, 22. (*Circ.* A.D. 700).

    Silv. ccxii-ccxiv.

    Parisian Homilies of St. Augustine on Papyrus. Silv. cvii.

6th or 7th cent.

    Gospels in B. M., Harley 1775, Pal. Soc. pl. 16.

    Parisian Augustine, No. 11,641. Pal. Soc. pl. 42, 43. (Papyrus and vellum).

7th cent.

    Charter of Hlothari of Kent, A.D. 679, Brit. Mus., MS. Cotton, Augustus II. 2.

    Charter of Hodilred of the East Saxons, A.D. 692, or 693.

ibid., II. 29.   *See* Facsimiles of Ancient Charters in B. M., pl. 1-2.

Homilies of Origen, B. M., Burney 340.

8th cent.

Hieronymian Gospels of Canterbury, B. M., MS. Reg. I. E. VI.   *See* Pal. Soc. pl. VII.

Charter of Æthilbalt, A.D. 736, B. M., Cotton, Augustus II. 3.   See Facs. of Anct. Charters in B. M., pl. 7.

9th cent.

Golden Gospels or *Codex Aureus*, B. M., Harley 2788.

Gospels of St. Medard.   See p. 15.

Hours of Charles Le Chauve, Silv. cxxv.

Gospels of Charles Le Chauve, Silv. cxxvi. cxxvii.

(*f.*) RUSTIC AND UNCIAL CHARACTERS MIXED.

7th cent.

Amiatine Bible, *see* p. 35.

Parisian Prosper, *see* p. 36.

8th cent.

Cotton Psalter, B. M., Vespasian A. 1.   *See* Pal. Soc. pll. 18, 19.   (*Circ.* A.D. 700).

(*g.*) RUSTIC AND MINUSCULE CHARACTERS MIXED.

7th cent.

Cambridge Gospels, *see* p. 38, and Westwood's *Palæogr. Sacra.*

7th to 9th cent.

Commonly abundant miniscule texts with Rustic rubrics, etc.

9th cent.

Aratus, B. M., Harley 647.   Rustic and minuscule duplicate text.

(*h.*) UNCIALS AND MINUSCULE CHARACTERS MIXED.

6th cent.

Cambridge *Codex Bezæ*, Pal. Soc., pl. xv.

7th or 8th cent.

Parisian Livy, Silv. cxxi.   (Uncials and semi-uncials.)

Lichfield Gospels of St. Chad.   Pal. Soc., pl. 20, 21, 35, (*circ.* A.D. 700).

6*

It is now necessary to pass on to a brief notice of the principal works on Western Palæography, a subject which has now for a long time been a favourite science, and a valuable assistance to the learned, whether in the branches of literature, history, or antiquity. As is most natural for us to expect, some of the productions which appeared at first respecting palæography do not exercise any very authoritative sway over opinions that have been formed at a later period and more recently, because these earlier lucubrations were in many cases the result of investigations carried on upon the basis of examination of imperfect or inaccurate facsimiles; and, on the other hand, more modern opinions have been matured upon the inspection of either the Manuscripts themselves, or, at the least, accurate photographic reproductions. And, indeed, without some such aid as permanent photography offers us in every step of this modern science of palæography, it would be impossible to arrive at correct conclusions, or to derive accurate deductions from the comparison of Manuscript characters resembling each other more or less generally. And of this a notable instance has already been adverted to, where the opinion of one, whose lengthy experience of Manuscripts demands very great deference, has been recorded to the effect that the writing of the Utrecht Psalter so closely resembles that of the Paris Manuscript 8084, *i.e.*, the well-known *Paris Prudentius*, as given in *facsimile engraving* by the authors of the *Nouveau Traité*, "that it is difficult to believe that the two Manuscripts were not written by the same scribe."

Whereas, on the contrary, it is far more difficult for any one who will examine the *published photographs*, to believe that the writing of the one could ever have been accomplished by the scribe of the other volume.

The earliest comprehensive treatise of any real importance upon the subject of palæography appears to be the immortal work of Jean Mabillon, a Benedictine Father of the last quarter of the seventeenth century. The title of this book, which must have occupied the unremitting attention and unwearied care of the author for a very long space of time, and which even now, two centuries after its production, continues to occupy a very prominent position in the literature and bibliography of palæography, by reason of the general soundness of its reasoning, is: *Jean Mabillon; De Re Diplomatica libri VI, in quibus quidquid ad veterum instrumentorum antiquitatem, materiam, scripturam, et stilum . . . . pertinet, explicatur, et illustratur. Accedunt . . . . veterum scripturarum varia specimina tabulis LX comprehensa, nova ducentorum et amplius monumentorum collectio, etc.* Folio, Lutetiæ Parisiorum, 1681-1704. A supplement was published in 1704-1709, and the volume contains upwards of sixty large plates of facsimiles of Manuscripts, besides a number of illustrations and woodcuts. It is immaterial to the student whether the book be of the first edition, 1681, or the second, 1709, provided copies of the work have the Supplement published in 1704, and the Nova Appendix (pp. 635-48) issued by Ruinart in 1709. By reprinting a few leaves and by inserting additions, the first edition was made conformable to the new one.

A well known bibliographical writer says of this stupendous monument of human energy: "Ce livre est regardé comme le chef-d'œuvre du savant bénédictin, qui en est l'auteur. Le supplément est beaucoup plus rare que le livre auquel il appartient, parceque, selon toute apparence, les exemplaires en ont été tirés à plus petit nombre."

In the year 1708 D. Bernard de Montfaucon published at Paris his celebrated work upon Greek palæography which has already been brought to the notice of the reader at page 2; and in 1715 the same author brought out his *Bibliotheca Coisliniana, olim Segueriana, MSS. Graecorum in eâ descriptio, aliaque ad Palaeographiam pertinentia*, in folio, published, also at Paris. This volume is especially valuable for the plates and facsimiles from Greek Manuscripts with which it is embellished. A few years afterwards appeared the following useful addition to the library of the palæographer: *J. P. Ludewig, Reliquiæ Manuscriptorum omnis Ævi Diplomatum ac Monumentorum adhuc ineditorum*, 12 volumes, 12mo. with many illustrations, Francof. Lips. et Halæ, 1720-41.

The great work of Schilter of which the following is the title—*Thesaurus Antiquitatum Teutonicarum, Ecclesiasticarum, Civilium, Litterarium, cum Glossario Teutonico non et Linguæ solum inservituro sed et Antiquitatibus abundanti*, 3 vols. folio, was published at Ulm, in 1727-1728, and contains many facsimiles of ornaments in ancient Manuscripts. Brunet, in his Manual, says of this production "Schilteri Thesaurus Teutonicus est un recueil rempli de documents précieux pour l'histoire civile et littéraire de l'Allemagne à l'époque Carlovingienne." Next in order of chronological arrangement comes another work from the pen of the indefatigable Montfaucon, which, although not strictly palæographical, yet contains so much that is valuable to the study of the Manuscript treasures of Italy, France, Germany, and other countries, that it deserves passing mention. The title of this monument of study is : *Bibliotheca Bibliothecarum Manuscriptorum Nova, ubi describuntur quæ innumeris Bibliothecis continentur*, etc. It was published in two folio volumes at Paris in 1739, and contains ample indexes, which augment its value and add greatly to its general utility. Hence it will always deserve, as it always finds, a place in a palæographical library.

The Florentine Virgil, already described at page 22, was added to the series of works on palæography by its publication at Florence in form of a quarto, in 1741, under the title—*Virgilius, Codex Antiquissimus a Rufo Turcio Aproniano, Consule Romano, Seculo V. Scripto, qui in Bibliotheca Mediceo-Laurentiana asservatur*.

In 1747 was published a very valuable folio, entitled, *Alphabetum Tironianum*, by Carpentier, which treats in a masterly manner of the Tyronian figures or short hand of the ancient Roman imperial scribes ; a practice which dates back to the time of the orator M. T. Cicero.

Mention may here be made of a dictionary of abbreviations and contractions found in Manuscripts, which was compiled by Johann Ludolf Walther, under the title of *Lexicon Diplomaticum abbreviationes syllabarum et vocum in diplomatibus et codicibus a seculo VIII. ad XVI. usque occurrentes exponens, junctis alphabetis et scripturae speciminibus,* etc. The folio edition of 1745 published at Göttingen has a useful preface by J. D. Koeler, and there are other editions, with a preface by J. H. Jung, which were printed at Göttingen in 1752, and at Ulm in 1756. In this Lexicon there are contained no less than 225 plates of alphabets and contractions, and twenty-eight plates of facsimiles. The palæographical writer, Ebert, considers the edition of 1752 to be the best for reference.

The best work on palæography and diplomatics is universally acknowledged to be the celebrated *Nouveau Traité de Diplomatique, où l'on examine les fondemens de cet Art, on établit des regles sur le discernement des Titres, et l'on expose historiquement les Caractères des Bulles Pontificales et des Diplomes, par deux Religieux Bénédictins de S. Maur* (Toustain et Tassin), 6 vols. 4to. Paris, 1750-1765. This noble and enduring literary production is enriched with a very large collection of carefully engraved facsimiles of every kind of ancient writing, specimens of Manuscripts, charters, diplomas, documents, and other illustrations bearing upon the subjects of the text;[1] and the principal point in the book is that the

---

[1] "The most comprehensive endeavour to systematise the science was made by the Benedictines of St. Maur in their *Nouveau Traité de Diplomatique.* The plates, however, though numerous, are insufficient for their purpose, for the specimens rarely extend beyond a few lines. Moreover, the subject of ornamentation and illustration is scarcely noticed."—*Prospectus of Palæographical Society,* 1873.

rules laid down by Mabillon and other previous writers, are carefully examined, tested, and explained; while at the same time, the forward state of the science of palæography, which had made rapid strides during the period which intervened between the publication of Mabillon's labours and this new treatise, a space of seventy years, is clearly indicated and the future of the science well prognosticated.

Next in order of time we have an Italian work on palæography by Giovan Grisostomo Trombelli, entitled *Arte di conoscere l'età de' Codici Latini ed Italiani*, 4to. Bologna, 1756. The same author produced a work closely resembling the above, with the altered title, *La Diplomatica, o sia L'Arte di conoscere l'età ed autenticità de' Codici Latini é Italiani*, 8vo. Napoli, 1780. And the important *Dictionary of Diplomatics* written by François Joseph de Vaines, which was printed in two octavo volumes at Paris in 1773, 1774, brings to a close the list of principal treasures on palæography issued to the world during the eighteenth century. The title of De Vaines' work is: *Dictionnaire raisonné de Diplomatique, contenant les regles principales et essentielles pour servir à déchiffrer les anciens Titres, Diplomes, et Monuments, ainsi qu'à justifier de leur date et de leur authenticité. On y a joint des Planches . . . . avec des explications à chacune, pour aider également à connoitre les caractères et écritures des différents âges et de différentes nations.*

In 1780 was published the *Escuela palæographica* of A. Merino de Jesu-Christo, at Madrid; and in 1784 the first edition of a popular book by Thomas Astle, entitled, *The Origin and Progress of Writing, as well*

Hieroglyphic as Elementary, illustrated by Engravings taken from Marbles, Manuscripts, and Charters, ancient and modern, etc., quarto, London ; the second edition was of folio size, and appeared in 1803. This treatise is adorned with numerous facsimile plates from early Manuscripts. There is also a curious and valuable addition to the list entitled *Calligraphia Graeca et Poecilographia Graeca, exaravit Johannes Hodgkin, sculpsit H. Ashby*, folio, London, 1794-1807.

The commencing years of the present century ushered in several literary productions concerning the art of palæography, and from the beginning of this period[1] to the year 1870 many important additions have been made to the bibliography of this interesting science. The valuable work *I Papiri Diplomatici, raccolti ed illustrati dall' Abbate G. L. Marini*, was published in folio at Rome in 1805. In 1817 appeared the well-known work of Ulrich Friedrich Kopp, bearing the title of *Palæographia Critica*, in four volumes of quarto size, printed at Mannheim 1817—1829. This production contains many new characters, especially struck for it, to represent the endless varieties of styles, contractions, and abbreviations, in early Greek and Roman writing. They are arranged in form of a Lexicon, explained in the regular Greek and Roman characters, and followed by reverse Indexes. The work also contains several large folding sheets of facsimiles. The cost of the publication amounted to several

---

[1] For some account of the voluminous labours of Cardinal Angelo Mai, the reader may consult with advantage a work entitled " *Palimpsest Literature, and its Editor, Cardinal Angelo Mai*, by C. W. Russell, octavo, 1863, in the fourth series of *Afternoon Lectures on English Literature. See also page 27.*

thousand pounds, and was entirely defrayed by the learned author, in whose lifetime only a few copies were circulated among collectors and public libraries. The same author published a work of enduring interest, entitled *Bilder und Schriften der Vorzeit*, at Mannheim, in 1819-1821, in two volumes, octavo, which, like the larger work mentioned above, contains numerous plates of facsimiles of early Manuscripts, and the text contains a variety of alphabets. In 1825 the labours of J. B. Gail on the subject of Greek palæography, as described above at page 4 were published ; and Friedrich Adolf Ebert wrote his treatise *Zur Handschriftenkunde*, in two octavo volumes, which were printed at Leipzig, in 1825-1827.

The year 1833 witnessed a very important addition towards the history of Manuscript illumination, in the publication of Henry Shaw's *Illuminated Ornaments selected from Manuscripts and Early Printed Books from the sixth to the seventeenth centuries.* This magnificent work was engraved on fifty-nine copper plates, all highly finished in opaque colours, and enhanced with very carefully prepared descriptions by the late Sir Frederic Madden, K.H., Keeper of the Manuscripts in the British Museum.[1] Although this work does not contribute very much that is new towards the elucidation of palæographical controversy, still the text and the illustrations taken together render the book an indispensable adjunct to a collection of works on palæography, and demand a place here. Nor must the *Viele Alphabete*

---

[1] A fine copy, with additions and corrections by Shaw himself, is in the Library of the British Museum, marked C. 43. i.

of Heinrich Joachim Jaeck, published at Leipzig, in a double folio size, 1833, be passed over without mention. A volume of great interest to palæography was published in 1836 under the following title : *Antiquissimus Quatuor Evangeliorum Codex Sangallensis Græco-Latinus interlinearis, nunquam adhuc collatus, accuratissime delineatus cura Rettig*, large quarto, *Turici;* being a facsimile upon 395 pages (with introduction and notes), of the original Manuscript, written in the ninth century by an Irish monk in Germany. The *Grammatographie du Neuvième Siècle,* by J. B. J. Jorand, a large folio full of most interesting plates from the " Bible of Charles the Bald," was published at Paris in 1837; and the same year produced at London *Alchuine's Bible in the British Museum*, in octavo. About the same time, 1837-1841 occurred the publication of M. Champollion's *Chartes Latines sur Papyrus du sixième siècle*, issued, like most of the previous valuable works on palæography, at Paris. This important contribution is full of plates which demand careful study and minute examination. Although partaking more of a bibliographical than a palæographical nature, mention must here be made of a work of indispensable utility, entitled, *Bibliographie paléographico-diplomatico-bibliologique: répertoire des ouvrages relatifs à la paléographie, à l'histoire de l'imprimerie*, etc., by J. P. Namur, in two volumes octavo, at Liége, in 1838. Place, too, must be accorded to J. A. Letronne's *Fragments d'anciens poëtes Grecs tirés d'un papyrus*, 8vo, Paris, 1838.

One of the most comprehensive summaries of the history and art of palæography is that of M. Natalis de Wailly, entitled *Éléments de Paléographie, pour servir a l'Étude des Documents inédits, sur l'Histoire de France, publiés par Ordre de Roi*, etc., in two volumes square folio, Paris, 1838. The opinions of this author are generally sound, yet there, are occasional indications of a want of carefulness in the dates assigned to some of the earlier Manuscripts, but as a rule the opinions expressed by Mabillon and the authors of the *Nouveau Traité* have been adopted. This work was illustrated with a considerable number of facsimiles of ancient handwriting. The student must not pass over this period without a view of the *Paléographie des Classiques Latines*, par M. Champollion-Figeac, which was published in folio, Paris, 1839; and a notice of the *Chartes et Manuscrits sur Papyrus, de la Bibliothèque Royale*, par M. Champollion-Figeac, large folio, Paris, 1840.

At page 4 the reader's attention has already been directed to M. J. B. Silvestre's magnificent work. The original work was published in 1841 at Paris under the following comprehensive title: *Paléographie Universelle. Collection de facsimile d'écritures de tous les peuples et de tous les temps, tirés des plus authentiques documents de l'art graphique, chartes et manuscrits existant dans les archives et les bibliothèques de France, d'Italie, d'Allemagne et d'Angleterre ; publiée, d'après les modèles écrits, dessinés et peints sur les lieux mêmes, par M. Silvestre, accompagnée d'explications historiques et descriptives.* This most beautiful work was published at Paris in 1841 in four volumes, atlas folio size, and contains several hundreds of specimens of every style of calligraphy and illumination; the miniatures from service books, of every style, country, and age, are especially numerous and most faithfully reproduced as far as colouring and general effect can go. The facsimiles are the finest that can be produced by hand, and they afforded the best medium of study and comparison of Manuscripts, at a time when the marvellous resources of photography, an art then in its very earliest and weakest stages, had not been sufficiently developed to be applied with any degree of success to the services of comparative palæography. This work led the author through all the principal libraries of Europe, which were liberally thrown open to his researches, and it was produced under the immediate auspices of Louis Philippe. It is now very rare, and may be fairly considered one of the finest pictorial books in the world, apart from the special nature of its contents. It has well merited the admiration that has been universally accorded to it as the best exponent of Manuscript literature of ancient and mediæval times, Of the translation, in 1850, into English by the late Sir Frederic Madden, K.H., one of the most learned palæographers that England has ever produced, notice has already been given, and the annotations and corrections introduced by the translator into the English edition give it a considerable advantage over the French text. The same year, 1841, produced at Rouen the large octavo work of Langlois, entitled, *Essai sur la Calligraphie des Manuscrits du Moyen Age et des Ornements des Livres d'Heures*, etc., adorned with plates of initial letters and miniatures. Le Comte Auguste de Bastard, another learned Frenchman of great taste and erudition, published at Paris, the seat of the palæographical school up to this time, 1843, his celebrated work on ancient Manuscript art, of which the title is *Peintures et Ornements des Manuscrits, classés dans un ordre chronologique pour servir à l'Histoire des arts du dessin, depuis le quatrième siècle*, etc. The book is a fitting companion to the productions of Silvestre, Shaw, Bastard, Westwood, and others, that have preceded or followed it.

The efforts of Madden to establish a native school of palæography in England, and thereby to share with the French the honours the savants of that nation had hitherto monopolised with respect to this science, resulted in the publications of Professor J. O. Westwood, an artist well known for his wonderful drawings and coloured figures of subjects connected with the many-branching sciences of Natural History, and for his literary labours which have done so much towards the correct classification of lepidopterous insects ;— an excellent study of minutely changing forms, and of colours blending and resolving themselves according to natural, but none the less hidden and mysterious, laws ; a study which especially fitted his eye for forming correct appreciations of the slowly changing forms of letters, and of the harmoniously sorted colours in which the semi-sacred scribes and artistic miniators of the early and middle ages for the most part found their own and only pleasures, whereby they evolved and codified a happy means of out-pouring their hidden, pent-up yearnings after the outward expression of a latent energy of thought, an inward spiritualism, which was not, alas! emancipated from the trammels of imperfect vehicles, and stern conventionalism, until the religious forces, which alone gave these men of art a political power and a means of life, had been shattered beyond all hope of rehabilitation. Professor Westwood's principal works in connection with the present subject are: *Palæographia Sacra Pictoria, being a Series of Illustrations of the Ancient Versions of the Bible, copied from Illuminated Manuscripts executed between the Fourth and Sixteenth Centuries*, published in 1843-1845, and adorned with fifty richly illuminated engravings; *Illuminated Illustrations of the Bible copied from select Manuscripts of the Middle Ages*, 1846, in imperial quarto, with forty excellent plates of a typical character; and *Miniatures and Ornaments of Anglo-Saxon and Irish Manuscripts*, illustrated in a series of fifty-four superb plates, most elaborately executed in exact facsimile of the originals in gold and colours, with a descriptive text to each plate, serving as a History of British Palæography and Pictorial Art, imperial folio, 1868. In addition to these printed masterpieces of reproductive skill, there is a Manuscript volume in the Egerton collection at the British Museum (No. 2263) which contains a large number of the original tracings and coloured facsimiles executed by the author of the above works during his researches into these subjects. Other works to be noticed are J. A. Letronne's, *Diplomata et Chartæ Merovingicæ Ætatis*, folio, Paris, 1844-1849; the *Schrifttafeln zum*

Gebrauch bei Diplomatischen Vorlesungen, of Georg
Heinrich Pertz, in large folio, Hanover, 1844-1869;
the *Éléments Carlovingiens Linguistiques et Littéraires*,
of Barrois, in quarto, Paris, 1846, with many plates
of characters ; the second volume of *Le Moyen Age et
La Renaissance*, quarto, Paris, 1849, with many fine
plates of early Manuscripts on vellum and papyrus,
to illustrate the article *Manuscrits ;* the work of the
Hon. R. Curzon, entitled, *Catalogue of Materials for
Writing, Early Writings on Tablets and Stones, etc.,*
folio, 1849, with several good coloured and illuminated facsimiles ; and Noel Humphrey's *Illuminated Books of the Middle Ages, with an account of
the Development and Progress of the Art of Illumination
from the IVth to the XVIIIth centuries,* folio, which
was published in 1849, and illustrated with full size
specimens, beautifully printed in gold, silver, and
colours by Owen Jones, after the originals, that
were collected from all the libraries of Europe. At
Vienna, in 1852, the labours of Paul Pretsch, on *Die
Buchschriften des Mittelalters* appeared in octavo
form ; and in 1856, at London, the *Photographic
Facsimiles of the Remains of the Epistle of Clement of
Rome, made from the unique copy preserved in the Codex
Alexandrinus,* were edited by Sir Frederic Madden,
and published in a quarto volume of remarkable
interest and importance. During the next year,
1857, the *Lectures on Illuminated Manuscripts from
the Eighth to the Seventeenth Centuries, and the Practice and Materials of Illuminators,* by Thomson and
Tite, were privately printed, in 8vo. ; and in 1860,
The Art of Illuminating as practised in Europe from

the Earliest Times, by W. R. Tymms, with an Essay,
etc., by M. D. Wyatt, small folio. Then come the
following publications:—*Grammatography, a Manual
of Reference to the Alphabets of Ancient and Modern
Languages*, octavo, London, 1861; *Dictionnaire des
Abbreviations Latines et Françaises*, 12mo, Paris, 1862,
a work containing about eight thousand contractions; *La Scuola di Paleografia in Venezia*, by
Cecchetti, in atlas quarto, Venice, 1862, with several
plates of facsimiles; *De l'Origine de la Signature*, par
M. C. Guigne, octavo, Paris, 1863; A. Kirchhoff's
Studien, in 1863, which has already been referred to
at page 4, where will also be found a note of the
Specimina of Bishop Sabas which was produced in
the same year; and of the *Philodemus* facsimiled by
T. Gomperz in 1864. Several useful *Facsimiles of
Greek Papyri* were published at Paris in 1865; and
of the same city and year is the *Notices et Extraits
des Manuscrits de la Bibliothèque Imperiale et autres
Bibliothèques*, with facsimiles of Papyri, Tom. XVI.,
2e partie. The writings of F. Trinchera, entitled,
*Syllabus Graecarum Membranarum, que . . . . jamdiu
delitescentes, et a doctis frustra expetitae, nunc tandem
adnitente impensius Francisco Trinchera, Neapolitanis
archivis praefecto, in lucem prodeunt*, large quarto,
Naples, 1865, follow next in order; and *Ornements
des Manuscrits du VIIIe. au XVIe. Siècle, reproduits
en couleurs par Mathieu, avec notice historique par Ferd.
Denis*, 2 vols., octavo, Paris, 1867, with numerous
facsimiles; and the *Compendio delle Lezioni Teorico-
Pratiche di Paleografia e Diplomatica* of Dr. Andrea
Gloria, published at Padua in 1870; although the

facsimiles in this last are not so strong and characteristic of their archetypes as they might have been in these late days of reproductive excellence, must not be omitted from this list. In 1871 some remarkable leaves of lead, inscribed with a peculiar and indeed unique handwriting of the north of Italy, and recording historical events of the eighth and ninth centuries, the period of Charlemagne, formed the subject of a treatise in the *Archæologia* of the Society of Antiquaries (Vol. XLIV., art. 10, pp. 123-136), by the present writer, and the treatise is illustrated with a facsimile of one of the inscribed metallic leaves of early date, which has been reproduced by permanent photography of the heliotype process. W. Wattenbach's *Anleitung* has been already noticed at page 4, having been published in 1872, and forming a valuable addition to the great quantity of literary material that has been hastily summarised in the preceding pages. In 1873 the trustees of the British Museum sanctioned the publication of a number of early charters, which were likely, it was feared, to suffer seriously before long from the effect of age and former careless treatment, and under the auspices of Mr. E. A. Bond, the present keeper of the Manuscripts, a volume in large folio was prepared by autotype permanent photography, and issued under the title of *Facsimiles of Ancient Charters in the British Museum, published by order of the Trustees*, 1873. These plates, seventeen in number, are of great value to the student, as they range in date between A.D. 679 and 838, and are entirely of English diplomatic character. Mr.

7*

Bond says very happily of them : " The palæo-graphic interest of the facsimiles will not be overlooked, although it is only incidentally connected with the present publication. The comparison of the Charters, one with another, and of all with other Manuscripts in similar characters, is most instructive. The variations in the style of writing of documents so nearly of the same age point to the prevalence of special forms in the different divisions of the island ; and if the examples had been drawn from the archives of monasteries in various districts, a very important classification of handwritings by localities would probably have been possible."[1] A second and more extended series of these charters is now in course of preparation, and in a very forward state. In the year 1875 a very fine series of early English Charters, preserved among the muniments at Exeter Cathedral were photographed by the silver positive process, but their size necessitated a slight reduction in the pictures which did not add to their useful-ness. In the same year, M. Léopold Delisle, of the Bibliothèque Nationale, gave to the world the facsimiles of Eugyppius, which have been mentioned in the Introduction, page xi. In addition to the numerous works already mentioned some substantial account must be taken of the publications of various societies in England and abroad, which, either from their connection with archæology generally, such as the Society of Antiquaries, the British Archæological Association, the Royal Archæological Institute, and kindred societies in many counties, or from their

[1] Pref. p. viii.

own special devotion to subjects of palæography,
such as the *École des Chartes*, and the Palæographical Society, naturally contain much that is
useful, necessary, and instructive with regard to the
careful examination of writings and Manuscripts of
bygone ages.

The formation of the Palæographical Society
dates from November, 1873, and, contemporary
with the establishment of this prosperous undertaking, must be taken the foundation of a new and
native school of palæography, which seeks by the
extensive employment of permanent photography to
extend the study, and by means of perfectly trustworthy facsimiles to collect useful data upon which
to build hereafter more correct general rules than
have as yet been laid down. Mr. Bond, in his
address issued at the date mentioned above, says of
its scope :—" This society has been formed for the
purpose of collecting materials for the study of a
branch of antiquarian science not yet established on
a satisfactory basis, though one in which it is
possible to attain to a very great exactness. That
palæography has hitherto been treated with imperfect success is owing to the incompleteness, both
in quantity and quality, of facsimile specimens of
ancient writing and ornamentation of Manuscripts,
on the evidence of which it has been attempted to
establish definite conclusions. And this deficiency
is most apparent for the more remote times, the
extant Manuscripts of which are few in number and
usually undated. As they are also widely dispersed,
the means of study of forms of characters and other

peculiarities by comparison of the original writings have been proportionately limited. . . . . It is by the mechanical autotype process of photography, by which permanent impressions can be produced, that it is proposed to work ; and by means of it to form an ample collection of facsimiles from pages of ancient Manuscripts and other early writings, exact in every particular except actual colours. The action of the Society will be extended to foreign countries; and the finest examples of writing and ornamentation will be selected."

And with this extract from the starting point of a Society which has now issued upwards ot sixty full-page plates of facsimiles of a very large variety of ancient writings, the reader may leave the consideration of abstract palæography, and pass on to the consideration of the lessons laid before him in the pages of the " UTRECHT PSALTER."

CHAPTER II.

IN the present chapter it is proposed to give the reader a carefully drawn description of the Manuscript, taken as an object of antiquity only; apart, that is, from the account of its artistic and palæographical contents, the contemplation and discussion of these being intended to form the subject of a subsequent chapter. It is also proposed in this place to investigate, as far as may be, the circumstances under which the Manuscript passed into the possession of Sir Robert Cotton, one of the most ardent and indefatigable collectors of Manuscripts whom any age or any country has the honour of having numbered among her men of mark and of worth; the probable manner of the abstraction of the Psalter from the Cottonian Library; and its deposition in the Library of Utrecht in the Netherlands, where it is now preserved in the manner due to its transcendent value and interest.

The volume, which measures as nearly as possible thirteen inches in height, by ten in breadth,

and may be called a large sized quarto, or small
folio, contains one hundred and eight leaves of
vellum, of which the quality and appearance has
been described in different terms by those who
fortunately have been enabled to examine it during
its brief sojourn in this country, and by those who
had the opportunity of inspecting it at the Utrecht
Library. According to some writers, " the vellum [1]
is leathery and wants the fine surface of a very
ancient Manuscript;" and, " though not thick, is not
of a fine texture. It is of a rather soft leatherlike
consistency which bends easily under its own
weight; and it has none of the smooth crispness
which one looks for in very ancient Manuscripts." [2]
On the other hand it has been recorded, that " the
vellum [3] on which the Psalter, the Canticles, the
Lord's Prayer, and the two Creeds are written is of
a delicate and uniform texture; so fine, indeed that
the writing and drawings on one side of the page can
be easily seen and read on the other. It is quite
different from that containing the fragments of the
Gospels, bound up in the same volume, and from the
vellum generally used in the eighth, ninth, and
succeeding centuries."

There is no doubt that a careful consideration of
the actual material upon which any Manuscript is
written is a positively necessary, and frequently very
valuable, element in the determining of the period of
the production of that Manuscript. It is, moreover,

---

[1] Report by Mr. E. A. Bond, keeper of the MSS. in the British Museum.

[2] Report by Mr. E. M. Thompson, Assistant keeper.

[3] Second Report of Sir Thomas Hardy, p. 10.

a well-known canon in the Science of Palæography, that every country, and every successive age, made use of a different species of the vehicle by means of which it was alone able to hand down its written productions to future times. The preparation and method of finishing vellum varied considerably, not only with the century during which, but with the kingdom, and even the very locality in which it was prepared; and an eye experienced in the examination of ancient vellum Manuscripts is enabled to distinguish quite as many subtle varieties in the quality, the substance, and—if such a term may be properly applied to it—the texture of the skin, as it can in the forms of the letters which that skin bears upon its surface, or in the density and colour of the ink with which those forms are written.

The vellum employed by those engaged in the *scriptoria*, or *writing schools* of England, as exhibited by the consideration of a large number of our ancient national Manuscripts—both books and charters—of the eighth, ninth, and tenth centuries, partakes of several natures. We may select, for example, from the vast repertory in the British Museum, the fine and smooth white skin of crisply sharp firmness; the white and glazy kind, of a thin and delicate softness; the brown, hard, leathery, and heavy sort, chiefly seen in the Charters and diplomatic documents of the regal chancery; and the rough, coarse, almost hide-like parchment that obtains in documents which may be unquestionably demonstrated to belong to an age contemporary with the finer and more beautiful qualities.

But the fineness, of the vellum of the eighth century, for example, differs specifically from the fineness of that of the tenth, and this again from that of the twelfth century ; and the roughness and coarseness of the thick and leathery parchment of the ninth century is easily distinguishable from the thick and leathery kind affected in the fourteenth, fifteenth, and sixteenth centuries. The vellum of Irish Manuscripts is remarkably thick, harsh, and dark-coloured ; that of Scotland, little less so ; but both differ very considerably from that of English Manuscripts of several periods. And these distinctions exist, too, in a very unmistakeable and self-evident degree. In fact there is hardly a single Manuscript which may not have a peculiar and appropriate epithet applied to its substance to distinguish it from all others. The terms *leatherlike* and *leathery*, which have been, as is shown, attributed to the vellum of the Utrecht Psalter, must be received with some degree of reservation and explanation. For while on the one hand it must be admitted that the vellum, when compared with other vellum of later ages, has a leathery feeling, yet it is far from meriting the indiscriminate application of this word. A better term would perhaps have been *hardened*, for while the parchment possesses a transparency, which is quite remarkable for its frequency throughout the volume, not a mere soaking through of inks and pigments, but a decided amount of translucency which occasionally permits the finest lines to be seen on the opposite side to that on which they have been drawn ; yet there is a hard and substantially firm and thick feeling of a smooth material when the page is held in the hand. And again, this property of transparency is by no means a characteristic of leather, and the term *leathery* can scarcely be rightly applied to this semi-lucent skin.

The volume is made up, by *quaternions* or gatherings, that is, quires of eight leaves of vellum folded one within the other in the way now employed ordinarily for books. The writing is between two lines, parallel, or at least intended to be parallel, for the equality of distance between the pairs of lines has not always been faithfully carried out. These lines are ruled with a dry point, or plummet, horizontally, between three pairs of vertical bounding lines, symmetrically arranged to carry within them the three columns of the writings. On the outer margins to the right and left of these columns, the space of an inch or sometimes more has been left; the two inner spaces are about half an inch wide; the upper margins are about an inch; and the lower margins are between two and three inches in width; but "all¹ the margins have been much clipped." In every page this three-fold arrangement of columns of lines has been preserved, but some of the columns, although they have been ruled, are not filled up with writing when the Psalm finishes well down in the lower half of the columns.

The initial letters of the sentences are written in uncial characters, and are placed outside the vertical lines which bound the column of text, and of this

¹ Mr. Bond's Report.

unusual position, as well as of the writing being placed between pairs of lines, we are told, " the writing ' is between double lines, not on single ones ; the ruling being close-set. This circumstance is significant ; supposing the scribe to be writing in an unaccustomed style, in which his hand would require guidance ; for the writing is not of that exact regularity which is found in ancient Manuscripts when written between lines. The arrangement of the initial letters of the verses, regularly placed beyond the margin of writing, is also a rather too artificial method to be consistent with great antiquity." There are about thirty lines of words in each column, the full lines being of fairly equal length, and containing from fifteen to twenty letters on an average. We may here take an example of this arrangement from Psalm CVI. [107] in the facsimiles appended to the Dean of Westminster's Reports.

> *CVI ALLELUIA*
> C *ONFITEMINI DÑO*
> QNM̄BONUS.ʔQNM̄INSAE
> CULUMMISERICORDIAEIUS ;
> D ICANTQUIREDEMPTISUNT
> ADÑO.ʔQUOSREDEMITDE
> MANUINIMICI.ʔDEREGIO
> NIBUSCONGREGAUITEOS ;
> A SOLISORTUETOCCASU.ʔ
> ABAQUILONEETMARI ;

CVI. Alleluia.
Confitemini *domino* quon*i*am bonus.ʔ quon*i*am in saeculum misericordia eius ;

' Mr. Thompson's Report, p. 6.

Dicant qui redempti sunt a *domino?* quos redemit de manu inimici? de regionibus congregavit eos ;

A solis ortu et occasu? ab aquilone et mari ;

107. 1. O give thanks unto the Lord for *he is* good : for his mercy *endureth* for ever.

2. Let the redeemed of the Lord say *so*, whom he hath redeemed from the hand of the enemy.

3. And gathered them out of the lands, from the east and from the west, from the north, and from the south.

Sir Thomas Hardy gives[1] other interesting examples of this nature transcribed from portions of the Athanasian creed.

The spaces which contain the pictures do not appear to have been ruled, although in some cases the lines of the drawings have extended over some of the straight lines intended for the reception of the words. No spaces or breaks are observed between the words, but these are written running together with blank intervals only where they are required to mark the terminations of the sentences ; and in these cases the fresh sentences always commence upon a new line. Mr. Bond says that " the words are run together, with only the necessary breaks to mark the alternations and terminations of the verses." But the word verse is apt to be misleading, because the arrangement of sentences in this version of the Psalms does not in all cases correspond with the original Hebrew metrical divisions, nor with later versifications.

The drawings with which that first and principal

---

[1] First Report, p. 14.

part only of the Manuscript that contains the Psalter, has been adorned, and which are intended to illustrate the subjects of the respective Psalms to which they have been attached, extend quite across the page, and are executed in brown or bistre, perhaps a black pigment that has now faded, with a pen or stylus ; perhaps indeed they may have been put in with a very fine brush. They are not enclosed in frames or panels as we observe in some of the older classical Manuscripts, as, for example, the Vatican Virgil alluded to in page 16 and the following pages. In all there are not less than one hundred and sixty-six of these illustrations, each of which has some sort of reference, more or less realistic, to the metaphorical language of the poet. These drawings, with the analysis of the artistic elements they possess, will form the subject of a future chapter.

It is curious to note that faint outlines of fleeting figures, and imperfect groups of shadowy forms, generally corresponding with some of the finished forms in the adjacent drawings, can be observed here and there, by close examination, upon the lower margins, and sometimes in the body of the drawing itself. It is difficult to decide whether these sketches really represent to us the first essays of the artist who was here trying the effect of certain compositions before he drew them fairly in their proper places, or whether they are mere scrawls which have been suggested to some contemporary idler who has whiled away his time in looking over the Manuscript and injuring it. One theory certainly has been recorded that "does' not consider the marginal drawings, which occur here and there, to be designs for, but rather sketches taken from, the illustrative drawings."

The contents of the Manuscript have been carefully summarised by Sir Thomas Hardy in his first Report,[1] and Mr. Bond has described the various details more briefly. It is not necessary to describe minutely in this place what the book really does contain, inasmuch as some account of the different pieces with which it is composed will be found in the chapter especially devoted to this subject. It is only needful to say for the present that in addition to the text of the Psalms, in Latin, of the version known as the Gallican, which forms the bulk of the volume, and has been the cause of the assignment of the distinctive title of THE UTRECHT PSALTER to it, the volume contains the several canticles of Isaiah, of Moses in Exodus, or *Cantemus Domino*, of Abacuc, of Moses in Deuteronomy, of the Three Children, the *Te Deum*, here called *Hymnum ad Matutinis* (*sic*), the hymns of Zacharias, of Mary, of Simeon, the *Gloria*, the *Pater Noster*, the Apostles' Creed, the Athanasian Creed, or *Fides Catholicam* (*sic*) and the apocryphal Psalm often termed the 151st Psalm. In addition to this collection of Biblical and Liturgical texts—which undoubtedly formed at the time of writing a separate and complete book, for the last leaf has been evidently left blank for a fly leaf, which has indeed, like the first fly leaf at the beginning of the volume, been used for

---

[1] Mr. Thompson's Report, p. 7.   [2] P. 13, 14.

trials of the pen of the scribe, and like the first, too, has several sketches of figures and ornaments, and a few words in various styles of handwriting—there are twelve folios at the end, written in firm strong uncials of a fine character, and containing several disconnected leaves of a copy of the Gospels, viz., Jerome's epistle to Pope Damasus, the concluding part of his second general Preface to the four Evangelists, the Preface of the Gospel of St. Matthew, with the contents of the chapters of that Evangelist; a title medallion, in the margin or space of which is inscribed an invocatory prayer to the B. V. Mary, in Greek; the commencement of the Gospel of St. Matthew, and portion of the first chapter of St. John. All these are comprised in the twelve folios, or twenty-four pages, of two columns each, which are written in fine uncial characters of a solid and excellently formed type.

We have now to trace, as far back as we can, the history of the Utrecht Manuscript, and to examine the various hypotheses that have been placed on record, as being borne out more or less by veritable facts, or by reasonable conjectures founded upon the appearance of the volume itself, and the internal evidence it offers to these ends in view.

It has been suggested by Mr. Howard Payn, in his most interesting letter to Sir Thomas Hardy, printed as *Appendix II.* to the Further Report (pp. 59-63), that the drawings at least of the Manuscript originated at Alexandria at some time between A.D. 373, the date of the death of St. Athanasius, and A.D. 638, "the year in which Alexandria was destroyed, the great library burnt, and the theological schools scattered. At this time, too, the Holy City itself was in the hands of the infidel, and pilgrimages, for a time at any rate, impossible. Had the artist lived then, and had he been compelled to fly to Europe, in the drawings of so accurate an observer we should not fail to find some indications of new objects and scenery among which he had come ; but as far as I can see, no such indications exist. The whole of the drawings show Eastern surroundings, and I think it is not unreasonable to conclude that he carried out his labour of love undisturbed by fire or sword." This, then, is the earliest conjecture that we are invited to consider, and it amounts practically to this, that, provided for the sake of argument we admit the early date which Mr. Payn would attach to the Psalter as correct, and we accept the deductions he has made respecting the perfectly native Eastern style which he observes throughout the drawings, the volume must have been executed by an artist and a theologian of the Alexandrian school ; and we may even go a step further and conceive that it formed one of the precious Manuscripts of the celebrated library at Alexandria,' which was destroyed, according to some, by the Christians ; according to others by the iconoclastic hordes of Mohammedan barbarians, who were addicted solely to war and the chase, and despised the arts and sciences ; under whose destructive hands the finest

---

' For a graphic and succinct account of the *four libraries* at Alexandria, the reader is referred to a Treatise "*On the Extent of Ancient Libraries,*" by W. F. A. Axon, in the *Transactions of the Royal Society of Literature*, Vol. X., Second series, 1874, p. 383-405.

monuments of the Greeks and Romans were levelled to the ground, the libraries reduced to ashes, the schools and seminaries of instruction annihilated, the feeble rays of learning that remained to the vanquished nations being powerless to enlighten or civilise their enemies; so that all arts and sciences unsupported by those ignorant conquerors fell into a contempt from which it took them two centuries or more to gradually extricate themselves.

How far this theory is likely to find favour, even with those who would throw back the date of the Utrecht Psalter to such a remote period, it is difficult to say; but it must be very much modified by the remembrance that Byzantine work was to be found not only in Alexandria, but all over the parts of the world then within the pale of Roman civilisation; and it would be difficult, if not impossible, to find upon any ancient objects, and not only in books, pictorial representations of scenes of similar character to those that have been selected to illustrate the Utrecht Psalter, which, had they been executed within the limits of the early period claimed by Mr. Payn, would not indicate Oriental, *i.e.*, Byzantine influence and treatment. Hence it follows that the fact of this Archaic Byzantine feeling which these drawings so plainly possess does not avail us anything materially towards narrowing the civilised area of possible production of the Psalter, or towards circumscribing the period of its execution.

The next point that we come to in the history of this book is a suggestion made by Sir Thomas

Hardy [1] to explain its importation into England; for it may be taken for granted that the Manuscript itself was not written in this island, because the style would have been so different, and because it contains liturgical pieces and versions not in use among us in the periods assigned throughout for its age. This suggestion is, that the Psalter "may have been brought into England by Bertha, daughter of Chariberct, King of France, and Queen of Athelberct, of Kent, who allowed her to retain the Christian religion, and maintained a bishop here as her spiritual guide, [2] before the arrival of Augustine in Britain." "It is clear," the report goes on to say, "to demonstration, that the Utrecht Psalter was prepared for some special occasion; and the extreme costliness of such a Manuscript in those early times would appear to indicate that the Psalter under discussion must have been the property of some noble or royal personage." "As it was written in some foreign monastery, and was brought into England by Queen Bertha, so I am inclined to think that it was bequeathed by her to the monastery at Reculver, in Kent." The argument proceeds to show that the king built at *Regulbuim, i.e.*, Reculver, a new palace, and it was there that the Queen and her bishop performed the ceremonies of their religion, having previously celebrated them at the old church of St. Martin, outside the eastern walls of Canterbury. That there was a religious body, probably of

[1] First Report, p. 33.

[2] Beda, lib. i. cxxv., states that Athelberct received Bertha from her parents upon condition that she should be permitted to retain her religion, with Bishop Luithard, who was sent with her as an assistant to preserve her faith.

8*

secular priests, perhaps, indeed, a mixed community of professed persons of both sexes, at Reculver, is not indeed stated by Beda, but in A.D. 669 King Ecgbert granted to Bass,' a nobleman who had turned priest, exchanging his sword for a cowl, lands for amplifying the establishment at Reculver. Moreover, ten years later, Hlotharius, king of the Cantuarii, granted other lands at Westanae, in the isle of Thanet, and at Sturry on the Stour, to Bercuald, presumably the abbot, and to his monastery. So that there is no doubt that there was a monastic establishment in a state of organization at this later date.

Curiously enough the Utrecht Psalter itself, at the time that it was in the possession of Sir Robert Cotton contained an exemplar of the very Charter recording this gift. With respect to this, Sir Thomas Hardy says, " this very Charter was *originally inserted* in the Utrecht Psalter." And in a footnote he says, " The *original Charter* is now in the Cottonian collection, Augustus II. 2, and seems to have been removed from the Utrecht Psalter by Sir Robert Cotton himself when the volume was re-bound." There is, however, no evidence to support the fact that the Charter was *originally* inserted into the Psalter. All the fact we have on record is that the Table of Contents, written by a librarian for Sir Robert Cotton in the fly-leaf at the commencement of the Manuscript indicates that in that collector's time, viz., the seventeenth century, there was an

---

¹ Bass, the mass-priest, occurs in the Saxon Chronicle as the founder of the Monastery of Reculver, *sub ann.* 669. See W. de G. Birch, *Fasti Monastici Ævi Saxonici*, p. 47.

original (?) Charter answering to this description, at the end of the volume. We cannot decide now whether the Charter was an insertion or not; whether it was an original document or a copy, for Cotton's opinion on this head is not worth much ; or whether the Charter now in the Cottonian collection under the numeration Augustus II. 2, is the identical document which was abstracted from the Psalter by the illustrious collector, or a duplicate which he acquired for his library from sources entirely independent of the Utrecht Psalter. Judging, as we have every right to judge, from the procedure of Sir Robert Cotton with regard to other Manuscripts in his enormous library, it is far more probable that he would have fallen into the opposite mistake of binding together two or more separate Manuscripts in one volume, a practice of which every one conversant with the contents of the Cotton collection is only too well aware, than of separating one volume of different contents into two or more. Even this very Utrecht Psalter has been by some adduced as an example of his method of grouping two codices of similar proportions under one cover, for Mr. Bond, in his report, writes, " The Gospel fragments . . . . are only accidentally connected with the Psalter by having been bound with it at some comparatively recent time—in all probability by Sir Robert Cotton." So that here, if we follow Sir T. Hardy's reasoning, we have to face the anomalous circumstances that Cotton finds the Utrecht Psalter without the Gospel fragments, but with the Reculver Charter, or, at any rate, that such is the state of the volume on its first passing into his hands ;—(it is certainly an indisputable fact that the last page of the Rustic Psalter has been at one time exposed to rough usage, and is well thumbed, as though the covers had been defective or altogether missing)—he then inserts the Gospel fragments of uncial writing between the Psalter and the Charter, causes a Table of Contents for the compound book to be written in this order: 1, Psalter ; 2, Fragments of Gospels ; 3, Original Charter of Hlothari, and finally, (and strangest of all), he withdraws the Charter and gives it a new place in another part of his library.

Before proceeding any further with this subject it is not out of place to put before the reader a correct transcript of the Augustus Charter itself, and this is due, not only because it, or a duplicate copy of it, certainly formed at one time a component part of the Utrecht Psalter, but also because it is incorrectly printed, not only in Dugdale, Stevens, and other repertories of monastic evidences, but also in Kemble's standard work upon Anglo-Saxon Diplomatics, entitled *Codex Diplomaticus Aevi Saxonici*, Vol. I., No. xvi. ; and in Sir Thomas Hardy's *First Report*, p. 34, note. The typographical transcript attached to the photograph of it in the *Facsimiles of Ancient Charters in the British Museum*, pl. 1, presents the nearest resemblance to the text of the original. It is in mixed uncial and capital characters, and runs as follows :—

+ .In n̄ . d̄[1] nostri saluatoris īhu xp̄i[2] . ego hlo tharius rex cantuariorum[3] pro remedium

---

[1] *Nomine domini*, Hardy.   [2] *Jesu Christi*, H.   [3] *Catnuariorum*, H.

animae meae dono terram . in tenid . quę[1] ap
pellatur . uuestan ⁀ ae[2] tibi bercuald . tuoque
monasterio cum omnib:[3] ad se pertinentibus
çampis pascuis meriscis . siluis modicis . fon
nis piscaris omnibus ut dictum est ad ean
dem terram pertinentia . sicuti nunc usq:[4]
possessa est . iuxta notissimos terminos
a me demonstratus et proacutoribus
meis . eodem modo tibi tuoque monasterio
conferimus . teneas possedeas[5] tu . poste
rique[6] tui inperpetuum[7] defendant a nu
llo contradicitur . cum consensu[8] archi
episcopi theodori et Edrico[9] . filium fra
tris mei necnon[10] et omnium principum .
sicuti tibi donata est ita tene et poste
ri tui :—quisquis contra hanc donatione̅
////[11] uenire temptauerit sit ab omni xp̅iani
tata[12] separatus . et a corpore et sanguini
dn̅i nostri ih̅u xpi[13] suspensus . manentem .
hanc donationis chartulam in sua nihil
ominus firmitate et pro confirmatione
eius manu propria signum sc̅e[14] . crucis
expraessi[15] et testes[16] ut subscribere
nt rogaui . actum in civitate recuulf .
in mense maio[17] inᵹ[18] septima :—In ipsa ante
memorato[19] die adiunxi aliam terram in

---

[1] *Que*, Kemble; *quœ*, H.   [2] *Uuestan ae*, K.; *westan ae*, H.

  [3] *Omnibus*, H.   [4] *Usque*, H.   [5] *Possideas*, K.

[6] *Qui*, altered into *que*, Facs.   [7] *In perpetuum*, H. and B. M.

Consenso, altered into *consensu*, F.   [9] *Edrico*, K., H.   [10] *Nec non*, K.

Donatione | m, but *m* erased and the line over the *e* inserted, F.; *donationem*, H.

[12] *Christianatata*, H.   [13] *Jesu Christi*, H.   [14] *Sancte*, H.

Express, H.   [16] Erasure here, F.   [17] Erased letter between *a* and *i*, F.

[18] *Indictione*, H.; *ind̄*, B. M.   [19] *Antememorato*, K., H., B. M.

sturia iuxta notissimos terminos
a me demonstratus[1] et proacutori
bus meis cum campis et siluis et pra
tis sicuti ante memorabimus[2] supra
dictam terram . ita ista sit a me donata
eodem modo cum omnibus ad se perti /////
///// nentia[3] in potestate ab̄b̄ sit . inperpe
tuum[4] . a me donata . a nullo contradicitur
quod absit: neque a me neque a parentibus
meis neque ab aliis . si aliquis aliter fecerit
a d̄o se damnatum sciat . et in die iudicii ratio
nem reddet d̄o in anima[5] sua :— ·
+ Signum[6] manus hlothari regis donatoris
+ Signum manus gumbercti : + Signū[7] manus[8]
gẹbredi :[9]— + Signum manus osfridi :—
+ Signum mạnus irminredi + Signum manus
aedilmaeri[10] . + Signum manus hagani .[11]
+ Signum manus aeldredi : + Signum manus
aldhodi :— + Signum manus gudhardi :
+ Signum manus bernhardi . + Signum manus
uelhisci :.—   :.—

Now, whether Sir Robert Cotton came into
possession of the Psalter and Charter contained
within the same covers, as Sir Thomas Hardy
thinks, or not, as Mr. Bond thinks, there is nothing in
the way of record left to bear directly upon the
subject either way. It is a well-known fact that Sir
Robert Cotton was commonly in the habit of

---

[1] *Demonstratos,* H.   [2] *Antememorabimus,* B. M.
[3] Originally *pertinen | tinentia,* but *nen | ti* erased, F.   [4] *In perpetuum,* K.
[5] *Inanima,* H.   [6] + *Signum* to the end of the text in a different hand, F.
[7] *Signum,* K., H.   [8] *Us* conjoined, F.   [9] *Gebredi,* K., H.
[10] *Aedibmaeri,* H.   [11] *Hacani,* H.

binding up into convenient volumes Manuscripts of
all ages, and on paper or vellum, provided only the
sizes fitted tolerably well together, although even this
necessary point of agreement was not always adhered
to. He even went further than this, and cut out
from illuminated Manuscripts and printed books
miniature paintings or engraved titles wherewith to
embellish, as he thought, other more precious Manuscripts. But we do not find any direct evidence of
his being accustomed to insert a separate Charter
into a volume. On the contrary there is every
reason to believe that his formation of a collection
of Charters, which now exists to the number of
upwards of thirteen thousand, was commenced about
the same time that he began to acquire his library
of Manuscripts; and, in addition to this separate
collection of Charters, two designations of his Manuscripts (*codices*), viz., Augustus II., and Nero C. III.,
appear to have been portfolios, or boxes, specially
arranged to hold Charters, and yet to range themselves, like books, in their places in the book shelves,
which, being surmounted by busts of the Roman
Emperors, took from these busts the distinctive
press-marks by which they are now known.

If this be so, there appears to be no necessity
for his binding up a Charter here in Claudius C.
VII., the Utrecht Psalter; nor for his pursuing a
similar course in regard to another deed in another
volume of which notice will be presently made.
Hence it must be conceded, that while there is no
doubt that the Charter and the Psalter were connected in some way before they passed into the

Cotton library, there is at the same time nothing as yet on record to show at what period, anterior to Cotton, this literary union had been effected. And, to endeavour to show that because a Reculver Charter (of A.D. 679) is bound up with the Manuscript, therefore it is to be accepted as a conclusion that the Manuscript itself is of that early date, and connected with that monastery, is as peculiar a reasoning as would be to say that because a man hangs up in his house an Italian picture of the fifteenth century, therefore the house is of that date and connected with that country. The most that can be admitted is, that the Charter was inserted into the volume previous to the joint acquisition of the two relics by Sir Robert Cotton; and it may be even imagined without difficulty that the volume passed into the possession of the monastery at Reculver when the head or librarian of that religious house, following a not uncommon custom, inserted into the sacred volume as it were into an impregnable sanctuary whence no sacrilegious hand should snatch it, so precious a title-deed of his house as this Charter undoubtedly is, at a time as late as the tenth or eleventh century. But the actual Charter, now numbered Augustus II. 2, bears no marks of having been stitched into the Utrecht Psalter or into any other book, and it is not of a size with the Psalter, for it measures (even in its mutilated state) 13 by 6 inches, although, on the other hand, it has been very closely cut in all its margins, so that perhaps the holes of the bookbinders' needles have been trimmed away.

We may also reasonably presume that if the removal of the Charter from any other location in the Cottonian collection had been carried out in compliance with the intention of Sir Robert Cotton, some record of its original numeration and position would remain, but there is nothing to indicate that such was the case. We may too, with equal reason, expect to find an explanatory note on the page containing the *elenchus* or descriptive title of the Utrecht Psalter (Claudius C. VII.), wherein the Charter is specified as existing in the volume. And we should certainly expect to find the words relating to the Charter scored out with a pen, but nothing of the kind has been done. So, too, should we expect to find some literary notice of the document being missing from the Psalter, in the writings of contemporary cataloguers and Manuscript readers, but it is not so.

Far different from all these are the circumstances surrounding a volume preserved in the same magnificent library, which presents so many points of illustration that we must of necessity take them into consideration. The Manuscript entitled *Vespasian A. I.* is a Roman Psalter most beautifully written in fine uncial character of about A.D. 700, with some pages in Rustic handwriting of somewhat later dates, prefixed and inserted into it. The Latin text has been interlined with Saxon glosses. The *elenchus* which was prefixed to this venerable Manuscript, during the lifetime, and in all probability under the immediate supervision of Sir Robert Cotton, runs as follows :—

" 1. Psalterium Romanum antiquo charactere cum interlineari interpretatione Saxonica, *cui præfixa est donatio antiqua regis Australium Saxonum Æthelbaldi*, et ad finem habetur symbolum Athanasii Saxonice etiam interlineatum cum aliis hymnis et precibus. Codex iste scriptus videtur Anno 700 a Nativ. Xpi." From the *italic* words in the above sentence it is clear that a charter of Æthelbald king of the West Saxons, was, at the time of composing this table of contents, prefixed to the Psalter, much in the same way as the Reculver Charter was suffixed to the Utrecht Psalter. Richard James, Fellow of Corpus Christi College, Oxford, a literary man of distinction in the seventeenth century, and contemporary of Sir Robert Cotton, who knew more about the Cottonian library in his own times than any one else, not even excepting Cotton himself, bears witness to the safety of the Charter in the Vespasian Psalter. But between his date and the compilation of Thomas Smith's Catalogue of the Cottonian Manuscripts, published at Oxford in 1696, the document had been abstracted, for we read in Smith's work (p. xxxv.) the following regretful words: " Donatio antiqua Æthelbaldi, Regis Australium Saxonum, quam libro Psalmorum olim præpositam fuisse memorat D. Jamesius, ... ab aliqua impia manu abscinditur."

The *impia manus*, nevertheless, has not carried the Charter very far off; it, too, rests at the present moment in the British Museum, only five paces distant from the volume which afforded it a sacred protection for so many centuries, for at some time during the period between 1696 and 1802 it was found in the portfolio which Cotton designated as Augustus II., placed the very next in order to the Reculver Charter, and numbered 3 in that priceless series of records of our Saxon history. On its discovery and ensuing identification, some hand, probably that of a Cottonian librarian, has drawn a pen and ink through the words in italics in the *elenchus* given above, and the same pen has inserted in the margin the note " V[*ide*]. Aug. II. 2," the 2 being afterwards corrected in pencil by a later hand into 3. In like manner the folio Parliamentary Catalogue of the Cotton Manuscripts, which was published in 1802, speaking of Augustus II. 3, says: " This Charter was formerly in the Psalter Vespasian A. 1 ;" and the same Catalogue gives the following account of the Psalter styled Vespasian A. 1 : " 2. Psalterium D. Hieronymi Romanum elegantissime litteris capitalibus, in Anglia, scriptum et illuminatum ; cui postea accedit interlineata Versio Saxonica ; folium primum, mala manu abscissum, continebat Psalmum primum integrum et secundi partem ; exscinditur etiam charta donationis Æthelbaldi R. Merciorum, quam hinc libro Psalmorum olim præpositam fuisse memorat D. Jamesius, *quæ autem hodie in codice August. I. [II.], No. 3, asservatur.*" And the same Catalogue, speaking of the Charter, in the description of the *Codex* Augustus II., says : " This Charter was formerly in the Psalter Vespasian A. I." The Charter itself, although it shows no marks of having been bound up, has been very much trimmed away on all its margins. It has been frequently printed, by Dugdale in his *Monasticon Anglicanum* under his account of Worcester Cathedral, Vol. I., Appendix, No. VII.; by Stevens in his *Continuation*, Vol. II., Appendix, p. 208; by Kemble in his *Codex Diplomaticus*, Vol. I., No. LXXX.; and a facsimile of it is given in autotype permanent photography, together with a printed transcript, in the *Facsimiles of Ancient Charters in the British Museum*, No. 7. It relates to the foundation of a religious house at Stour, or Stourminster, generally identified with Kidderminster, and probably one of several which were impropriated and absorbed into the more extensive establishment at Worcester; and it bears the date A.D. 736.

From the above consideration it is perfectly clear that while the removal of the Mercian Charter of Æthelbald from Vespasian A. I. was discovered and noted before 1802, yet the removal of the Reculver Charter from the Utrecht Psalter, under identically similar circumstances, was certainly not known in that year, for in that case a note would have been given to that effect in the Catalogue printed in that year, under the description of Augustus II., 2, its present and its then position.

Another instance of a very similar procedure (but where no removal has been practised) will be noticed in a third Cottonian Manuscript, Otho. C. I. pars I., a tenth century copy of the Gospels in Anglo-Saxon, where on two leaves, (folios 68, 69), the first of which contains four lines concluding the Gospel of St. Luke, there is an Anglo-Saxon translation of a Latin Bull or Rescript of Pope Sergius I., *circ.*

A.D. 701, in favour of the Abbey of Malmesbury. The Gospel of St. John begins on folio 70. And Mr. N. E. Hamilton, the learned editor of the *Gesta Pontificum* of William of Malmesbury, for the Master of the Rolls' Series of Chronicles and Memorials, in printing this Anglo-Saxon translation for the first time, deduces from this fact of the insertion of this Charter, that it seems " probable that the Manuscript Otho. C. 1. belonged to the monastery at Malmesbury." No doubt other examples of similar treatment might be adduced from the Manuscripts in the Cotton collection. But enough has been said to show the practice of English monasteries before the Conquest by the Normans with respect to inserting original deeds or copies of them into Biblical Manuscripts, or transcribing their Charters into spare leaves in the body of the books themselves.

It is necessary now to revert to the concluding considerations of the theory adopted by Sir Thomas Hardy regarding the preservation of the Utrecht Psalter in the monastery of Reculver. It has been already shown that he would rely upon the finding of this Charter in the volume as the principal, indeed only reason for associating the volume with that ancient monastery. It has also been shown how weak and insufficient that evidence, taken by itself is to support such a theory. We have, however, to hear the remarks of Sir Thomas in his *Further Report*[1] upon this head. These remarks are so valuable and so instructive upon the subject that they must be repeated here. " It was the custom to

---

[1] P. 39, 40.

place royal and other Charters in valuable books and chartularies for preservation, for it was not every monastery that possessed means of recording gifts. The smallness of Reculver would almost determine that it did not possess any ; what then would be more natural than the abbot should place such a valuable document as the Charter of king Lothair in the highest place of honour with which he was acquainted ; and what higher would occur to him than in a valuable Psalter presented to his house by Queen Bertha ? . . . The Abbey of Reculver had been dissolved[1] centuries before the reign of Henry VIII. ; what then became of this strip of parchment during all the centuries which passed between these two dates ? was it kicked about somewhere or other until the time of the suppression of monasteries ? Then why was it placed in that particular Psalter, if there had not been a tradition that it had belonged to Reculver ? . . . I may ask where the Charter had been kept between the time of the suppression of monasteries and when Sir Robert Cotton placed it in this Psalter. Why did he select this particular Psalter ? I would also ask . . . whether it is probable that Sir Robert Cotton would himself have placed the Charter of Lothair in the Psalter, and then have removed it to Augustus II., where it now is ? I am inclined to believe that the Charter was in the Manuscript when it came into possession of Sir Robert Cotton, and that he removed it to Augustus II." After further observa-

[1] The Abbey was founded for Benedictines in A.D. 669; they were removed, *circ.* A.D. 949; but deans occur, *circ.* A.D. 1030, showing that the secular clergy had replaced the regular monks.

tions, tending to show that there was no necessity for the Charter to be *bound* in the volume, although there placed, the *Further Report*,' referring to the *First Report*, proceeds :—" I conjectured that it (the Utrecht Psalter) was written in some monastery where the Gallican Ritual obtained, and accompanied Bertha, daughter of Chariberct, King of France, when she came here to be united in marriage to Athelberct, King of Kent, who, though himself a Pagan, allowed her to retain the Christian religion under the guidance of Luithard, who accompanied her, before the arrival of St. Augustine in Britain. I then stated that the Utrecht Psalter was in all probability prepared for some special occasion ; and the costliness of such a Manuscript in those early times would appear to indicate that it must have been the property of some noble or royal personage, and I added that it is evident that the Manuscript was not written for an Anglo-Saxon personage, or it would have had an interlinear translation into that language ; that Bertha, being a French Princess, would not require such assistance." Sir Thomas then goes on to quote an independent confirmation of his opinion that it was written for Bertha's mother, who presented it to her daughter on coming into Britain, which has been conveyed to him, and by him to us, in these words :—" You trace it to Bertha—let me give some further links. The Kentish queen was brought up by her mother, Ingolberga, at Tours, after the desertion of the latter by Chariberct, in the strictest seclusion, under the eye of Gregory of Tours, who has recorded her

last moments.   But Gregory had another friend and
protégé living at Tours at this period, viz., Venantius Fortunatus, to whom (on independent grounds)
Muratori has assigned the compilation of the Athanasian creed.   The occasion for this is indicated by
Pope Pelagius' letter to Childebert, showing the
increasing progress of Eutychianism in France.
And here a fresh link appears.   Avitus, Bishop of
Vienne, (who died in 523,) had written letters against
the heresies of Sabellius, Arius, and Eutyches, at
the instance of King Gunebald, which were so
highly valued that they were read in the church of
Tours as a safeguard against these dangers. . . . .
Might we not suppose that Fortunatus, who was a
Christian poet, was led by his patron Gregory to
give these letters a hymnal and antiphonal form for
the purpose of chanting ?"

   Having now before us the whole of the evidence,
for and against the theory that the Reculver
monastery was the first home of the Utrecht Psalter
in England, and having shown how weak is the
evidence which connects it with that monastery, it
remains for us to adopt some theory to account for
the insertion of the Reculver Charter, by binding or
otherwise, into the volume.   For there is little
doubt that the connection between Charter and book
took place before the suppression of monasteries.
It would appear that in seeking to connect Queen
Bertha with the Psalter, and so begging the question
of its date, there has been a departure from, and a
rejection of the evidence of, material facts, and a
simultaneous flight into the realms of fancy, un-

fettered by any evidences or proofs wherewith to check or moderate theories which are certainly as interesting and alluring as they are improbable and inconsistent. And in this flight of fancy where we can imagine the deserted Queen Ingolberga solacing her woes at Tours with contemplating the materialism of the pictures in her Psalter, and alternately wondering at the incongruities they would represent to her, and admiring the facility with which the pen of the artist has sketched out the ideas which the language of the Psalmist has conveyed to his simple soul; where we can imagine the royal daughter, Bertha, reverently depositing the precious volume in the monastery of Reculver, and bequeathing it to the Abbey at her death; in these misty reveries, and in the glamour of these surroundings we have allowed ourselves to be carried away unnecessarily from the consideration of one or two facts which are very important, and entirely do away with the necessity of connecting the volume with Reculver, while at the same time they reasonably account for the presence of the Reculver Charter in the pages of the book.

The theory that appears to be more consistent with established facts, and less dependent upon conjectures, is briefly this. To commence: the Charter is a grant by Hlothari, King of the Cantuarii, "to thee Bercwald, and to thy monastery," "with the consent of the Archbishop Theodore," and is witnessed by a number of nobles, not of bishops, abbots, and other dignitaries of the church. There can be no doubt that these circumstances point to very remarkable proceedings which the Charter chronicles, between the lines, yet manifestly, if one will only take the trouble to accept the hidden meaning it plainly conveys. A careful inspection of the Charter points undoubtedly to the fact, that it is not the *original Charter*, but a copy, executed after a considerable interval of time. This is borne out by the presence of innumerable proofs. If we turn to the facsimile published for the British Museum, or, better still, to the Charter itself, Augustus II., we shall see that a number of the words are wrongly divided, and portions of two consecutive words frequently conjoined; for example, the words " Uuest-anae tibi " are actually written ". Uuestan ⁀ aetibi," a stop intervening between two parts of the word designating the place, and the final letters run on to the following pronoun. There is the phrase " sicut-anteme morabimus," where three words are made into two, thus, two and part of the third form the first, and the remainder of the third forms the last. The clerical errors of the text have been corrected, and yet while the eye of the corrector has not been offended by the foregoing examples, it has been offended by the final letter of *donationem* being set upon a new line, and so he has erased the *m* and added a mark (~) over the *e*. The corrector has also emended some clerical blunders which he has left to stand in their amended form thus, " ettest es ut sub scribere nt" for "et testes ut subscriberent." His eye has also detected the blunder of *pertinentinentia* and erased the first *nenti*. All these point invincibly to this, that the deed is a copy of the original document. Another very strong proof of this is that the clause containing the attestations is written in another hand, very closely resembling, but yet in general *ensemble* unmistakeably different from the handwriting which is shown in the body of the text. This would not have been the case with the original deed, which would have been drawn up by the royal scribe at one consecutive sitting, the names of the nobles who were present being entered in their proper order, the *signum manus* merely being a conventional form of signifying their concurrence with the object of the Charter, and not their actual subscription, as it came to mean in after years, to which we must assign the date of this copy which by a change of hand seeks to convey to us that the subscriptions are genuine autographic representations. By thus showing that the deed is not original, we by no means desire to assert that it is a fabrication. The practice of the earlier Anglo-Saxons, as is indeed well known, was to multiply examples of their title-deeds, for there was no royal registry or chancery wherein to enrol or to deposit them. Hence those whose property depended upon the ability to produce immediate documentary evidence of their right to holdings of territory, took good care to provide against loss of their Charters by fire, theft, carelessness, or decay. It is to this custom that we owe the fact that so many duplicate copies of Saxon Charters are yet extant, some of which, when tested by the scientific examination of palæography, have evidently been prepared as late as the twelfth century, a hundred and fifty years

after the domination of that dynasty. It is a significant point in this deed, that although the grant is
made with the consent of Theodore, Archbishop of
Canterbury, his name has been omitted from the list
of subscribing witnesses. This is very suspicious,
for although Theodore frequently appears in the
Charters of this period, whether his name is introduced into the text or not, I only find one instance
where allusion is made to the Archbishop (or his
predecessor perhaps) where Theodore's name does
not appear among the witnesses, and this, an
undated Charter of Osuuini, king of the Cantuarii,
has been marked as doubtful by Kemble, who has
edited it in Vol. I., No. x. of his celebrated *Codex*.

It is curious, but it will be profitable, to conjecture,
if we may, the reason why the consent of the Archbishop of Canterbury was required under the circumstances of the case. The king is giving to a
monastery in his dominions certain lands over which
he enjoys absolute power. There is no doubt that
Theodore, the head of the Church in the province,
would be consulted, but we may go further than
this, and without travelling out of the path of
possible facts, believe that there was a very close
bond of union between the great house at Canterbury, and the unpretending little monastery presided
over by Bercwald at Reculver, a few miles nearer
to the sea. It is well known that monastic establishments, generally but not necessarily of the same
order, were in the habit of entering into confraternity
with each other (not in any way connected with their
revenues, which were always distinct), not only,

like Wearmouth and Jarrow, when they were situate in close proximity one with the other, as was the case with Canterbury and Reculver, but we find long distances, such as those which lay between Worcester, and Evesham, and Chertsey; between Durham and Chertsey; Durham and Pershore; Durham and Westminster; Malmesbury and Gloucester; Evesham and Whitby; Evesham and York; Cirencester and Bruerne; bridged over by the fraternization of the houses,[1] whereby the members of the one entered into close compact with those of the other, to share its joys and its fears, to lean mutually upon each other for moral and

[1] Hickes in his *Dissertatio Epistolaris* gives the Anglo-Saxon text and Latin translation of a mutual compact of fraternization between Wulfstan, Bishop of Worcester, and the Benedictine houses of Evesham, Chertsey, Bath, Pershore, Winchelcombe, Gloucester, and Worcester, from a Manuscript at Corp. Chr. Coll., Cambr., *Miscell.* G. p. 55.

In the Cotton Manuscript, Titus D. xxvi., folio 17 *b*; an early eleventh century book belonging to the Abbot of Newminster, is a formula of the agreement entered into by fraternising monasteries at that time, see *English Cyclopædia, Arts and Sciences, Supplement,* col. 1069.

The Cotton Manuscript, Domitian vii. ff. 33 *b*, 44, records similar agreements between Durham Cathedral and Chertsey Abbey, between Durham and Gregory of Bermondsey, a professed writer of Manuscripts; between Durham and Wlfravenus, Canon of St. Paul's; between Durham and Pershore Abbey; between William, Bishop of Durham, and Vitalis, Abbot of Westminster for themselves and their respective monks. Gloucester, Lastingham, Winchester, Coventry, Canterbury, Fécamp and Caen in Normandy, Glastonbury and Hackness entered into similar fraternity with Durham, attracted probably by the fame of St. Cuthbert.

William of Malmesbury in his *Gesta Pontificum*, Ed. Hamilton, p. 293, says that St. Oswald's Priory of Austin Canons at Gloucester was conjoined "affinitate arctissima" with his own Benedictine monastery of Malmesbury.

The Abbey of Evesham (in its Register, MS., Cotton, Vespasian B. xxiv., folio 11) was in fraternity with Malmesbury; with St. Mary's Abbey York (folio 12 *b*), and of Whitby, it says, "quod hēē due congregationes quasi una erunt."

The Cotton MS. Vitellius E. xvii. belonged to a religious house, now not identified, which was leagued by conventions with Peterborough, Worcester, Gloucester, Reading, Tewkesbury, Chertsey, Burton, Ely, Abingdon, Glastonbury, Lewes, St. Albans, Durham, Merton, Malmesbury, Bury, Westminster, Wherwell, Romsey, Bec, and Battle.

For the text of the agreement between Cirencester and Brueria, see Madox's *Formulare Anglicanum,* p. 301.

Further remarks on this interesting subject may be found in Silvestre's *Account of the Mortuary Roll of St. Vitalis,* pl. clxxxii.; and see B. M., Add. MS. 28,107, f. 239 *b*.

spiritual support, and to benefit by the spiritual exercises and worldly experiences of their fellow-workmen in the field of Christ. Although there is no direct evidence that can be brought to bear upon this assumption, it is a very natural solution of the question raised concerning the consent of Theodore being required to the gift of land to Reculver. It is quite possible that at those early times the Arch-bishop was considered the natural head of all monasteries within his province; but the unsettled state of both lay and ecclesiastical rule in England would require that we should receive such a pro-position with great reserve; whereas from analogy there is nothing to militate against the idea of a confraternity being in operation between the Bene-dictine houses of Canterbury and Reculver.

But be this as it may, it is sufficient for the argument to indicate, that there was a connection either as between two brothers, or in the light of head and branch, between these two establishments: and this resulted in the very example of Bercwald himself being raised from the comparatively unim-portant position of Abbot of Reculver (perhaps for his services to the Queen Bertha) to the all-powerful office of Archbishop of Canterbury, in A.D. 693, on the death of Theodore. What could be more natural under these circumstances than to conceive the ties of brotherhood drawn more closely around the monastery of Reculver and the Cathedral of Canterbury when the Abbot of the one is elevated to the dignity of Archbishop of the other?

It is this fact which more reasonably explains the

connection of the Reculver Charter with the Kentish Court in these early years, than any other yet adduced. Indeed, it almost ceases to be conjectural that the favoured Abbot, on the occasion of his election, 1st July, A.D. 692, to the vacant archiepiscopate, or on that of his ordination by Godwine, the Archbishop of Lyons, which was solemnised on the 29th of June, A.D. 693, or, finally, on the ceremony of his enthronement at Canterbury on the 31st of August[1] in the same year, removed, together with other documents of a more private and personal nature, this royal Charter addressed to himself by name, as well as to the Abbey of which he was the head. At any rate, it is quite likely that he had a duplicate copy of it for his own use. There must undoubtedly have been a very close connection, even at this early period, between the Abbey of Reculver, wherein, as we have already observed, members of the Royal Family were sometimes domiciled, and Canterbury, the capital city of the kingdom of the Cantuarii : and this connection was assuredly in some measure contributory to the elevation of the Abbot to the dignity of the Archiepiscopate. In addition to this, the harmony of feeling which existed between Archbishop Theodore and Abbot Bercwald in respect to the peculiar and novel proceedings of Wilfrid of York may have had something to do with it.[2] And this very elevation, as it is equally reasonable to believe, operated by drawing

[1] Beda, *Historia Ecclesiastica*, v. 8.

[2] See William of Malmesbury's *Gesta Pontificum*, Ed. Hamilton, Index s. v. *Berhtwald, Theodore, Wilfrid*.

even yet more closely the bonds of a spiritual fellow-
ship, should we reject the probability of an organised
and definite fraternisation having arisen between the -
two religious and ecclesiastical establishments.

Another valuable evidence of the close affinity of
these contiguous churches is afforded by a passage
in Dugdale's *Monasticon Anglicanum*,' where it is
stated "that in a Manuscript Chartulary of the
Archbishopric of Canterbury in the Bodleian
Library at Oxford, several grants of lands and
privileges to this monastery (of Reculver) are
recorded, as well as the substance of them, in the
Evidentiae Ecclesiae Christi Cantuariae, printed in the
*Decem Scriptores*ᵃ by Twysden."

Yet stronger still is the historical fact, that in the
year 949 the monastery of Reculver and its posses-
sions were annexed to the Cathedral of Christ
Church, Canterbury, by a special Charter of King
Eadred, which has been frequently printed; and,
curiously enough, there was evidently some peculiar
interest attached to the transfer, for no less a personage than St. Dunstan himself composed and
wrote out the words of the Charter "propriis digitorum articulis."ᵃ It is worthy of remark in this
place that at times somewhat later, the text of the

---

¹ Vol. I., p. 454.

² Part II., col. 2207, 2220, from a Manuscript in Corpus Christi College, Cambridge.

³ *V.* Dugdale, *Monasticon*, I. 455 where it is printed "Ex ipso autographo in
Bibliotheca Cottoniana," viz., Augustus II. 57; another record from the *Codex
Augustus II.*, which has been alluded to already on several occasions. The following
sentence occurs in the Charter, towards the end:—"Ego Dunstan . . . . propriis
digitorum articulis perscripsi." Kemble, also, in his great work on *Anglo-Saxon
Diplomatics* prints the Charters (vol. 2, No. ccccxxv., page 293) from another exemplar
Antiquæ Cartæ Cantuarienses, R. 14, collated with the Augustus II. 57. But the
clause concerning Dunstan is not in this Canterbury specimen which bears signs of
injury at the place.

Charter (which is too long for insertion here) became corrupted and very sensibly curtailed, until we find[1] that it reached the following laconic form: " + Anno dominicae incarnationis . DCCCCXLIX. Ego Eadredus Rex, praesente venerabili viro Odone archiepiscopo, patre tocius Britanniae, et Eadgiva regina matre mea, *dedi aecclesiae Christi in Dorobernia* (Canterbury), *monasterium Raculfense cum tota villa et omnibus ad eam pertinentibus* liberam ab omni saeculari servitute, exceptis tribus, expeditione pontis et arcis constructione. Et ego Dunstan, abbas indignus, cartulam, inde imperante domino meo rege Eadredo, composui, et propriis digitis meis perscripsi." Both the full and the abbreviated Charter indicate that the grant of Reculver to Canterbury was made in the presence of Queen Eadgiva, the king's mother, and of Archbishop Odo. Notwithstanding this, the convent was not entirely dispersed, although in all probability the Rule practised by its inmates underwent a fundamental change ; and there was some kind of establishment still kept up until at least a few years before the advent of the Normans, for in a grant or demise of portion of the demesne lands of Reculver monastery, made by Archbishop Agelnoth (the period of whose archiepiscopal life extended from A.D. 1020 to 1038), to Alfwold and Aldred, his *ministri*, the gift is made " ex consensu fratris nostri Givehardi *decani ejusdem ecclesiae* Sanctæ matris Dei, ut illam terram habeant

---

[1] Kemble, v. 354, No. mclxvi. MS. Lambeth, No. 1212, page 323. Twysden, *Histor. Angl. Scriptores* x., 2220. There is also an abbreviated form of the Charter of Hlotharius in Dúgdale's *Monasticon*, i. 424.

non longius quam ipsi placuerit decano, vel ejus successori,"[1] showing that the Reculver was then, and likely, for some time to come, to be, under the management of a dean : whether this deanery was collegiate, or attached to the Cathedral, is of course a matter of speculative research. After this, nothing more is found relating to this Abbey. It is supposed to have ceased as a religious house, and to have lapsed to the crown in the time of William the Conqueror, by whom it was restored, with its revenues, to the Archbishop Lanfranc, *as having been given to Canterbury Cathedral;* and, Dugdale says, " soon afterwards, on the separation of the estates of it, between the Archbishop and the priory of Christ Church there, the manor of Reculver with its demesnes, of which the ancient Abbey was esteemed part, and the church appurtenant, was allotted to the former."[2]

On the dispersion of the monastery at Reculver, it is equally possible that all the muniments and documents relating to the erection and maintenance of the house were transferred to the larger Cathedral foundation at Canterbury ; and hence we may argue, that even if Bercwald did not take the Charter itself with him to Canterbury, nor absorb it into the muniment-room of the Cathedral during his prolonged Archiepiscopacy of nearly forty years,[3] which terminated in A.D. 731, the Charter which found its

---

[1] Dugdale, *l. c.* Somner, *Antiq. Cantuar. Appendix,* xxxix., fol. Lond. 1703.

[2] Hasted, *History of Kent,* iii. 632. Compare also the account of Reculver in *Domesday Survey,* i. 3 *b.*

[3] He sat longer than any previous prelate, and died in January, 731, Beda. *Hist. Eccl.,* v. 23. He was buried in St. Augustine's Abbey, Canterbury. *Anglo-Sax. Chron.*

way into the Utrecht Psalter may have been copied
for him for purposes of reference, it may be the
duplicate which was deposited with Theodore, the
Archbishop, who was a consenting party to it ; or it
may have been placed in the hands of the Cathedral
registrar when the removal of the monks from
Reculver to Canterbury (and of course their library
and records with them) was accomplished in A.D.
949.

However these things may be, and to whichever
of the three alternatives which are here proposed
better credence is due, let us consider what
evidence there may be, if any, of the connection of
the Utrecht Psalter into which this Charter was
inserted at an early period, with the capital city of
the Kentish kingdom.

If the Utrecht Psalter had been brought from any
other place and deposited in the library of the
Cathedral, or written there in the *scriptorium*, or
writing-school attached to that Church, we should
not fail to find some facts that would indicate its
existence there, for it is hardly likely that so
uniquely beautiful a Manuscript could long remain
in any monastic library without attracting the
attention of some one connected with its fortunes.
And this is the very thing that we do find.
For in the library of Trinity College, Cambridge,
there exists a Manuscript, entitled the " Psalterium
Tripartitum Eadwini," the tripartite Psalter of
Eadwine, a folio volume of 280 leaves (18 inches × 13)
in which is written in three columns of parallel text
to each page, the Hebrew, Roman, and Gallican

versions of the Psalms. Each Psalm is illustrated
with a drawing embodying the subject of the text in
a singularly quaint but expressive manner; and
many, almost all indeed of these drawings, are so
closely alike to those in the Utrecht that no one can
deny that they have been minutely imitated from
the illustrations in the Utrecht Psalter. Westwood,
in his *Palæographia Sacra*, has given a plate (No. 43)
and a short description of this book; and the additional Manuscript, 29,273, in the British Museum,
contains a few photographic pictures derived from
the same volume. That this Eadwine was a monk
of Christ Church, Canterbury, is easily deduced
from the finding of two pages at the end of the
Psalter which contain a bird's eye view of Christ
Church, Canterbury, with all its buildings and
grounds. This was published in the *Vetusta Monumenta*, London, 1747. In the calendar contained
also in the book is an entry of the day of the death
of Archbishop Anselm, (21 April, A.D. 1109,) and of
the day of the dedication of Christ Church. There
is also a full-length portrait of Eadwine himself,
pen in hand, with verses and a prayer relating to
him, wherein he calls himself the *famulus* of God, an
expression demonstrating his connection with the
church by profession. These facts are sufficient to
indicate the name and position of the compiler, the
place and date of the execution of the Psalter,
which could only have been made by one having the
Utrecht Psalter before his eyes at the time.
Another point is that the Cotton Manuscript Galba,
E. IV., which contains a list of the library of

the Cathedral in A.D. 1315, alludes to this very volume as the "Tripartitum Psalterium Edwini," as suggested by Wanley. (Hickes' *Thesaurus*, Vol. II.) The other copy of the Psalter which forms a Manuscript in the Harley collection, No. 603, will have its date and place discussed, and its probable connection with Canterbury determined in the ensuing chapter, which will treat of the Bibliographical history of the Utrecht Psalter.

The few remaining incidents in the history of the Utrecht Psalter are soon told, although they too are blended with a certain amount of conjecture and uncertainty. Wherever it was preserved prior to the dissolution of the monasteries by king Henry VIII., it probably fell into the hands of one of the branches of the great family of Talbot, viz., shortly after that date, for Mr. Bond reports that "in the lower margin of folio 60*b*, an entry in a hand of the middle of the sixteenth century, can be made out, of the name ' Mary Talbott,' now nearly obliterated." This may tend to show that the Manuscript passed from the library of whatever dissolved house owned it in or about A.D. 1540, and was very shortly afterwards accessible to, or in the keeping of the lady who has recorded her name in this page.

It would be impossible to positively assert to what lady this signature, and with it the possession of the Utrecht Psalter, is to be assigned. It may be that the name refers to *Mary Talbot*, the eldest daughter of Gilbert Talbot, seventh Earl of Shrewsbury, who occupied the earldom from A.D. 1590 to 1616. She married William Herbert, who became third Earl of

Pembroke, 1600, and died in 1630. This lady was one of the three heiresses to the baronies of Talbot, Strange, Badlesmere, and Furnival.

Another lady, whose name and time correspond with the signature, is *Mary Talbot*, third daughter of Sir Gilbert Talbot, the second, of Grafton, co. Worcester. Her father died in A.D. 1542, and she was married to Sir Thomas Astley, of Patteshall, in Staffordshire.

But another, and infinitely more interesting method of accounting for this name, remains to be proposed, and this, if conceded, adds yet another link to the chain of evidence in favour of the Canterbury origin of the book itself. In the Cotton Manuscript, Julius C. VI., there occur, after some of Leland's *Collectanea*, several pages of extracts, written in a hand of the middle of the sixteenth century, relating to affairs in connection with Christ Church Cathedral, Canterbury, and at the side of the first page of these extracts is written, in a hand somewhat bolder than the body of the text, the words " *Master Talbot of Norwiche*," as if the extracts had been made from information supplied by him to the compiler of the extracts. Among these very extracts, at pp. 98-100, there is one section headed " E quodam registro sive indice bibliothece Cantuarie." This is a list of books belonging to the Cathedral library, and among them occurs the remarkable entry " Mr. Talbot made this anotation in the fronte of Oresius historie that he lent me, translated out of Latin into Saxon tonge : Rex Ælfredus Oresium interpretatus est et boetium et

bedam de historia Ecclesiastica Anglorum." Here
the explanation is manifestly this : "Master Talbot"
acquired in some way a great portion of the library
of the Cathedral; out of some of the records he
supplied the matter of the extracts to the writer of
Julius C., VI., pp. 90, etc. "Master Talbot" also
had possession of the Anglo-Saxon translation of
Orosius by king Alfred, a Manuscript thus known to
have been preserved at Canterbury before the dissolution, and lent the Manuscript as stated in the
quotation already made. Now, if we admit these
plain facts, it follows naturally that the name of *Mary
Talbott* which is written in the Psalter is that of Master
Talbot's wife or daughter, who has inscribed it while
the book was in the possession of Master Talbot,
its first lay owner. This very volume of Orosius, a
fine Manuscript of the eleventh century, is now in
the Cotton library, Tiberius B. 1., and contains, *in
Master Talbot's writing*, the very words " Rex Al-
fredus Orosium interpretatus est, et Boetium et
Bedam de histo. ecclesiastica . . . . . ." which are
stated by the compiler of Julius C. VI., page 99, to
have been written in the volume lent to him by
Talbot. This evidence connects the MS. Tiberius
B. 1, with the library of Canterbury Cathedral, a
fact never yet before known, and a very valuable
one in the history of that unique Manuscript.

A careful search for information regarding
" Master Talbot of Norwiche," has resulted in
identifying him with Robert Talbot, A.M., who
was Rector of Birlingham St. Peter's, co. Norfolk,
and installed in the second Prebend of Norwich

Cathedral on the 9th of April, 1547. Blomefield (Vol. III., p. 663) says, "He was a most ingenious and industrious antiquary, and what by love or money, he collected a *valuable collection of rare Manuscripts*, most of which are now in Bennet College library, where also remain, of his own handwriting, a treatise of the ancient Charters of the kings," etc.

From this private depository the volume passed into the library of Sir Robert Cotton, but in what way, whether by purchase or gift, and from whom, has not been recorded. In this collection it received the number 207, and subsequently, the distinctive appellation, or press-mark, Claudius C. VII.

The written catalogue of the collected Manuscripts belonging to Sir Robert Cotton, which was prepared in his time, in the year 1621, and which now forms Harleian Manuscript, 6018, contains the following description of the Psalter, as No. 207: "Psalmi dauidis latine literis Romanis (que in usu circa Imperii inclinantis tempora) exarati, iisque majusculis, cum schematis non impari vetustate passim intertextis." It will be noted that there is no reference to the charter of Hlotharius, but whether this escaped the notice of the cataloguer, or was intentionally not referred to, cannot now be determined.

Mr. Bond's report supplies succeeding links in the history of the book, "Archbishop Ussher, in his treatise 'De Romanæ Ecclesiæ Synodo,' published in 1647, speaks of having examined the Manuscript when [it was] in the Cotton library. And, in fact, a letter from him to Sir Robert Cotton, dated on the 12th of July, 1625, is extant (Cotton MS., Julius

C., III., f. 1509 *b*.) in which he speaks of having borrowed four Latin Psalters, three of which were of Gallican use; and no doubt this Manuscript was one of them, and that he examined it at this time. But he returned it to Sir Robert; for among some later memoranda at the end of the catalogue of 1621, already referred to, under a general heading of 'A note of such bookes as have been lent out by Sir Robert Cotton to divers persons and are abroad in their hands att this daye the 15th of January 1630' [1631], is a list of volumes lent 'to my Lord the Earle of Arundel' (fol. 173 *b*) among which occurs the Psalter, under the description of 'An Ancient Coppie of the Psalmes literis maiusculis, in Latin, and pictures: bound in redd leather with Sir Robert Cotton's Armes, fol.'"

The next record that comes under our notice with regard to the lending of books from the Cotton library is the Manuscript called "Cotton Appendix, XLV., art. 13," which contains notes of Manuscripts lent by Sir Thomas Cotton between the years 1637 and 1661, but in this there is no notice of the Psalter, and we are left to conclude that it had been returned at some time during the period 1630-1637, or that, if still wanting, its absence from its place in the library was not noticed, or that this Cotton Appendix does not represent a complete list of books lent out during the years it embraces.

In the classed catalogue of the Cotton Manuscripts made in the year 1674, the Psalter is not entered; and in the catalogue called Smith's Folio Catalogue, published at Oxford in 1696, its number is marked " Deest," indicating that it was wanting at those periods.

It would appear, therefore, from the above records, that the Psalter had been borrowed by the Earl of Arundel between the years 1625 and 1631 ; that it might have been returned before 1637 ; that at any rate it was missing in 1674 and in 1696.

Smith, in his erudite prefaces, takes good opportunity to inveigh bitterly against those who borrowed Manuscripts from this renowned library, but never cared to return them; and his remarks are so apposite, and so well represent the abhorrence in which he did, and indeed all lovers and collectors of Manuscript antiquities rightly should, hold such a course of conduct, that they are well worthy of reproduction here.   He says, for example :—" Mecum dolebis, et pariter obstupescendum ac deplorandum videretur, tot libros, quod ex vacuis locis in catalogo cuivis facile apparet, hodie desideravi, nisi thesaurum quoque literarium peculatui obnoxium esse, et pro summis beneficiis non semper bonam gratiam rependi solere, crebris exemplis constitisset.   Non ita egregia Cottonorum humanitas, quæ illorum gentilitiæ dignitatis peculiare decus est, tam male, et præter omne jus fasque, multari debuit. Utinam illorum, qui mutuo acceperunt, aut heredum, in quorum manus pervenerint, fides vel paria fecisset ! . . . . . . Crimen, quasi sacrilegio proximum, omnes boni quibus inest justitiæ et æquitatis amor, execrantur, et non minimam religionis partem in ablatis vel mutuo acceptis restituendis collocant : *nec exceptiones de jure possessorio, qualicunque prætextu acquisito, contra vindicias veri Domini, a quo ejusmodi res sacræ, quæ hæreditatem sequuntur, abalienari non possunt, sunt admittendæ.* Utinam vero ii, qui codices Cottonianos apud se retinent, imitarentur exemplum cujusdam probi viri, qui, antequam moreretur, sollenni verborum formula illic inscripta, amicos superstites obnixe obtestatus est 'ut propter amorem Dei librum istum, quem apud se habuit, Bibliothecæ Cottonianæ restituendum curarent.' "

After its disappearance from the temporary possession of the Earl of Arundel, or at least after 1661, the Psalter seems to have fallen, by unknown means, into the possession of D. de Ridder, and of this Sir Thomas Hardy says :—" We[1] are in ignorance when or by what means it became dissevered from that far-famed repository (the Cottonian collection) ; there is, however, evidence that, as early as the year 1718, it had happily become the property of Monsieur D. de Ridder; I say happily, for by this means it escaped the fire which destroyed so many precious volumes in the Cottonian library." The contemporary entry on the first fly leaf is " Bibliothecae urbis Trajectinae donavit D. de Ridder," where the letter D. appears rather to stand for *Dominus,* than for the initial of a Christian name. With regard to this, Mr. Bond says: " Nothing more is heard of it from this time [1631] till the year 1718, when it was presented to the library of the University of Utrecht, as recorded in a memorandum on the fly leaf of the Manuscript." The credit of the rediscovery of the volume has been

[1] First Report, p. 7.

very properly accorded to Professor Westwood, who, in 1859, communicated to the Royal Archæological Institute a paper entitled "Archæological Notes of a Tour in Denmark, Prussia, and Holland," which was printed in the *Archæological Journal*, Vol. XVI., pp. 132-145, 236-252. Professor Westwood, from his opening sentence, which says, "A desire long entertained . . . to examine a remarkable Manuscript of the Psalter preserved at Utrecht, which had once formed part of the Cottonian library led me to Hamburgh in the course of last August," appears to have known of the existence of this Manuscript for a long time previous to his inspection of it at Utrecht, and this is confirmed by a note in his paper (p. 247), whence it appears that in a detailed account of the Psalter by Herr Kist, printed at Leyden in 1833, the Cottonian press mark, Claudius A. 7, is mentioned as being found in the book. This is really an error for Claudius C. 7, but the principle of the fact remains the same. We are, nevertheless, indebted to Mr. Westwood for supplying and circulating this early and interesting information respecting the Utrecht Psalter.

The chain of history is now completed, and we have been enabled to trace back the Utrecht Psalter and its Charter, the former to Canterbury, the latter to Reculver. At Canterbury the union probably took place, and thenceforward we have the Canterbury monk Eadwine certainly copying from the book in the twelfth century; at the dissolution, we see the precious library of the Cathedral ransacked, the Psalter finding its way, along with Ælfred's

Orosius, and other books, into the possession of Prebendary Talbot, when "Mary Talbott" inscribes her
name in a page of the Psalms.   Then we find Sir
Robert Cotton acquiring it in *c.* 1621 ; lending it to
Archbishop Ussher in 1625, and to the Earl of
Arundel in 1631 ; and losing it altogether before
1674.   Finally we have " D. de Ridder " presenting
it to the University of Utrecht in 1718, where it
finds a final resting place, having thus fortunately
escaped from the Cottonian conflagration in 1735.

CHAPTER III.

BEFORE asking the reader to follow us in the description of the pictorial and palæographic art which the UTRECHT PSALTER exhibits, we must ask his patience and forbearance awhile, in order that some account of the bibliography which the book itself has called into being may be laid before him. For without this, the ideas which should be impressed upon his mind would be less vividly conveyed, and apt to become imperfect and fugitive. Whereas, on the other hand, when he sees how great a value has been set upon the Psalter from early times; how the volume itself forms an important link and occupies a prominent position in the history of several other priceless Manuscripts; and how great an interest has been created, exerted, and sustained regarding the many points which this book illustrates, he will be led, imperceptibly perhaps, but more or less irresistibly, towards admitting, in the main, the conclusions which have been rationally and carefully deduced from a protracted investigation of the devious paths into which the Psalter takes us. In this chapter, therefore, some notice will be given of the bibliography of the Utrecht Psalter, that is, of the mediæval copies of the Manuscript, of the tracings and facsimiles which have from time to time been made of it, of the dissertations, reports and treatises which have been written concerning it, and of the literature which has been built up around it, and under the shadow of its transcendent surroundings.

It is hardly necessary to say much here of the facsimile published by the Palæographical Society in 1875, because it is upon that work that the great part of this present treatise is founded. And to that work, of which a considerable number of copies have been successfully produced by permanent photography, and dispersed among the principal libraries and collectors of Manuscripts both in the kingdom and on the Continent, principal reference is made, because the means of access to the Manuscript itself must necessarily be very limited, and, to many, impossible; whereas the facsimile copies are not only very accessible, but, should demand arise, could be easily acquired. The title prefixed to the facsimile by the Palæographic Society is, *LATIN PSALTER. In the University Library of Utrecht (formerly Cotton MS., Claudius C. VII.). Photographed and Produced in Facsimile by the Permanent Autotype Process of Spencer, Sawyer, Bird & Co., London.* There is no preface or introduction placed in the facsimile, so that the Palæographical Society prudently abstained from putting on record any opinions in this place respecting the date, or circumstances surrounding the origin of the Manuscript.

It was however necessary to speak of the facsimile here, because it represents in a great measure the original volume. Let us now consider the various works to which the Utrecht Psalter itself has given rise. To whatever age that volume may be ascertained to belong there is no doubt that the Harley MS., 603, in the British Museum, is connected with it in the light of an inspired copy, although the differences are remarkable and extensive. The description of this MS. is thus given in the Harleian Catalogue, folio, London, 1808 : " No. 603. Codex Membranaceus in folio quadrato, circa tempora Regis Eadgari scriptus et inluminatus. In eo continebatur Psalterium Divi Hieronymi Romanum, Iconibus Sacrum Textum illustrantibus ornatum. Quas, etsi rudiori penicillo delineantur, dignas tamen judico, quæ a venerandæ Antiquitatis amatoribus, intentis oculis, perlustrantur. Notandum quod plurimis foliis, flagrante forsan Bello Danico, a Codice abscissis, medicam manum adhibuit pius quidam vir, temporibus Eadwardi Regis aut Wilhelmi Conquestoris ; destinatum vero opus, quod dolendum, non perfecit." This is practically a correct description of this beautiful Manuscript, which deserves to be, and no doubt will, hereafter, be a subject for reproduction by some method of photography.

There is one, and as far as I can say, only one intrinsic clue contained in this Manuscript, which, if rightly investigated, could give to it a more exact date than as yet has been recorded. In the pictorial explanation prefixed to Psalm 119—a picture differing entirely from that which occurs in the Utrecht Psalter at this passage—there is a figure of a winged bowman, shooting arrows towards an uncertain object in the centre of the illustration; over his head, written in minute letters, of about the middle of the tenth century, is the word *ægelmund*, and this is evidently so written to point out thus by name some individual personage for whose portrait the writer considers this figure to stand. Now, if we can search the yet remaining documents of a period coeval with the time of King Eadgar (who assumed the royal dignity in A.D. 957, and died in 975), and if we can find any conspicuous person whose name and position agree with what we have on this picture, it will go far towards establishing the date of the composition of the Manuscript. Strange to say, there are frequent attestations of an Anglo-Saxon *dux*, or military leader, of the name of *Æðelmund*, occurring in the royal documents issued between the years 956 and 965, and when we consider that *Ægelmund* is merely a local variant form of the more correct word *Æðelmund*, it is not beyond fairness to conjecture that the Ægelmund of the picture, with his bow and arrows, is the same individual as the *Æðelmund dux* of the charters and dates here subjoined :—

Kemble's Codex.

No.	448	A.D.	956
„	451	„	„
„	453	„	„
„	456	„	„

No. 457	A.D. 956
,, 471	A.D. 958
,, 1218	,, ,,
,, 1219	,, ,,
,, ʻ1221	A.D. 959
,, 1225	,, ,,
,, 481	A.D. 960
,, 485	A.D. 961
,, 486	,, ,,
,, 487	,, ,,
,, 488	,, ,,
,, 1230	,, ,,
,, 1235	,, ,,
,, 1236	,, ,,
,, 493	A.D. 962
,, 1246	A.D. 963
,, 1247	,, ,,
,, 521	A.D. 965

There is no doubt, and there never could be to any reasonable person, that where drawings occur having subjects in common, those of the Utrecht Psalter are older and more original, if such an expression may be rightly used, than the corresponding pictures in the Harley Psalter, which, from their manner of treatment, their multifarious details, their grouping and their whole expression and *ensemble*, must have been copied from the pictures of the Utrecht Manuscript. There is no other escape from this position unless we care to conceive that the draughtsmen of the two Manuscripts copied, each one in his turn, from some third Manuscript of a

date earlier than the Utrecht itself.   But although
this is quite possible, it is very improbable that such
a Manuscript should have existed without some
signs of its existence, some proofs of its employment
as a copy by the inmates of mediæval *scriptoria*.   A
great many observations have been put on record
with regard to this Harley MS., and many com-
parisons have been made between it and the
Utrecht Psalter.   For example, Mr. Bond's report,
speaking of the pictorial contents of the Utrecht
MS., says : " Many of these illustrations are found
in the Psalter of the 11th century in the Harley
Collection, No. 603,   Some are exactly similar in
design, but generally additions are introduced in the
later copies with differences in costume ; and it is
remarkable that many of the series in the Harley
MS. are altogether different from those in the
Utrecht Psalter."   The real fact is, that from the
beginning of the volume at Psalm 1, down to Psalm
113, more than two thirds of the whole series, the
resemblance is so great, that when allowance is
made for the difference of age, the caprice of the
individual artist in filling up small parts and subordinate details after his own fancy, no one will
venture to deny that the most intimate connection
between the two Manuscripts exists in a very
prominent and self-asserting manner.   Canon
Swainson, in his report to the Trustees of the
British Museum, arrives, by a peculiar method of
reasoning, at the unique conclusion that the
Harleian pictures must be regarded as earlier than
the Utrecht drawings.   This opinion is so much at

distinct variance and diametrical opposition to all
the recorded opinions of palæographers, that it is
necessary to repeat the exact words he uses: " But
a comparison," he says, " in another respect must
be drawn between this Manuscript and the Harleian
603, which is considered to belong to the tenth or
eleventh century, and which contains a large
number of illuminations similar in outline to those
which occur in the Utrecht Psalter. It has been
considered that the Harleian pictures must have
been imitated or copied from the Utrecht drawings.
On careful examination I discovered some time ago
that this could not be; because of the drawings in
the Utrecht Psalter to which I have on another
occasion begged attention as belonging to the ninth
or tenth century or later, not one occurs in this
Harleian Psalter; thus, taken as a whole, the
Harleian pictures must be regarded as exhibiting
an earlier type than the Utrecht drawings; and if
the former are of the tenth or eleventh century, the
latter must be brought down much lower." This
passage contains very much that is calculated to
mislead the studious enquirer, who cannot for a
moment endorse the canon's statement concerning
the similarity of outline of the illustrations, for this
is one of the points where the Utrecht Psalter and
the Harley Psalter diverge, the drawings of the
one being of an infinitely freer and less conventional
character than those of the latter, which, in their
outline indicate an entirely different method of
treatment, the grouping and essentials only being
common to both. Sir Thomas Hardy very justly

criticises in severe terms the passage quoted above, and says:[1] " Observe the cogency of Canon Swainson's arguments. Because the Harleian MS. (said to have been written in the tenth or eleventh century) does not contain some of the drawings in the Utrecht Psalter, which have been assigned to the ninth or tenth century or later, therefore the Harleian pictures must be regarded as exhibiting an earlier type than the Utrecht drawings; and if the former (the Harleian) are of the tenth or eleventh century, the latter (the Utrecht) must be brought down much lower. I should have thought that most men would have drawn exactly the opposite conclusion; but I may leave Canon Swainson to settle this knotty point . . . . . When he shall have convinced any one . . . that the Utrecht MS. is a later production than the Harleian Psalter, that is, later than the tenth or eleventh century, it will be time for me to canvass more seriously this extraordinary paradox of his. There may be doubts whether the Utrecht Psalter is as old as the sixth century; there can be no doubt, whether or not, it is older than the Harleian; and the very arguments which lead Canon Swainson to so absurd a conclusion are sufficient to show their unsoundness."

It has been said that there is no evidence to connect this book with Canterbury, and it would of course be very difficult to prove that the Manuscript originated at that city, but there are at least two very strong grounds for reasonable supposition that

[1] Further Report, p. 48.

the book was written there; the first being this, that
it was undoubtedly made, as far as illustration goes,
from the Utrecht Psalter, down to Psalm 113. And
we have shown conclusively that the Utrecht Psalter
has considerable claims to Canterbury for its place
of deposit. Whence the artist of the Harley Psalter
obtained the specimens of the latter portion of the
pictures, and whether they are copied from older
exemplars, or the result of his own original and
unaided efforts, and what is the real reason of the
marked divergence of the pictorial element at the
place indicated, are questions which would involve
too much labour, and demand too much space if the
attempts to investigate them were made on the
present occasion, because they require special
and independent treatment.

The second ground for connecting the Harley MS.
with Canterbury lies with this very occurrence of
the name of *Ægelmund*, for if the conjecture that
Ægelmund, the bowman of the Manuscript, is *Æðelmund*, the *dux* of the Saxon documents, be admitted
as feasible, then we must allow that his frequent
attestation of so many royal documents yet extant,
(and probably a much larger number no longer in
existence) presupposes his frequent presence in the
royal court of the king in the ecclesiastical capital
of his kingdom, in Dorobernia or Canterbury, the
chief city of the Cantuarii, or men of Kent.

The next bibliographical object in connection with
the Utrecht Psalter is the volume which is entitled
The Tripartite Psalter of Eadwine, preserved in the
library of Trinity College, Cambridge. Of this

Manuscript, which resembles the Utrecht Psalter more closely (as regards its illustration) than the Harley MS., inasmuch as its pictures are copied, with few exceptions, from the Utrecht Psalter alone (as far as I am able to gather from the description I have obtained of it), some account has already been given.[1] There is an excellent facsimile of a portion of it in Westwood's *Palæographia Sacra;* and, with this exception, there is no published illustration of it.

The peculiarly beautiful drawings of the Utrecht Psalter attracted more attention even than that which found vent to its expression by the preparation of the Harley MS. 603, and the *Psalterium Eadwini;* for Professor Westwood, in his *Archæological Notes,*[2] speaking of the Utrecht Psalter, says :—" Moreover, each Psalm is illustrated with an elaborate pen-and-ink drawing, running entirely across the page, in which the subjects are treated exactly in the same manner as in the Harleian Psalter, No. 603, a MS. of the end of the tenth century ; in the Cambridge Psalter of Eadwine, a work of the twelfth century ; in another early copy of the Psalter, which I am informed is in Lord Ashburnham's library ; and in the Paris MS. Suppl. Latin. 1194, date *circa* A.D. 1250." From this interesting passage we are now cognizant of the fact that the Utrecht Psalter gave rise to at least four copies executed with more or less faithful adherence to its archetypal teaching, in the tenth, twelfth, and thirteenth centuries. Of the

---

[1] See p. 101-103.
[2] Published in the *Archæological Journal* for 1859, p. 245.

copy stated to be preserved in the Ashburnham library, I have no means of recording any definite description, and probably Professor Westwood would have given more precise information concerning the Manuscript had it been in his power to do so.' The Paris Manuscript, however, furnishes an excellent facsimile plate to Silvestre's monumental work, to which so much reference has been made in the foregoing pages of this book. A reference to plate CLXXXIV. shows that the text is of the thirteenth century, and is arranged, like the Cambridge MS., in triple columns of Hebrew, Roman, and Gallican versions, whereas the Cambridge MS. has its columns arranged thus: Gallican, Roman, and Hebrew.

Passing on from a contemplation of these most interesting early Manuscripts, we come down to the opinions of cataloguers and others in the seventeenth and succeeding centuries, which have already been discussed, and to the bibliographical accounts of the Utrecht Psalter which were drawn up in the present century. The first notice in manuscript to which it is necessary to advert, is the additional Manuscript, 26,104, in the British Museum, which was purchased of Messrs. Boone, in January, 1865, from the sale of A. D. Schinkel, at the Hague, in November, 1864. It is thus described in the original sale catalogue :—

' The Catalogue of Lord Ashburnham's Manuscripts contains references to the following Psalters, among which may be found the one alluded to in Professor Westwood's *Notes* :—(1) *Psalmorum Liber, Latinè, litteris uncialibus,* folio, 5th (?) cent., No. L, 5; (2) *P. L., cum versione Anglo-Saxonica,* folio, 8th cent., No. S, 843; (3) *P. L., cum glossa,* folio, 9th cent., No. L, 54; (4) *P. L., notis Tyroniis,* quarto, 9th cent., No. L, 94; (5) *P. L., cum glossa,* folio, 14th cent., No. L, 980.

" 10. Facsimile de' 166 Dessins contenus dans le Codex Psalmorum, de R. Cotton, MS. du VII. Siècle, qui se trouve dans le bibliothèque de l'Université à Utrecht, (MSS. lat. No. 58) folio oblong, etc."

" 101 de ces dessins sont faits sur papier végétal sous les auspices du Prof. C. J. C. Reuvens, par M. Hooiberg, à Leide ; les 65 autres sont d'une autre main, (voir la Notice jointe à ce volume). Ces dessins sont d'une très-belle exécution ; et ont surtout une grande valeur, pour la connaissance des costumes, des arts et des sciences du VII. siècle."

The following extracts are from the account by Schinkel, prefixed to the facsimiles :—

" *Facsimiles der Teekeningen, voorkomende en het Codex psalmorum in de Utrechtsche Boekkerij berustende.*

" Deze Facsimiles komen op de Catalogus der nagelaten Boeken van wyle den Hooggeleerde Heer Proffessor C. J. C. Reuvens,—waar van de veiling op den 8e. Octob. 1838, en volgende dagen heeft plaats gehadt aldus omschreven voor :—

" No. 53. 101 Tabulae in charta tenuissima (papier végétal), picturas exhibentes, quibus Psalterium secundum Septuaginta interpretes ab Hieronymo emandatum etc. ornatur (Cod. MS. in perg. Biblioth. Acad. Ultraject. MSS. Latt. n. 58).

" Tabulas has summa cura ac diligentia delineatas sibi describendas curaverat Reuvensius, quoniam imprimis utiles esse ei videbantur ad ritus populorum prioribus saeculis et medio aevo cognoscendos.

" Adduntur annotationes MSS. Reuvensii et viri nob. van Westreenen van Tiellandt dissertatio de Codice illo Ultrajectino, prouti edita est in op. Arch. v. Kerkel. Gesch. door Kist en Royaards, vol. IV. pgg. 231-246, ipsius Westreenii manu descripta."

Then follows a long statement in Dutch, to the effect that Heer Fredrik Altheer, a bookseller of

Utrecht, acquired the facsimiles from Professor
Reuvens, and at the death of the former the book
was sold by auction under the following head :—

"Alle afteekeningen of doortrekken op papier végétal der
150 oud Romeinsche teekeningen in bister uit het handschrift der Utrechtsche Bibliotheek, No. 280, contin. 'Psalterium sec. 7ᵉ, vers. ab Hieronymo emend,' en der 16
toekeningen¹ uit het daaraan gebondene 'Fragmentum
Evangelii sec. Matheum de translatione Sⁱ Jeromini,' welk
handschrift en teekeningen volgens het oordeel van Z. Excell.
Baron W. H. J. Westreenen van Tiellandt te's Hage, uit de
6ᵉ eeuw dagteekenen. De stukken door Z. Excell. en Professor J. Geel, in het archief voor kerkgeschiedenis, 4ᵉ dl.
medegedeeld over dit allebelangrijkste handschrift en teekeningen zijn hier bijgevoegd. Het geheel is gebonden in rijk
vergulden rood maroq. band. etc."

This Manuscript is interesting from the fact that
until the publication of the *Autotype Facsimile*, it was
the only complete copy of the drawings in the
original Psalter possessed by the British Museum ;
but the tracings are by no means executed with
sufficient exactitude to render the Manuscript
available for reference or research.

Another record of value and importance in the
series of notices regarding the volume under consideration is the additional Manuscript, 22,291, in
the British Museum, which contains the following
pieces relating to the Utrecht Psalter :—

1. A letter from M. Suermondt (to Mr. Bond),
dated from Utrecht, October 1, 1857, in which is
said : "As far as my recollection of your Psalter

---

¹ These facsimiles are no longer in the volume, which, however, shows the marks
of their removal.

(Harley, 603) goes, it is evident that ours is a copy from yours or yours from ours ; and as far as I am a judge in these matters, ours is the original, the drawings in ours are much better, more spirited, they bear the stamp of being original. The writing of the London Psalter on the contrary is better and done with more care. . . . . In our Psalter all the drawings are completed and no blank space left."

2. Then follow carefully executed tracings of the drawings prefixed to Psalms 6, 58, and 102; and the drawing and text of the last page of the Rustic part of the volume, consisting of the Psalm 151. " Pusillus eram," etc.

3. To these has been appended an extract from the *Archief voor kerkelijk geschiedenis, inzonderheit van Nederland*. Vezameld door N. C. Kist en H. J. Royaards. 4.de Deel, te Leiden, 1833, 8vo., entitled, *Naspeuringen nopens zekeren Codex Psalmorum in de Utrechtsche Boekerij berustende*. Door W. H. J. Baron van Westreenen van Tiellandt. As this account is probably the earliest independent notice we have, of the Utrecht Psalter, in the shape of a detailed description, it is well that it should be placed before the reader entire. Sir Thomas Hardy, in the first report he made, gives the translation of Baron Westreenen van Tiellandt's description written in Dutch, but omits the prefatial remarks of Royaards, which are as follow :—

"Onder de Oude HSS. die in die Akademische Boekerij te Utrecht gevonden worden, en welke tot dus ver weinig bekend zijn, behoort een overoude Codex der Psalmen, of

Psalterium, hoogstbelangrijk om de wijze, waarop dit geschrift der vroegste eeuwen bewaard is. Het staat op den vroegeren Catalogus der Utrechtsche Bibliotheek (P. 455, 155) onder de HSS. aangetekend als :—*Psalterium secundum septuaginta, sive Psalmi Davidis, Latine cum aliis Hymnis et Canticis sacrae Scripturae, Oratione Dominica, Symbolo Apostolorum et Athanasii. Quae omnia illustrantur Romano habitu, figuris et antiquitate. Imperatoris Valentiniani tempora videntur attingere.* No. 280a.

"Deze titel is ontleend uit de aantekening, op een der voorste schutbladen geplaatst, alwaar echter de eerste regel : *Psalterium, secundum septuaginta Interpretes, ab Hieronymo emendatum, sive,* door een later hand, is bijgevoegd. Daarenboven vindt men dáár, behalve het hoofd *Elenchus Contentorum in hoc Codice,* na het woord : *attingere* het volgende : *Ffragmentum,* etc.

" Daar dit alles, behalve den aangeduiden eersten regel, met oude letters geschreven is, zal het welligt zoodanig uit de Cottoniaansche Bibliotheek in Engeland alhier zijn overgekomen.

"De Leipziger geleerde, Dr. Gustavus Haenel, die voor eenige jaren, op zijne Bibliographische Reis door verschillende landen van Europa, ook de Utrechtsche Bibliotheek bezocht, geeft in zijne *Catalogi*[1] van dit Handschrift aldus berigt.

"*Psalterium Latinum, literis uncialibus et semiuncicialibus, saec. VI exaratum, c. delineatione ejusdem temporis ; Salomonis fragmentum eodem charactere, quo celeberrimus Codex Theodosianus, qui Romæ in ædibus vaticanis asservatur, scriptus est, membr. 4.*

" Deze Codex trok voor eenigen tijd de aandacht tot zich van onzen geleerden Landgenoot, den Baron van Westreenen van Tiellandt, wiens eigene Bibliotheek, rijk, zoowel in

---

[1] Catalogi Librorum MSS. qui in Bibliothecis Galliae, Helvetiae, Hispaniae, Lusitaniae, Belgii, Brittaniae M. asservantur. Editi a D. Gust. Haenelio, Lips. 1829, 4to.

boeken, als Handschriften, die van publieke instellingen op zijde streeft, en gaf denzelven aanleiding tot eene korte zaakrijke beschrijving, door hem aan onze Bibliotheek medegedeeld.

"Dezelve scheen mij te belangrijk toe om alleen bij de papieren der Utrechtsche Bibliotheek bewaard te worden, en geschikt om ter meerdere bekendmaking van den Codex te kunnen dienen. Het is met volvaardige taestemming van den Heer van Westreenen van Tiellandt, dat ik meende dezelve in ons *Archief* te moeten opnemen, vertrouwende daarmede kenners van oude Handschriften eene dienst te bewijzen.

"Ik meende echter ter algemeene opheldering, en in overeen-stemming met hetgeen buitenslands vroeger van zoodanige Codices gedaan is, een Facsimile te moeten mededeelen, hetgeen door der Heer van Westreenen werd aangedrongen.

"Wij hebben daarop tevens geplaatst die unciaal letters en andere typen, waarheen in het Berigt verwezen wordt, en welke gemakkelijker door Steendruk, dan door de drukpers, konden worden medegedeeld.

"H. J. ROYAARDS."

Then follows the *Naspeuringen nopens zekeren Codex Psalmorum in dee Utrechtsche Boekerij berustende*, by Baron van Westreenen van Tiellandt, of which Sir Thomas Hardy has given an English trans-lation in his report, *Appendix*, pp. 41-43. The principal points in the Baron's *Investigations* are that the version of the Psalms is "not made after the *Versio Itala*, or Greek Translation of the Septuaginta, but after the common translation, the so-called *Vulgata*, by Jerome, about the end of the 4th century." He points out several errors com-mitted by Haenel in his description of the Manu-script; he speaks of the initial B in the word

Beatus (Ps. 50. 1.) as of "Anglo-Saxon form." Of the illustrations, the Baron gives the following account: "All the representations, both in the style of houses, temples, and altars, and in the dresses, armours, furniture, etc., are evidently derived from the time of the low Roman Empire, in which not a shadow of the Gothic occurs, but which, in general, have a striking resemblance with the representations in the celebrated Virgil of the Vatican Library, published in 1741 ; as also, concerning the buildings, with several diptycha of the Low Empire. (See for instance, Gori, *Thesaurus Diptychorum*, III., 22.) With regard to the date, he says, "every thing concurs to justify the estimation of Haenel, who places it in the sixth century as an intermediate epoch."

The Manuscript 29,273 in the British Museum, to which reference has already been made, comprises several pieces of very great interest to the UTRECHT PSALTER. Among the letters, facsimiles, photographs, and reports which it contains are—

1. A lithographic plate of the two pages containing the Athanasian Creed, prepared originally for the Rev. J. Jones, of St. Beuno's College, at St. Asaph, and presented to the British Museum by the Rev. C. A. Swainson, Canon of Chichester.

2. Notes on the Organ, a picture of which is found in the UTRECHT PSALTER, from the *Penny Cyclopædia*, Vol. XVII., p. 1.; from Mersenne's *Harmonie Universelle;* Hawkin's *History;* Augustine; William of Malmesbury ; and *L'Art du Facteur des Orgues.*

3. Positive photographs by the nitrate of silver process, taken, apparently somewhat reduced in size, from the illustrations in the *Psalterium Eadwini* at Cambridge:—for· Psalm 11, " Salvum me fac, domine," etc.; Psalm 63, " Exaudi Deus Orationem meam," etc.; Psalm 139, " Eripe me, domine," etc.; Psalm 150, " Laudate dominum in sanctis ejus," etc.; the illustration and first page of the " Quicumque Vult;" a part of a page containing Psalm 80, " Qui regis Israel intende," etc.

4. A facsimile executed by hand, in colours, of the initial B in *Beatus*, Psalm 1. i., contained in a Manuscript in the library of St. Gall, in Switzerland, a Psalter of the ninth century, No. 27, page 20. This letter resembles in several respects the initial letter B in the corresponding place in the UTRECHT PSALTER.

5. Photographic plates of parts of the Athanasian Creed, from a MS. not named, but apparently of the eleventh century.

6. A copy of the translation of a report, presented by P. J. Vermuelen, librarian, 10th August, 1872, to the curators of the University of Utrecht, on the Psalter there preserved. In this report the learned librarian propounds two questions: 1. " Can any information be given to prove that the MS. belongs to the sixth century?" 2. " Are there reasons to suppose that the miniatures and illuminations are of later date than the writing or text of the creed?" The first of these questions is thus answered:—

" With respect to the first question I must observe at once that it is not possible for me to afford any proof that the Manuscript belongs to the sixth century, for the simple reason that I have always assigned it to the eighth or ninth (750-850), and my opinion is unaltered." . . . . . "All who of late years have examined the Manuscript, have always embraced my opinion about the age of it. This opinion is, however, at variance with that of other persons." The writer then quotes Usher's reference of the Manuscript to the period of Pope Gregory I., and Haenel's erroneous statement that it is a "Beau manuscrit du VI. Siècle en lettres onciales, et semi-onciales, et miniatures !" The report continues : "My opinion that our MS. belongs to the age of the Emperor Charlemagne rests on a comparison of the character of the writing with that of other MSS. (as is believed) of that age, ... the contents of our MS. certainly give no sufficient proof at all for exactly determining its date." After deploring the inadvertence of removing the older binding of the book, which, had it remained, would have helped the question of date, notice is taken of the method of gathering the leaves of vellum into *quaternions*, and the writer says, "It is this regular putting up the leaves of the MS. together which has made me sometimes suspect that our MS. must be only a copy of an earlier one."

The second question is answered with better reason than the first : "As is well known, the ornamentation [and] the work of the illuminator did not begin until that of the writer was completed, and it was generally entrusted to other persons skilled in that art. Now the already-mentioned uniformity of the writing and parchment proves most certainly that our MS. was written from the beginning to the end continuously by the same hand. But then the writer must have left above every Psalm or other portion the room or space required for the drawing or ornamentation ; and he must have been able to calculate this room or space when he was writing, for it depended on the greater or less extent or development of the illustration of the subject, and of the emblems of the text that followed upon it. And for this it was necessary that the drawings or illustrations must have been already executed when the writer began his work, either by themselves or in an earlier MS. which served him as a model. This may be the explanation why costumes, arms, household furniture and utensils, instruments, etc., are represented, which point to an earlier period, and which have given occasion to the MS. being ascribed to an earlier age than that to which it actually belongs. In this view of the case it is worth while observing the drawings of two organs . . . . whose construction probably does not admit of their being assigned so far back as to the sixth century." Sir Thomas Hardy prints this report entire, as an appendix to the first report he himself prepared.

Then follow other reports referring to the transmission of photographs and enclosures ; and, finally, four photographic plates, by the silver process of 1. the Fides Catholica (two plates) ; 2. the page containing the *Canticum Simeonis*, and *Gloria in excelsis*, with two illustrations ; 3. the page containing the *Oratio Dominica secundum Matheum*, and the *Symbolu(m) Apostolorum*, also with two illustrations.

The Egerton MS. 2263, a volume containing a collection of original facsimiles, by Professor Westwood, contains a page from the Gospels at the end of the Utrecht Psalter, in uncial characters, but not any example of the Rustic writing of the Psalms, although it has a specimen of the fine Rustic character of the *Leyden Aratus*, a Manuscript of great beauty, and probably of the sixth century, which may be compared with those tabulated at page 41.   These appear to have been executed in or about the year 1873.

Having now carefully examined and noticed all the salient points of Manuscripts appertaining to the bibliography of the UTRECHT PSALTER, the next duty is to examine the printed books connected with the subject, before passing on to the description of the Manuscript itself.   The account of the bibliography of the Athanasian Creed belongs to a subsequent place.

The first notice we have concerning the UTRECHT PSALTER, other than in the catalogues of the Cottonian Manuscripts and works already described, appears to be in the work of James Ussher, Archbishop of Armagh, entitled *De Symbolis*, London, 1647, 4to. It is not a separate account of the Psalter, but the Manuscript is mentioned by him in a letter to Gerard Voss, a theologian and critic of celebrity, dated February 8, 1646.   Sir Thomas Hardy[1] gives a quotation of the passage in which the opinion of·

[1] In his *Report*, p. 8.

the Archbishop, respecting the age and contents of the book are recorded, the date of it being placed, "Gregorii I. tempore non recentius:" "not later than the time of Gregory I.," who occupied the pontifical throne from A.D. 590 to 604.

Daniel Waterland, the author of the *Critical History of the Athanasian Creed*, Cambridge, 1728, 8vo., criticises this statement of Ussher, and concludes a long examination[1] into the conjectures of "Comber, L'Estrange, Tentzelius, Tillemont, Le Quien, Muratorius, Natalis Alexander, and Montfaucon," writers either on theological or historical subjects, by stating his prescient conviction, "that Bishop Ussher had seen some other Manuscript, which has since that time, like many more, been lost or stolen from the Cotton Library . . . . . I conclude therefore that there really was such a Psalter as Ussher describes, with the Athanasian Creed in it, such as he judged to be of the age of Gregory I., from more marks than one; and how good a judge he was in those matters is well known to as many as know anything of that great man. But how far his judgment ought to sway, now the MS. itself is lost, I must leave with the reader."

Gustave Haenel, who compiled a catalogue of Manuscripts in European libraries, as has already been stated, in 1830, places this Manuscript in the sixth century: "Saec. VI Exaratum;" but as he also states that it is written in uncials and semi-uncials, he evidently examined it with insufficient accuracy.

[1] See the whole passage in Hardy's Report, p. 8, 9.

Baron van Westreenen van Tiellandt wrote a treatise entitled, *Investigations about a certain Codex Psalmorum preserved in the Utrecht Library.* The original, in Dutch, was printed in 1833, with prefatial remarks by Professor H. J. Rozaards, in the *Archief voor kerkelijke Geschiedenis.* Sir Thomas Hardy prints the translation of the Baron's account. The original preface of Royaards, with further accounts of this work has been already given under my account of the Add. MS., 22,291.

Next in order is the notice of the Manuscript contained in Professor Westwood's *Archæological Notes of a Tour in Denmark, Prussia, and Holland.*[1] In the account of the Manuscript which he inspected at Utrecht, he says: " The Psalms are written throughout in triple columns on each page in Roman Rustic capitals, very similar in size to those of the celebrated Virgil of the Vatican, but with as much elegance in the letters as in the Paris Prudentius. In this respect a date not more recent than the sixth or seventh century ought to be assigned to the Manuscript; but the initial letter of the first Psalm is a large golden uncial B, ornamented in the genuine interlaced Saxon style." . . . " I made careful copies of many . . . drawings, and others have been sent to the British Museum. I copied, for sake of comparison, the illustration of Psalm 54, of which I had published the corresponding subject from the Eadwine Psalter in my *Palæographia Sacra*. These I found identical." . . . . . " Others also equally agreed with those in the

[1] In the *Archæological Journal,* Vol. xvi., 1859, p. 132-145, 236-252.

Harleian Psalter. At the same time there are many entire drawings which are either wanting in the Harleian MS., or only very rudely indicated, and from some of these I have copied various details which are so beautiful in their style and subject that one is tempted to believe that this must have been the original from which not only the Harleian, but also the later Eadwine Psalters were copied. One peculiarity I observed with respect to these drawings which is worthy of note. Spaces were left by the scribe across the whole pages, cutting through the triple columns of texts, for the insertion of the drawings by the artist, and in several instances the space was not sufficient, the drawings running close to, or even upon the line of text below. From this fact I infer that the drawings even in this Utrecht Psalter were copied from some earlier MS., and that they were not composed expressly to fill up the spaces which had been left for them." . . . . . .

" Supposing the drawings to be later additions by an Anglo-Saxon artist copying from an early classic series of drawings, we should have no difficulty in referring the text to the fifth or sixth century. The initial of the first Psalm, however, precludes us from assigning it to so early a date, and would bring it to the seventh or eighth at the earliest, ranging it with the Psalter, so-called, of St. Augustine, in the Cottonian Library, Vespasian, A. 1. In this case the drawings may have been added in the ninth or tenth century." The account concluded with a notice of the fragments of the Gospels bound up with the Psalter.

In 1868, Professor Westwood's grandest work, entitled, *Facsimiles of the Miniatures and Ornaments of Anglo-Saxon and Irish Manuscripts,* was published, as has already been described at p. 56. In this he gives a plate of some of the writing and pictures of the Utrecht Psalter, and a further description of the book, from which I select the following extracts :—

" I have not been able to obtain any information, either documentary or otherwise, when or how it reached Utrecht, although it cannot be doubted that such a volume could hardly have been separated from the remainder of the Cottonian MSS. except by undue means ; neither ought there, as it seems to me, to be any question as to the justice of its restoration to the library from which it must have been improperly removed, unless its present location can be satisfactorily accounted for."

Professor Westwood then goes on to give a very careful description of the contents of the Psalter, and he points out the principal peculiarities in which its writing may be contrasted with the other known examples of Rustic writing, and its illustrations may be compared with those in the Harleian Psalter, No. 603, and the Eadwine Psalter at Cambridge. Some portions of his descriptive paragraphs are identical with those already alluded to as occurring in the *Archæological Journal* for 1859. It is, of course, with the illustrations that the learned author has principally concerned himself in this his monumental work on *Miniatures and Ornaments of Manuscripts ;* and his remarks on the subject of the pictures in the Utrecht Psalter, many of which he describes in detail, are of the greatest value towards correctly appreciating the peculiar beauty of the style adopted by the draughtsman of the original sketches. Reference will, therefore, be made hereafter to several passages in this portion of Professor Westwood's essay. The pieces selected by him for facsimile reproduction are the commencement of the 1st Psalm, and the page containing Psalm 149. The date for the facsimile is expressed thus (VI? IX? century), which sufficiently indicates the doubts which were then present in the writer's mind with regard to the true age of the volume.

After this magnificent volume of *Facsimiles*, we must turn to one of the most interesting and critically valuable contributions to the bibliography of the Utrecht Psalter, viz., the work entitled *The Athanasian Creed in connexion with the Utrecht Psalter, being a Report to the Right Honourable Lord Romilly, Master of the Rolls, on a Manuscript in the University of Utrecht.* By Sir Thomas Duffus Hardy, D.C.L., Deputy Keeper of the Public Records. There is no date on the title page or in the introductory letter addressed to Lord Romilly, but the colophon on the back of page 43, shows that the printing was completed in December, 1872. The main issue of this work (in which the theological aspect is more prominently placed than the palæographical interest) is that the Psalter was written in the sixth century; but the numerous and perplexing points which arise in the course of Sir Thomas Hardy's most rigorous examination are treated in a manner such as we should naturally expect from the literary acumen of so illustrious a master of record-palæography. The learned reporter defines his position succinctly, and yet clearly, when he says in his introductory letter to Lord Romilly : " I could have given my opinion that the MS. contained a Gallican Psalter, written in the sixth century, without assigning arguments for my belief, leaving it to those who entertained a different opinion to give their reasons for their dissent ; but I was sure that such a course would not be satisfactory to your lordship." . . . . . . " I am fortunate in being able to lay before your lord-ship the chief objections which have been urged against the age I assign to the Utrecht MS., at least so far as they have been communicated to me. Without entering more fully than I have done into all the liturgical phases of the question, it was sufficient for me to show that the Utrecht MS., which contains both (the Athanasian and the Apostles') Creeds, is a Gallican Psalter, and was written in the sixth century. I have also shown that the Gallican Ritual was used in Britain before the arrival here of Augustine ; but by whom the so-called Athanasian Creed was composed I have not ventured to give my opinion, though there is no doubt in my own mind that the " Fides Catholica," since called the Athanasian Creed, was acknowledged in the Gallican church long anterior to the com-position of the Utrecht Psalter." This extract explains the object of the report, which is, in point of fact, an endeavour to ascertain the first appear-ance of the text of the Athanasian Creed, its connection with the Utrecht Psalter, and by what appellation it was known, as far as these facts can be decided on palæographical grounds, rather than the result of any intention to describe exclusively the volume of Psalms under present consideration.

Sir Thomas Hardy sums up the age, origin, and first outlines of the Creed or *Symbolum*, and indicates, in his terse and vigorous language, the principal controversies respecting it; and says, in the course of unfolding his theories: " The earliest copy of the Creed, at least the earliest with which I am acquainted, is found in a very ancient volume belonging to the Academical Library at Utrecht, that is, the Utrecht Psalter." The learned reporter proceeds to recapitulate the various notices and descriptions of this Manuscript, and deduces his opinions at this stage from a variety of photographic and lithographic facsimiles, for he had not then seen the volume itself. His description, nevertheless, of the contents of the Manuscript agrees closely with the photographic facsimile which was afterwards published by the Palæographical Society. The peculiarities of handwriting, the fewness of the abbreviations, and the almost unique kind of *quasi-*punctuation are all carefully examined; and the individual features of a variety of early Rustic and other illustrative Manuscripts are not inaptly compared with corresponding peculiarities in the one here under consideration. The powerful objection that the Rustic writing of the Psalter is a later imitation of an earlier hand, that is, that the writing is of the style of the sixth or seventh century, but, at the same time, that it is a copy made in the

ninth or tenth century, "and that the writer pur-
posely imitated the handwriting of the sixth century,"
is carefully met and combated ; and the peculiar
relationship of the Harleian MS. Psalter, No. 603,
to this Utrecht Psalter (namely, its partial
resemblance as far as illustration goes, and its
divergence from the *Gallican* text into a *Roman*
version of the Psalms), is exhibited with great dili-
gence.   Of the initial *B* at the commencement of
the first Psalm, Sir Thomas Hardy says :—" It is in
reality *an Irish letter*, commonly found in Irish
Manuscripts from the sixth to the ninth century."
He quotes, in support of this opinion, the words of
Mr. Brian O'Looney, an able Irish scholar, who
" thinks it may be referred to the early part of the
sixth century," and thereby adds another name to
the phalanx of " sixth-century men."   After re-
capitulating the peculiarities of MSS. of the sixth
century, and branching off into a most instructive
digression concerning the punctuation of sentences
and separation of words in early Manuscripts, the
reporter carries on his arguments with an able
examination of the illustrations, of which he says,
" the age probably belongs to the end of the fifth or
beginning of the sixth century.   The suggestion,
found on one of the fly-leaves of the Psalter, which
would make them as old as the time of the Emperor
Valentinian (the younger), and therefore of the end
of the fourth century, is somewhat exaggerated."
Sir Thomas is manifestly here unwilling to admit
that these *illustrations* were made before the *writing*
of the Psalter.   Of his conjectural explanation of the

occasion of the Psalter coming to England, notice has already been made, and the theory critically examined, and a more probable modification proposed in the preceding chapter containing the external history of the volume. The report, which we are loth to leave so hurriedly, concludes with a summary of arguments in support of the various propositions; and the opinions of Ussher, the theologian, Haenel, the cataloguer of European Manuscript libraries, Baron van Westreenen, and Professor Westwood, to the effect of the date being of the sixth century or thereabouts, are tabulated and corroborated by conclusions arrived at in the course of the report. In the appendix are placed the Dutch original and English translations of P. J. Vermuelen's Report to the University of Utrecht, August 10, 1872; and the English translation of Baron van Westreenen's *Investigations* (*Naspeuringen*). The volume fittingly terminates with a transcript of the Athanasian Creed, and facsimiles of, 1. The Creed, two pages; 2. Two pages, containing the *Canticum Simeonis*, the *Gloria*, the *Oratio Dominica*, and the *Symbolum Apostolorum*; and 3. The lithographic plate of the commencement of the 1st Psalm, in gold and colours.

The next bibliographical work is an essay, entitled *Facsimile van den Ersten Psalm en het Quicumque, of Symbolum van den Heiligen Athanasius, naar het Psalmboek van Robert Cotton's Codex Claudius A. 7., thans in de Academische Bibliotheek te Utrecht vervaardigd op last van* J. Arntz, Leerar aan het Seminarie te Kuilenburg. Utrecht. *n. d.*

This contains a Dutch translation of the *Quicumque* or *Symbolum*, and a *Beknopt Historisch overzigt*, or short historical review, divided into, 1. The authority of the *Quicumque*; 2. Difference of opinions concerning its antiquity; 3. Ecclesiastical proceedings; 4. Notice of the literary labours of Canon Swainson; and, 5. of E. S. Ffoulkes, in connection with the Creed; 6. Account of Archbishop Ussher's description of the Manuscript when it was yet in the Cottonian library, its discovery at Utrecht, and of the reports concerning its condition and age by G. Haenel, Baron van Westreenen van Tiellandt, P. J. Vermuelen, J. O. Westwood, and others; 7. Description of Facsimiles that have from time to time been made of parts of the Manuscript. In this portion of the essay, the writer says, "Met het Handschrift leerde ik Waterlands werk, Van Westreenens verhandeling over het Handschrift, de twee Catalogussen van Cotton's verzameling: die van Th. Smith in 1696, en die van J. Planta in 1802 verwaardigd, kennen; ik kon dus, althans eenige inlichting geven, en besloot, op raad van den Boek- en Steen- drukker P. W. van de Weijer te Utrecht, bij hem van het *Quicumque* een Chromolithographisch Facsimile te laten vervaardigen. Ik meende niets te moeten sparen, om dit zoo volmaakt mogelijk op het oorspronkelijke te doen gelijken; zoo dat het tot nog toe de schoonste der thans bestaande kopiën is. Daar ik inzag dat de hoofdkwestie over den ouderdom des Psalmboeks liep, deed ik uit eigen beweging, en in navolging van Van Westreenen, den in dit opzigt zeer belangrijke aanvang en de merkwaardigste

letters bij het *Quicumque* voegen ;" 8. An account of
the proceedings of Convocation on the 2nd of July
(1874 ?) ; 9. Notice of Sir Thomas Hardy's report,
already described, and of the main issues contained
in it ; 10. Principal points illustrated by the Psalter
itself. In this part, mention is made of the capital
letter *B* of the first Psalm ; and of the uncial letters in
the headings, and the remainder of the text "in zwarte
ruwe kapitalen," *in black rugged capitals.* Of these
the writer says, " Dat nu het gros van den tekst
in ruwe capitalen geschreven is, wordt als een teeken
van hoogen ouderdom opgegeven. Als dagelijksch
schrift komen deze ruwe kapitalen hoogstens tot in
het begin der 8ste eeuw voor.. Later vindt men ze
nog wel in titels of aanhalingen, in eene van het
overige des geschrifts, verschillende taal. Uit dit
laatste echter volgt, dat ze nooit geheel vergeten
werden, wat overigens reeds daaruit blijkt, dat ze
maar weinig van onze thans gebruikte kapitale druk-
letters verschillen. Professor Swainson telt daarenboven verscheidene handschriften van later tijd op,
van welke een groot gedeelte in ruwe kapitalen
geschreven is. De sierlijke aanvangletter is wel
eens als een bewijs aangehaald, dat het Psalmboek
niet ouder dan de 7de eeuw kon zijn, daar men ze
als Angelsaksisch aanzag." The description of the
166 illustrations follows ; and, 9. The *Besluit,* or
conclusion in which the present state of the palæographical and theological position regarding the
evidence offered by the Utrecht Psalter is put forth
in a few but pertinent sentences. The facsimile of
the commencement of the first Psalm, and of the

two pages containing the Athanasian Creed, conclude the work.

In 1874 by far the most important treatise, speaking simply in a palæographical sense, respecting this Psalter, was published under the following title: *Reports addressed to the Trustees of the British Museum on the Age of the Manuscript, by E. A. Bond, E. M. Thompson, Rev. H. O. Coxe, Rev. S. S. Lewis, Sir M. Digby Wyatt, Professor Westwood, F. H. Dickinson, and Professor Swainson. With a Preface by A. Penrhyn Stanley, D.D., Dean of Westminster.* These reports are framed principally to represent the respective answers of the eight reporters to the question of date. Whereas, Sir Thomas Hardy's report, as we have seen, treats the finding of the date, that is, the literary aspect of the Manuscript, as subordinate in interest to the liturgical element wrapped around the Athanasian Creed, of which the volume contains, it is believed, the earliest copy. Dean Stanley's Preface puts the true state of the case with clearness and brevity. He says: " In the discussions occasioned by the proposed permission to disuse in the English Church the recitation of the Confession of Faith, commonly called the Creed of St. Athanasius, a subordinate controversy arose amongst scholars as to the probable date of the creed. This date had been variously fixed from the middle of the 4th century to the beginning or the middle of the 9th. One of the elements of this chronological question was felt to be the age to be assigned to the . . . . Utrecht Psalter. . . . Inasmuch as this Manuscript contained what was supposed to be the earliest copy of the Creed, considerable attention was attracted towards the document." Accordingly, at the request of Dr. Ellicott, Bishop of Gloucester and Bristol, Lord Romilly, then Master of the Rolls, through the assistance of Earl Granville, Secretary of State for Foreign Affairs, obtained from the Utrecht Academical Library, photographs of several portions of the Manuscript. With the aid of these illustrations, and from examination of tracings and lithographic facsimiles already alluded to, Sir Thomas Duffus Hardy prepared his elaborate essay which has just been described. But the opinion which he laid down, that the date of the Manuscript is to be referred to the close of the sixth century, and the remarkable historical circumstances which he attributed to its originally finding a royal English home, "led to further enquiries, which issued in an application on the part of the Trustees of the British Museum to the authorities at Utrecht to allow the Manuscript itself to be transferred for a time to the British Museum, and there deposited for inspection." This was done, and by these means archæologists and students of palæography and church history have, for the first time since the Manuscript was separated from the Cottonian Library, had an opportunity of examining it at pleasure. Hence, all praise is due to the liberality of the Utrecht University authorities for so promptly lending the book, to the Trustees of the British Museum, for their judicious consideration in placing it temporarily before English scholars, and, finally, to the Palæographical Society for undertaking to reproduce it by one of the most faultless and enduring processes of photography, and thus practically recovering to permanent English uses the literary treasure of which our national library and its numerous students had been so long and so strangely deprived. It was during the brief depositing of the Manuscript in the British Museum that the opinions expressed in the reports were arrived at, and put into the shape in which they were laid before the Trustees; and, during this period, the photographic copy of the book was prepared. These reports, in respect to their conclusions respecting the date of the Psalter, range from the eighth to the ninth century only, and they are illustrated with three autotype facsimiles of the second page of the text showing the employment of golden uncial characters in the first line of the Psalm, "together with the manner of work of perhaps the best draughtsman of the illustrations." The second gives the drawings for Psalms 95, 96, and the text of the latter: in this page are shown various forms of the marks of contraction alluded to in Mr. Bond's report, and the abbreviation of *t* for *tur*, which is of frequent occurrence. "The drawing," we are told, "exhibits the jagged outlines of the draperies referred to as characteristic of English work of the tenth and eleventh centuries, and the classical origin of the design in the river God." The third facsimile is of the page containing the concluding lines of the Psalm 105; the picture and commencement of the text of the Psalm 106. This illustration has been chosen for the many interesting points it presents. The sun and moon, treated in a peculiar style of most ancient art, ships, temples, and towered buildings, and oxen at the plough.

The first report is that drawn up by Mr. Bond, Keeper of the Department of Manuscripts. It contains an accurate and exhaustive account of the volume, pointing out for special notice that it contains two distinct Manuscripts, the *Psalter*, and imperfect *Gospels*. To the Gospel portion the date of the seventh or beginning of the eighth century is attributed. The punctuation is full throughout, by simple points and by the virgule and point, in form of a semicolon (;) or reversed semicolon (⸵). There are frequent abbreviations as well of such words as *Deus*, *Dominus*, *Jesus*, *Christus*, *sanctus*, as of more constantly recurring words as *quoniam*, *noster*, *omnes*, *terra*, *pater*, *non*, *neque*, *sunt*, and parts of words, as *con-*, *-tur*, *-runt*, *-bus*. The arguments which have been used to arrive at the date are, that although the use of Roman Rustic capitals, and the tri-columnar arrangement of texts in themselves indicate a time prior to the seventh century, yet the abbre-viations, contractions, punctuation, and golden uncial letters in first lines, "are unmistakeable evidences of a date so late as the end of the eighth century." Mr. Bond proceeds to show, by reference to the Harley MS. 647, an early tenth century copy of Cicero's metrical version of the Treatise of Aratus on Astronomy, with the commentary of Hyginus, written in Rustic capitals, a MS. ascribed by Ottley[1] to the extremely early date of the second

[1] In the *Archæologia*, Vol. xxvi. 47-214.

or third century; and by reference to the additional MS. 24,142, a Bible of the ninth or tenth century, written in three columns in imitation of the older exemplar from which it was transcribed, that the earlier characteristics which the Utrecht Psalter contains, may be, and are indeed found to be carried on in more recent ages. But the use of so many late forms, that the Manuscript constantly exhibits, cannot be thrown back to an earlier age.

The weakness and irregularity of the Rustic writing; the employment of the two forms of semicolon; the occurrence of numerous abbreviations; the dotted $\dot{y}$, found throughout the Manuscript, with rare exceptions; the illuminated initial letter at the beginning of the first Psalm; the thin and sketchy figures of the illustrations, where, "if compared with acknowledged works of the tenth and eleventh centuries, the connexion . . . in style of execution with this later manner of representing the figures is equally apparent;" the full representation of the Crucifixion; the Saviour's form uncovered to the waist; comprise the principal grounds on which Mr. Bond considers it impossible to refer the Psalter to an earlier time than the end of the eighth century, and dispose him rather to assign it to the ninth.

The report continues by remarking upon the position of the apocryphal Psalm, which would have been placed after the last Psalm, not after the canticles and creeds, if the Psalter had been copied from one of higher antiquity. With regard to the arguments for early age which have been founded upon the Gallican text of the Psalter, it is shown that the greater number of Psalters of the ninth, tenth, and eleventh centuries, contained in the British Museum, are of the Gallican version, of English use, and with English glosses. The theory respecting the introduction of the Psalter into England by the French Princess Bertha is carefully examined, and the history of the inserted Charter to Reculver, and of the added Gospel fragments, laid down and illustrated from corresponding treatment of other Manuscripts by Sir Robert Cotton. The report closes with the later history of the volume and some notices of its mention by Archbishop Ussher. This account is certainly the best written of any separate history of the Utrecht Psalter extant. The remarks are forcible, pertinent, and completely to the point, recording no discursions into recondite subjects which affect the true history of the book, if at all, yet in a very slight degree; no ventilation of theories which, however attractive, have no solid basis of fact or strong probability to rest upon. The keynote is evidently this, that in judging the age of a Manuscript, we must place it to the date of the latest style it exhibits, not to an earlier or to an age intermediate between its youngest and its oldest aspects. Mr. Bond's remarks in the *Athenæum*, No. 2468, for February 13, 1875, may be taken as additional proofs and illustrations of his theories respecting the age of the writing.

Mr. Thompson's report is practically and substantially the same as that which precedes it. It goes further, perhaps, in some points, where it draws attention to the imitative appearance of the writing;

"the weakness and uncertainty about the strokes which force one to feel that the scribe is writing in a character to which he is not habitually accustomed;" the too artificial arrangement of the initial letters of the verses which are set beyond the margin of the writing, so that, to use a technical term, the text appears *indented;* the absence of stops or use of the full point only in ancient Manuscripts; and the constant use of contractions. "With respect to the drawings," it continues, "it may be observed that the hands of at least three artists can be traced. There is no reason to suppose that they are later insertions, yet they approach more nearly in style to the light sketchy drawings of English Manuscripts of the tenth and eleventh centuries, than to that of such Manuscripts as the Vatican Virgil, or the Cotton Genesis, where the classical element is so strong. They therefore tend to support the opinion that the Psalter is not of so great an antiquity as has been represented."

The statement respecting the volume made by the Rev. H. O. Coxe, Bodleian Librarian, is to the effect that he can see no reason to conclude that it was written before the commencement of the ninth century, and that he has never seen a Manuscript, save the one in question, written throughout in the character and tricolumnal form by which it is distinguished.

The Rev. S. S. Lewis, Librarian of Corpus Christi College, does not feel warranted in assigning it to an earlier date than the ninth century.

Sir Matthew Digby Wyatt makes some very

interesting remarks about the illustrations, the
majority of which, he considers, "give every indication of having been copied from a much earlier, and
probably less profusely illustrated, *painted* Psalter,
produced under a decidedly Classical influence." He
compares the Harley Psalter and the Aratus Manuscripts, to which the reader's attention has been
directed on several previous occasions, and dates the
Utrecht Psalter at about the middle of the eighth
century.

Professor Westwood's notes are of high interest.
They refer to his previous opinions expressed in the
Archæological Journal and his great work on *Miniatures and Ornameuts*, which have already been pointed
out. He brings forward, however, other circumstances which induce him to refer this Manuscript
to the eighth or ninth century at the earliest. These
are, the space for the large initial B; the style of
the ornamentation and the use of gold in the initial
itself; the mixture of Rustic text with uncial first
lines; the division of each verse by the semicolon (?);
the Anglo-Saxon character of the drawings which
accord with those of the tenth century Oxford
Pseudo-Cædmon,[1] the Cotton Julius A. VI., and
may be compared with Cotton MS. Titus, D. XXVII.;
the opposition that would have been given to the
pictures previous to the second council of Nice
(A.D. 787). "The use of the Rustic writing," he
writes, "was common from the sixth to the twelfth
century; scarcely a good Manuscript of that long

[1] See the plates, and description by Sir Henry Ellis, 1832, in the *Archæologia*,
Vol. xxiv. 329.

period exists in which some portion is not in that character. ⁘ . . . . ; it is childish to affirm that because an entire Manuscript is so written it must necessarily be of the fourth, fifth, or sixth centuries." There are also letters from Professor Westwood to the *Athenæum*, dated July 11, and Sept. 15, 1874, in which the ivory carvings on the cover of the Psalter of Charles le Chauve, a Manuscript of the middle of the ninth century, are compared, in a remarkable manner, with the Utrecht drawing for the 56th Psalm (Latin Version), and the corresponding picture in the Harley Psalter, and with the Utrecht drawings for the 26th Psalm (Latin Version). But we are not told whether the carvings are coeval, or older, or younger, than the writing contained in the Manuscript, whose covers they adorn.

Canon Swainson's report does not profess to partake of a palæographical character. It deals with the Gallican version of the Psalms ; the Harley Psalter, of which the pictures exhibit, he thinks, an earlier type than the Utrecht drawings ; the Apostles' Creed, the text of which was not definitely fixed even in the ninth century ; the *Te Deum*, the text of which, as it is in the Utrecht Psalter, was not fixed before the time of Charlemagne ; the *Gloria in Excelsis*, which therein occurs in its modern, and not in its older form ; and the indications of a daily use of the *Te Deum*, which had not come into practice even in the ninth century. The ancient Cotton Psalter, Galba, A. XVIII., is compared in some points ; and the report concludes that the contents of the Psalter could not have been arranged, nor the Psalter written long before the year 800.

Sir Thomas Hardy prepared an elaborate reply to these evidences collected by Dean Stanley, and published it under the title of *Further Report on the Utrecht Psalter ; in answer to the eight Reports made to the Trustees of the British Museum, and edited by the Dean of Westminster.* Like the first, this *Further Report* bears no date on the title, but the colophon shows the date of May, 1874. It is not proposed on this occasion to enter very deeply into the consideration of this report, which is one of the most exhaustive accounts ever written respecting any Manuscript whatever, and necessarily examines, weighs, and sifts every thing that has been advanced in the work to which it stands as an answer. It points to the exceeding scarcity of Manuscripts of the age of the Psalter, and the difficulty of comparing the style with any other example of cognate workmanship ; and states that the age of the Athanasian Creed is not affected by the age of the Psalter, and that absurdities are involved in the hypothesis that the Manuscript is of the ninth century. The Psalter is again described minutely and at length, the peculiarities of the writing pointed out, and some similarity of orthography claimed for it to the inscriptions in the catacombs of Rome, and the *Virgil* and *Prudentius* already mentioned in a former chapter. The age of the drawings is equally criticised, their execution being attributed by the learned reporter to an artist well acquainted with Oriental objects, scenery, and customs ; while they have no peculiarities of the well-known delineation of the Anglo-Saxon era in England. For "the buildings, furniture, costumes, weapons, armour, musical and agricultural implements do not belong to Britain." In support of this line of argument, it is stated[1] that "these drawings are conceived and executed by a highly intelligent artist who . . . . derived the forms . . . there portrayed from actual knowledge, and was personally acquainted with the scenes and objects he depicts. I think it impossible that he could have been indebted to some earlier delineator as has been suggested." This passage must be compared with another in the *First Report*,[2] with which it appears to clash, viz., "it is not unlikely" that "the draughtsman had in his possession many specimens of former art, and selected those which he considered suitable to his purpose; and having determined what his drawing was to represent, he delineated temples, houses, costumes, and armour, similar to those in use in his day."

A lengthy dissertation from the gifted pen of Mr. Howard Payn, given in full as an appendix to the *Further Report*, and referred to at length by Sir Thomas Hardy at this part of the text, sustains the idea of the familiarity of the artist with the scenes and details he depicts, and points out how powerful are the probabilities " of the drawings being executed by a dweller in Alexandria, well acquainted with Syria," and with details found repeated in the wall subjects of Egyptian tombs at Beni-Hassan and Thebes. The total absence of

[1] P. 13.   [2] P. 25.

monastic forms is also, and with great weight, brought forward in proof of the early age of the drawings; but here we may ask, "Where' are the Roman chariots, deities, helmets, sandals, ceramic and metallic utensils, bucklers and broadswords, which the classical theory as peremptorily pre-supposes?" There is undoubtedly a very strong Eastern character in these drawings, as will be seen hereafter; and this branch of the report is ex-ceedingly interesting, and demands very careful perusal from all who wish to examine these points exhaustively, and thus to see "how each of them has a direct and definite reference to the Psalm it is intended to illustrate, and which could, by no possibility have served for any other purpose." The report proceeds to examine the different positions and various propositions assumed, raised, or debated by the reporters whose opinions have been published by the Dean of Westminster; and in doing so a very great amount of research is exhibited, and an equally great power of discrimination and logical reasoning is brought to bear upon the numerous points which arise during the enquiry. To the initial B, Sir Thomas Hardy denies an Anglo-Frankish origin, or an Anglo-Saxon prototype, and refers it to an Irish style. With regard to the "leathery" vellum; the alleged weakness of the handwriting; the peculiarities of the ruling; the punctuation; the arrangement of matter; the marks of contraction and abbreviation; the accents; the breaks in the text; and the dotted y; the report

' See *Athenæum*, Nos. 2434, 2436, 2438, June and July, 1874.

enters into full discussions calculated to upset all previous determinations arrived at by the Westminster reports.

The history and surroundings of the inserted Charter of Reculver are treated in the way already shown in the previous chapter; and the report, which is deserving of all the good things that can be said of it, as far as ingenuity, energy, and powerful theoretical reasoning carries us, concludes with three appendixes: (1.) *The Concurrence of the Historical and Palæographical arguments on the date of the Utrecht Psalter, in the matter of the Athanasian Creed*, a letter to Sir Thomas Hardy by the Rev. Robert C. Jenkins, M.A., Rector of Lyminge and Honorary Canon of Canterbury, dated December 31, 1873; (2.) The letter from Mr. Howard Payn, March 2, 1874, mentioned in a previous page; (3.) The comparison of the text in the Utrecht Psalter with those in the Gallican, Roman, Vetus, Vulgate, Hebraic, and Conciliatum versions, as far as Psalm 50, and Psalm 95. In this, the complete coincidence of the Utrecht text with that called the Gallican, and the general coincidence of both with the Vulgate and Conciliatum, and occasionally with the Vetus, is demonstrated.

The principal treatises upon the Psalter have now been brought before the reader, who may, in furtherance of his study of the subjects which this remarkable book affords, consult at will the literary journals of the last four or five years to gather up other more or less correct opinions which have from time to time been expressed upon the same great centre of palæographical attraction. It is necessary, however, to pass on to the description of the art-work itself which the Utrecht Psalter contains.

CHAPTER IV.

THE account of the external view of the Utrecht Psalter, which has been given in Chapter II., naturally preceded the independent examination of the contents of the volume that will be found comprised in the present chapter, which is devoted to this description, and to an enquiry into the peculiar styles of handwriting in which those contents have been committed to the Manuscript. This will prepare us for that division of the present work containing the detailed notices of the pictures, which, although undoubtedly of older conventionality than the execution of the text, and so, apparently, claiming a priority of investigation, yet may not unduly be taken in hand subsequent to the characters of the words they purport to illustrate, because they undoubtedly are additions of a less remote antiquity, notwithstanding that they approach, perhaps very nearly in point of time, to the same period.

It will therefore be necessary here to take account of the Rustic capital writing, the plain capital, and the uncial letter as found in the Psalter; the abbreviations and contractions of words; the division and punctuation of verses or sentences; the bisection of words in the middle and at the end of lines; a variety of circumstances which seem to indicate that the scribe was ignorant of, or at least imperfectly acquainted with the Latin tongue; the particular version of the Psalms and subjoined liturgical compositions; the headings and descriptive sentences attached to the respective Psalms; and a quantity of evidence produced by, dependent upon, or connected with the above points.

For greater convenience, and for simplicity's sake, the Psalms will be referred to according to their number as given or implied by the Manuscript itself, and the Latin quotations will be from the text of the same; the English equivalents, where quoted, will be from the English translation of the Bible dedicated to King James I. As the numeration of the Utrecht and the English Psalms does not entirely correspond, it will be useful to bear in mind that the *ninth* Psalm of the Vulgate[1] and of the Utrecht or Gallican version is broken up into the *ninth and tenth* of the English version: so that, roughly speaking, from the numeration, *Psalm* 10, to the end of the series, the English figures are in advance, by one, of the Latin versions.

Nevertheless, the numeration of the Utrecht Psalter is by no means uniform; sometimes the number is omitted altogether; sometimes the number

---

[1] "Biblia Sacra Vulgatæ Editionis," *Vesontione*, 1839. And so also "Biblia impressa Venetiis opera ... Nicolai Jenson, mcccclxxvi;" Vitellius E. xviii., with Saxon glosses; and MS. Reg., 1. E. viii., a fine MS. of the 10th cent.

given is incorrect; hence the following table will be found useful :—

ENGLISH.	VULGATE.	UTRECHT.	FIRST WORDS.
I	I	Not numbered	Beatus qui.
2	2	,,	Quare fremuerunt.
3	3	,,	Domine quid.
4	4	,,	Cum invocarem.
5	5	v.	Verba mea.
6	6	vi.	Domine ne in.
7	7	vii.	Domine deus.
8	8	viii.	Domine dominus.
9 } 10 }	9	viiii	{ Confitebor tibi. { Ut quid domine.
11	10	x.	In domino.
12	11	xi.	Salvum me.
13	12	xii.	Usque quo.
14	13	xiii.	Dixit insipiens.
15	14	xiiii.	Domine quis.
16	15	Not numbered	Conserva me.
17	16	,,	Exaudi domine.
18	17	,,	Diligam te.
19	18	xviii.	Cæli enarrant.
20	19	xviiii.	Exaudiat te.
21	20	xx.	Domine in.
22	21	xxi.	Deus Deus.
23	22	xxii.	Dominus regit.
24	23	xxiii.	Domini est.
25	24	xxiiii.	Ad te domine.
26	25	xxv.	Judica me.
27	26	xxvi.	Dominus inluminatio.
28	27	xxvii.	Ad te domine.
29	28	xxviii.	Adferte domino.
30	29	xxviiii.	Exaltabo te.
31	30	xxx.	In te domine.

ENGLISH.	VULGATE.	UTRECHT.	FIRST WORDS.
32	31	xxxi.	Beati quorum.
33	32	xxxii.	Exsultate justi.
34	33	xxxiii.	Benedicam dominum.
35	34	xxxiiii.	Judica domine.
36	35	xxxv.	Dixit injustus.
37	36	xxxvi.	Noli emulari.
38	37	xxxvii.	Domine ne in.
39	38	xxxviii.	Dixi custodiam.
40	39	xxxviiii.	Expectans expectavi.
41	40	xl.	Beatus qui.
42	41	xli.	Quemadmodum desiderat.
43	42	xlii.	Judica me deus.
44	43	xliii.	Deus auribus.
45	44	[x]liiii.	Eructavit cor.
46	45	xlv.	Deus noster.
47	46	xlvi.	Omnes gentes.
48	47	xlvi.	Magnus dominus.
49	48	xlviii.	Audite haec.
50	49	xlviiii.	Deus deorum.
51	50	l.	Miserere mei.
52	51	li.	Quid gloriaris.
53	52	lii.	Dixit insipiens.
54	53	liii.	Deus in nomine.
55	54	liiii.	Exaudi deus.
56	55	lv.	Miserere mei.
57	56	lvi.	Miserere mei.
58	57	lvii.	[S]i vere.
59	58	lviii.	Eripe me.
60	59	lviiii.	Deus repulisti.
61	60	lx.	Exaudi deus.
62	61	lxi.	Nonne deo.
63	62	lxii.	Deus deus.
64	63	lxiii.	Exaudi deus.
65	64	lxiii.	Te decet.

ENGLISH.	VULGATE.	UTRECHT.	FIRST WORDS.
66	65	lxv.	Jubilate deo.
67	66	lxxi.	Deus misereatur.
68	67	lxxii.	Exurgat deus.
69	68	lxviii.	Salvum me.
70	69	lxviiii.	Deus in adjutorium.
71	70	lxx.	In te domine.
72	71	lxxi.	Deus judicium.
73	72	lxxii.	Quam bonus.
74	73	lxxvii.	Ut quid deus.
75	74	lxxiii. ·	Confitebimur tibi.
76	75	lxxv.	Notus in.
77	76	lxxvi.	Voce mea.
78	77	lxxvii.	Adtendite populus.
79	78	lxxvii.	Deus venerunt.
80	79	lxxviiii.	Qui regis.
81	80	lxxx.	Exsultate deo.
82	81	lxxxi.	Deus stetit.
83	82	lxxxii.	Deus quis.
84	83	lxxxiii.	Quam dilecta.
85	84	lxxxiiii.	Benedixisti domine.
86	85	lxxxv.	Inclina domine.
87	86	lxxxvi.	Fundamenta ejus.
88	87	lxxxvii.	Domine deus.
89	88	lxxxviii.	Misericordias domini.
90	89	lxxxviii.	Domine refugium.
91	90	xc.	Qui habitat.
92	91	xci.	Bonum est.
93	92	xcii.	Dominus regnavit.
94	93	xciii.	Deus ultionum.
95	94	xciiii.	Venite exultemus.
96	95	xcv.	Cantate domino.
97	96	xcvi.	Dominus regnavit.
98	97	xcvii.	Cantate domino.
99	98	xcviii.	Dominus regnavit.

ENGLISH.	VULGATE.	UTRECHT.	FIRST WORDS.
100	99	xcviiii.	Jubilate deo.
101	100	c.	Misericordiam et.
102	101	ci.	Domine exaudi.
103	102	cii.	Benedic anima.
104	103	ciii.	Benedic anima.
105	104	ciiii.	Confitemini domino.
106	105	cv.	Confitemini domino.
107	106	cvi.	Confitemini domino.
108	107	cvii.	Paratum cor.
109	108	cviii.	Deus laudum.
110	109	cviiii.	Dixit dominus.
111	110	cx.	Confitebor tibi.
.112	111	cxi.	Beatus vir.
113.	112	cxi.	Laudate pueri.
114	113 1-8	cxiii.	In exitu.
115	113 1-18	runs on with the above.	Non nobis.
—	new numeration of verses.		
116	{ 114	cxiiii.	Dilexi quoniam.
	115	cxv.	Credidi propter, verse 10.
117	116	cxvi.	Laudate dominum.
118	117	cxvii.	Confitemini domino.
119	118	cxviii.	Beati inmaculati.
120	119	cxviiii.	Ad dominum.
121	120	cxx.	Levavi oculos.
122	121	cxxi.	Lætatus sum.
123	122	cxxii.	Ad te levavi.
124	123	cxxiii.	Nisi quia.
125	124	cxxiiii.	Qui confidunt.
126	125	cxxv.	In convertendo.
127	126	cxxvi.	Nisi dominus.
128	127	cxxvii.	Beati omnes.
129	128.	cxxviii.	Sæpe expugnaverunt.

ENGLISH.	VULGATE.	UTRECHT.	FIRST WORDS.
130	129	cxxviiii.	De profundis.
131	130	cxxx.	Domine non est.
132	131	cxxxi.	Memento domine.
133	132	cxxxii.	Ecce quam.
134	133	cxxxiii.	Ecce nunc.
135	134	cxxxiiii.	Laudate nomen.
136	135	cxxxv.	Confitemini.
137	136	cxxxvi.	Super flumina.
138	137	cxxxvii.	Confitebor tibi.
139	138	cxxxviii.	Domine probasti.
140	139	cxxxviiii.	Eripe me.
141	140	cxl.	Domine clamavi.
142	141	cxli.	Voce mea.
143	142	cxlii.	Domine exaudi.
144	143	cxliii.	Benedictus dominus.
145	144	cxliiii.	Exaltabo te.
146	145	cxlv.	Lauda anima.
147	146	cxlvi.	Laudate dominum.
	147	cxlvii.	Lauda Hierusalem, verse 11.
148	148	cxlviii.	Laudate dominum.
149	149	cxlviiii.	Cantate domino.
150	150	cl.	Laudate dominum.

By this it will be seen that the 9th and 10th English form the Utrecht *ninth*. The errors occur of XLVI. for XLVII.; LXIII. for LXIV.; LXXI. for LXVI.; LXXII. for LXVII.; LXXVII. for LXXIII.; LXXIII. for LXXIV.; LXXVII. for LXXVIII.; LXXXVIII. for LXXXIX.; CXI. for CXII.; the 114th and 115th are combined to form CXIII.; the 116th is divided at verse 10, making CXIV. and CXV.; the 147th similarly divided at verse 11 to make CXLVI. and CXLVII.; and hence the total number of one hundred and fifty Psalms is brought up at the end.

With regard to the character in which the bulk of the text is written, it has already been stated that it is written in that letter which is distinctively called the Roman Rustic capital. The term *Rustic* is applied to denote the crooked branch-like appearance which some of the component parts of the letters exhibit when compared with the regular square capital that preceded this modified form. The particular kind of Rustic lettering adopted by the scribe of the Utrecht Psalter undoubtedly betrays a certain debility of formation not seen in the Rustic hands of the Vatican Virgils, Terence, and Sallust, the Florentine Virgil, or the Prudentius of the Bibliothèque. No one can compare these forms together for a moment without perceiving the instability and weakness of the one, the firmness and power of the other. Mr. Bond points this characteristic out, where he says, in his report, " That the Rustic capitals are not genuine characters of the sixth century is evident from their comparative weak form and irregular setting. The first aspect of the writing conveys this impression most forcibly." Another report, too, considers " the impression which the writing conveys to the eye is that, though the style is old, the forms of the letters are not true. There is a weakness and uncertainty about the strokes which force one to feel that the scribe is writing in a character to which he is not habitually accustomed. This impression amounts to a conviction that the writing is an imitation. An examination of the letters in detail will show, in the Rustic (? Utrecht) letters, certain deviations from original forms, which would not be found in genuine writing. The few leaves in the Augustine Psalter (Vespasian A. 1), which are written in this character, and which are themselves probably not older than the eighth century, impress the eye far more favourably." But to this Sir Thomas Hardy objects that the character of the handwriting belongs to the sixth century, and that these Rustic capitals shown in the Psalter, " were prevalent in Europe from the third century, or earlier, to about the end of the seventh century. In titles and colophons it appears still later ; but never, so far as I have been able to discover, in the full text of later Manuscripts."

These Rustic letters in themselves are, nevertheless, of regular and shapely appearance, being all of uniform height, with exception of the F, L, and Q, which respectively project slightly above or below the line.

The A is formed of two wavy strokes or arms without the cross bar ; the left stroke is thinner than the right, and the bases are finished off each with a small and short horizontal notch or spur.

B has its upper loop not so prominent as the lower loop, but the lower loop is sometimes shorter in height than the upper one ; the commencement of the upper loop, and the finish of the lower, project on the left side of the vertical bar.

C has a well defined spot at the top, and the bend is upright, thickened as it approaches the base, and curled up very slightly towards the concluding part of the letter. The curve is of an elliptical rather than circular shape. This letter resembles the G very much, except that the finish is made differently.

D is formed in a remarkable manner. The vertical bar has a horizontal stroke at the base, slightly projecting on the left, but prominently so on the right side. The loop is commenced slightly on the left of the bar at the top, rapidly thickened, and brought down to a fine stroke to meet the horizontal stroke on the base. Hence the letter does not represent that symmetry with which we are familiar, but appears to have a right-angled base, but not a right-angled summit, which is, on the contrary, more acute.

E is also curious for the short and abrupt nature of its three bars, all of which are of the same size and shape : the one in the base projects, however, more distinctly over the left side of the upright stroke.

F is one of the three projecting letters, and Sir Thomas Hardy considers that it possesses " scarcely any cross lines."[1] But a careful inspection shows that its cross lines are of distinct and peculiar style. The upright line is about one fifth longer than the corresponding line of other letters, and so overtops the bounding line of the two parallel lines ruled with a dry point, between which the letters of the text are ranged. The upper cross line is commenced slightly to the left hand of the vertical line, and,

[1] Further Report, p. 11.

after beginning with a thick stroke, finishes off thinly and with a curved point. This bar is not horizontal, but obliquely placed, and points upwards, thereby contributing to the additional height of the letter.

G is closely similar to C, but has a sort of shortened comma or *cedilla* added vertically downwards at the end of the curl, which seldom passes below the range of the other letters. Another form of G has no cedilla, but the curve of the C is enriched with a thick and short curve within it. The two forms are seen on column 1 of the second page of the Psalter, a facsimile of which is given in the Dean of Westminster's collection of Reports. In this page, the G with cedilla occurs seven times, and the G without cedilla, five times.

H also possesses two forms; the first is made up of two vertical and one horizontal stroke, the former having at their bases short spurs; the second kind, which is by no means so constantly recurrent, is somewhat like K.

I has a spurred base as large as that which is given to the E.

K does not appear to occur.

L is remarkable for the additional length bestowed upon its upright stroke, which is at least one fifth above the bounding line; its base stroke is very short, and scarcely longer than the base strokes of the E, F, and I.

M has the first and third strokes thin; the second and fourth, thick; the summits of the upright bars cut off obliquely; the bases embellished with spurs. The interior angle, formed by the junction of the second and third strokes, almost touches, and in many cases does touch the lower bounding line of the writing.

N has two thin upright bars, a thick interior line, curved in a distinct and decided manner towards the base, that is, the outer edge of the curve is towards the left hand; the second upright has no basal spurs; the first has a distinct one.

O is formed of two curved strokes, containing an elliptical space; the thick parts of these curved lines are opposite to each other obliquely, viz., the thickest part of the left hand stroke is near the bottom of the curve; but of the right hand curve it is near the upper part of the bend.

P has an upright stroke, framed according to the usual wavering Rustic form, a spur or base line of distinct dimensions, and a short and small loop, which commences slightly on the left of the vertical line, and is not continued so far as to finish in contact with the stem upon which it is built.

Q resembles O, with an oblique stroke jutting out downwards below the line, and pointing to the right hand. There are three forms of Q, the stroke being straight, curved, or elongated.

R is a fine and well shaped letter. The upright stem has a strong spur at the bottom; the upper loop resembles that of the B; the acute finishing stroke is thick, and produced far beyond the limit indicated by the loop. This also has a Rustic shaping, produced by a horizontal turning given to the pen when it reaches the bounding basal line.

S is not a thick and firm letter, but poor and thin

in its curves ; the middle and ends thicker than the other parts.

T resembles I very closely, with the single exception that the upper horizontal line is a trifle more distinctly expressed, whereas in the I the vertical line is abruptly cut off by imparting an oblique motion to the pen.

U, or V, is a very interesting letter. It is formed of an oblique thick stroke, slightly curved in the same way as the central stroke of the N, but more distinctly bent. The second stroke resembles the last upright of the N ; it is thin, and has a horizontal spur at the top. In this respect this letter may be compared with the uncial U, which has a curved stroke conjoined with the second stroke, that is upright and strongly marked.

X is very characteristic of the Rustic lettering. The oblique line from left to right is thick, strong, and cut off cleanly and abruptly without spurs. It is, however, slightly curved downwards. The cross-stroke from right to left is thin, weak, and (*f*) shaped, the spurs in this letter taking rather the form of a thickening in the line, that at the summit being on the right, that on the base being on the left of the stroke to which they perform the part of finial embellishments.

Y of the Rustic alphabet has attracted much attention, because it has been strenuously asserted, and as assiduously denied, that this letter is adorned with a dot or point above it. For example : " The' letter y in the Utrecht Manuscript is very seldom

---

' Sir Thomas Hardy, *Report*, p. 20.

pointed, and the point seems to have been added by
the scribe himself when he has made the letter look
something too like the V." "Of' individual letters,
the y (in the Utrecht Manuscript) is almost always
dotted." This letter is certainly of remarkable shape,
and does not seem to accord with pure Rustic
shapings. It is formed of a large and thick curve,
very boldly drawn, bulging towards the right, and
commences fully three fourths of the height of an
ordinary letter above the line. On reaching the
base the stroke is carried upwards thinly, and ends
off with a sharp but small and thick curve. The
dot is by no means always placed over it, and we
may compare this (Y) form as it occurs, with a dot,
in Ps. XXXII. 2, in *cythara*, with the form without
the dot in Ps. XXXV. 6, in *abyssus*.'

In the "*Canticum Moysi Prophetae*," or *Cantemus
domino*, verses 5, 8, the word *abyssi* occurs twice
with a dotted y̆, which does not project at all above
the row of letters.

Z does not occur very often. The oblique stroke
is thin; the horizontal strokes thick, short, and of
true Rustic waving form. The reader may for
instance, compare *Zabulon*, Ps. LXXII. 29, with a
variant form in *Zib et Zibeae*, Ps. LXXXII. 10;
Zelaveris, Ps. XXXVI. 1; *Zelavi*, Ps. LXXII. 3;
Zelus, Ps. LXVIII. 12; LXXVII. (for LXXVIII.)
5; *Zona*, Ps. CVIII. 18.

The addition of the point or dot over the y in this

' *Report* by Mr. Bond, p. 1.

' See also *tympano* (Ps. 148); *moÿsi* (Ps. 76, 102); *cÿmba, cÿthara* (Ps. 150);
tÿru (Ps. 82); *martÿrum* (Te Deum); *egypto* (Ps. 79); *aegypto* (Ps. 113, 114);
Moyses (Ps. 98).

Rustic alphabet has been instanced by some as a decided mark of late age; by others it has been asserted that in Manuscripts of the sixth century this letter is often dotted; but it is pretty well acknowledged that the dotted y seen in Manuscripts of the sixth down to the twelfth centuries affords no test of age, and must be ascribed to the fancy of the writer, and not to the conventionalism of any age in particular. This fact is so amply borne out by the facsimiles of pages of early MSS. selected and published in the issue of the Palæographical Society, that it is unnecessary here to recapitulate any evidence respecting it.

We have now to glance at the two other styles of writing which are found in the Utrecht Psalter. The uncial characters, in which the rubrics or headings of the Psalms, as well as the first line of the text of each Psalm (and in the case of the 118th, some of the first lines of subdivision) are written, differ naturally somewhat considerably from the Rustic capital, which is in this Manuscript a more interesting modification of the ancient capital. These uncial titles or headings are written in red-coloured ink, the first lines of the earlier Psalms in gold. The initials of the divisions or verses are also given in uncial letters, coloured, and stand out to the left of the text; but the *first letter of each Psalm* is plain and uncoloured, about half an inch square, and partakes of the capital form.

This capital alphabet may be briefly described as thick, massive, and solidly set, about half an inch high, and many of the letters quite of that breadth.

The generality of the letters are armed with spurs or projecting notches. The A, which commences Psalms XXIV., XXVII., XXVIII., XLVIII., LXXVII., CXVIII. (*daleth* and *tav*), CXIX., CXXII., has a thin left line and bar, a thick right line and firm bars or spurs both above and below. B occurs in Psalms XXXI., XXXIII., XL, LXXXIV., XCI., CII., CIII., CXI., CXVIII. (*aleth* and *teth*), CXXVII., CXLIII., and is of a fine Roman square or set form, such as may be seen on the inscriptions of the best period. C occurs in Psalms IV., IX., XV., XVIII., etc., in all seventeen times, and has a bold and well formed curve. D is of most frequent occurrence, being found in Psalms III., VI., VII., VIII., XIII., XIV., XVII., etc., forty-four times, or nearly one third of the whole number. This letter is beautifully made, with well marked spurs, and has a strong and solid shape, very unlike the rustic D. E is also of frequent use, being placed at the head of Psalms XVI., XIX, XXIX., XXXII., etc., for seventeen times altogether. It has a thick standard and well lengthened spurs; but the three horizontal arms are rather more short and thin than we might perhaps expect. F only occurs twice, in Psalms LXXXVI., and CXVIII. (*ain*). In these instances it resembles the E, but without the lower bar. G and H do not occur at all. I is met with in Psalms X., XXV., XXX., XXXIV., etc., fifteen times. Its upright line, which is strong, is thickened still more as it approaches the summit and base, and it has thin flat spurs extended prominently on either side. K does not occur. L is

the commencing letter of twelve Psalms or subdivisions, being found in Psalms CXII., CXVI.,
CXVIII. (*he* and *nun*), etc. M begins Psalms
XLVII., L., LV., LVI., etc., and is met with ten
times. Two fine examples, Psalms L., LVI., show
that it is of a very massive shape, the first stroke
thickened as it approaches the base, the second and
fourth stroke very broad, the spurs fine and thin.
N occurs five times, in Psalms' XXXVI., LXI.,
LXXV., CXXIII., CXXVI. Of these examples
two are very good, Psalms LXXV. and CXXVI.,
showing that the first and third strokes, which are
thin, gradually thicken as they approach their spur,
and the oblique line, which is very strong and broad,
is cut off at the top horizontally where it meets the
first vertical line; but at its junction with the third
stroke it forms an acutely pointed angle, set somewhat below the line of the writing, so that the third
stroke is longer downwards, in a corresponding
degree, than the first. O is only to be seen once, in
Psalm XLVI., and the photograph unfortunately
does not reproduce the whole of the letter, although
there is enough to show that the thickest parts of
its shapings do not stand horizontally, but obliquely,
opposite to each other. P is to be seen thrice, in
the initial letters of Psalm CVII., CXVIII. (*Heth*,
and *Sin*, or, as the Utrecht Psalter write these
words, *Eth*, and *Sen*). These three examples of the
capital P are of different dimensions, but all have
the same peculiarities, the broad upright stem,
strengthened towards summit and base, the distinctly expressed spur, and the swelling curve of the

loop, which falls short by a very little of meeting the vertical line in the middle, and so leaves the loop open by about the sixteenth part of an inch. Q is an interesting character, because it also appears to possess more than one magnitude. Altogether this letter occurs nine times, in Psalms II., XLI., LI., LXXII., LXXIX., LXXXIII., XC., CXVIII. (*mem*), and CXXIV. It is very similar to the O, already described, with the addition of an oblique line or finishing stroke with acutely pointed end. R only occurs in Psalm CXVIII. (*gimel*), and in this example is rather to be ascribed to the uncial than the capital alphabet, by reason of its smallness and the peculiar arrangement of the spur at the base of the upright line. This spur is very fine and thin, and points directly *downwards*. S is the initial letter of five Psalms, viz., XI. [LVII.], LXVIII., CXXVIII., CXXXVI. The curves in this letter are perhaps not so bold as we should expect to see in comparison with those of the C, D, O, P, Q, and R. T is found only at the commencement of Psalm LXIV., and of this, too, the photographic facsimile does not give a perfect reproduction. Its characteristics are, however, in keeping with the other members of this capital alphabet. U, or V., is seen in seven Psalms, V., XII., [LXXVII. for] LXXIII., LXXVI., XCIV., CXVIII., *resh*, CXLI. The first stroke is thick, and the second stroke by no means so thin in comparison as some in the series. X, Y, Z do not occur.

The added pieces, canticles, and prayers, do not fill up many vacancies. The T of the *Hymnum ad*

Matutinis is imperfectly reproduced. There is, however, a very fine capital G in the *Gloria in Excelsis*. This letter has a fine curve, and is finished with a strong short upright line, with spurs at the top and bottom of very handsome proportions.

The uncial alphabet, which is employed, for initial letters of verses, first lines except the letter at the beginning, and rubrications of Psalms, affords, naturally, far more specimens for examination. There are two types of this alphabet, a large kind, which is used as initials to the first words of head-lines, as well as initials to the first words of verses or divisions ; and a small kind that is employed in the sentences of the head lines. But the only variation appears to be in the size of the individual letters, and not in their shape, and we may, therefore, consider these two types together as one character. Of this alphabet, the letters have spurs or short notches where the forms present an opportunity for their employment. The A has a thick stroke from left to right, but its first stroke is thin, and its second stroke, or bar, rises obliquely from the base of the first to the middle of the third stroke. B resembles a capital B. C also is very like its capital equivalent, but is spurred at both extremities; the upper finish appears to project slightly beyond the lower end. D is a round letter made with two curves, that on the left rising upwards to form the up stroke of the letter, which resembles an O roughly made, and disconnected at the top. E is also nearly a circular letter, completed with a horizontal bar, the two ends of the curve approaching the end of the bar very closely, and all three ends have spurs. F has a thick upright, which is prolonged below the line, where its spur is added to it, curiously enough, not at right angles, but in the form of a thin stroke carried out perpendicularly downwards on the left hand plane of the thick stroke. G resembles C, with a thin stroke added below the line perpendicularly, and terminated with a dot or thick spot. H is not unlike a Roman minuscule (h) with thick upright, and curved bow thickened in the middle, and not spurred at the end as is the upright. I has a thick stem, a spur to the left only at the top, and a perpendicular spur like that described for the F, at the base. K does not appear to be found. L rises above the line, and has three spurs. M is very similar to a broken *figure of eight* lying down, being formed of two imperfect circles, or curved lines. N is of the rustic type, but with the first base spur not so strongly formed or altogether omitted, and of stouter build. O is round and firm, and has the same characteristic as that described for the Rustic alphabet. P is well shaped, but has the peculiar vertical spur already found on the uncial F and I. Q is of a distinctly uncial type, differing materially from the Rustic and the capital equivalents. This letter closely resembles an uncial C conjoined to an uncial I, the tail passing below the line, and being armed with the perpendicular spur. R is not unlike a capital letter, but has the distinguishing spur projecting downwards. S and T are similar to capital letters,

but not strong and firm.   The latter of these letters
does not always bear its upper spurs.   The spur at
the base, of the T should, to be uniform, be perpendicular, but in this letter the horizontal spur is
always used.   U and V, *in words*, have but one
form, a broadly swelling curved line united to a
straight line with short spurs.   But V, *in numerals*,
is of the capital form, made up of two straight lines
meeting at an acute angle.   X has a thick bar from
left to right, a thin and weak bar, bent, and with
only the upper spur, from right to left.   (See Psalm
LXXXIV., and the *Gloria in Excelsis*.)   Y resembles
a, capital V, with a thin vertical tail added, which
has a thick spot at the end, turning up slightly to
the left.   (See Psalms LXXI., LXXV., and the
Symbolum Apostolorum.   Z is like a capital Z, with
thick transverse line.   (See the *Canticum Zachariæ*,
and Psalms LXXXVII., CXLV., CXLVI.)

The abbreviations and contractions, which a
careful examination of the Utrecht Psalter enables
one to gather together, have been variously esti-
mated by different writers.   Sir T. D. Hardy considers
that "the rarity of abbreviations in Manuscripts is
generally in proportion to their antiquity, and this
is the case in the Utrecht MS.;" Mr. Bond, on the
other hand that the "abbreviations are of frequent
occurrence."   Mr. Thompson finds that "contractions are used throughout the Manuscript; and
these are not limited to the abbreviations of sacred
names and titles which occur in the most ancient
Manuscripts, but comprise many forms which are
only found in the eighth or subsequent centuries."

The following words occur in the text and headings with an abbreviated or contracted form :—

aetni	for aeterni.	nrs	for nostris (*Ps.* 77).
aetnu	„ aeternum.	propht	„ propheta (*Ps.* 50)
aut	„ autem (*Ps.* 33).	psal	„ ⎫
-b ;	„ -bus, *commonly.*	psalm	„ ⎬ psalmus, *com-*
xps	„ Christus (*Fid. Cath.*)	psl	„ ⎭ *monly.*
c-	„ con-, *commonly.*	oms	„ omnes, *commonly.*
dd	„ David, *commonly.*	omps	„ omnipotens.
dm	„ Deum, *commonly.*	ort	„ oratio (*Ps.* 101).
ds	„ Deus, *commonly.*	pat	„ pater.
defcit	„ defecit (*Ps.* 118 caph.)	propt	„ propter.
di	„ Dei, *commonly.*	qd	„ quod (*Ps.* 69).
dns	„ Dominus, *etc., commonly*	qm	„ ⎫ quoniam, *com-*
		qnm	„ ⎭ *monly.*
domu	„ domus (*Ps.* 95).	-r	„ -runt (*Ps.* 42).
e	„ est, *commonly.*	repudad	„ repudiandum, (*Apocryphal Psalm*).
ei	„ ejus (*Ps.* 70, 72, 96, 104, 108, 115, etc.).	-rnt	„ -runt, *commonly.*
f	„ fine (*Ps.* 73)	scs	„ sanctus, *and so for cases, commonly.*
ihs	„ Jhesus (*Fid. Cath.*).	scuarium	„ sanctuarium (*Ps.* 72, 77, etc.).
inscription	„ inscriptionem (*Ps.* 56).	seper	„ semper (*Ps.* 18).
		sps	„ Spiritus, *etc., commonly.*
long	„ longe (*Ps.* 55).	spuit	„ sprevit (*Ps.* 77).
(*overline*)	„ m *final, commonly.*	st	„ sunt, *commonly.*
ml	„ millia (*Ps.* 59).	tabernacul	„ tabernaculi (*Ps.* 28)
ms	„ meus (*Ps.* 42).		
n	„ non (*Ps.* 43).	-tr	„ -tur (*Ps.* 62, etc.).
neq ;	„ neque.	tra	„ terra (*Ps.* 77).
nost	„ noster (*Ps.* 105).	usq ;	„ usque (*Ps.* 27).
nr	„ noster, *commonly.*		etc., etc.

The mark used for indicating an abbreviated word is in all cases a line, more or less curved, according to the Rustic style, over the word from which a portion has been omitted. This line is, in the majority of cases, obliquely drawn from left upward towards the right, and may have a small hook at either or both ends, so that it appears to be a long but small *s* reversed. Sometimes, however, it nearly approaches a straight line, and is so given in the list on page 179.

Mr. Bond, however, in his Report, distinguishes three forms of the marks of contractions, " 1st, a horizontal slightly curved line, fine, and raised a little at the extremity; 2nd, a line turned in opposite directions at the ends, and slanting upwards obliquely to the right; 3rd, a modification of the same in which the ends are both turned inwards."

Another form of contraction is found for the letters U R, when they occur after T, forming the final syllable -TUR. This is found of pretty frequent occurrence, and in most cases at the ends of lines. It generally resembles a small figure of 2 obliquely disposed, but is not altogether unlike an *r*. A great deal of controversy has arisen with respect to this form of contraction: some maintaining that the constant use of the expression is alone conclusive evidence of the late date of the Psalter; others, again, being unwilling to concede any inference from the employment of this peculiarity.

In addition to the abbreviations pointed out, the letters N T, where they occur in following order at the end of a word, are conjoined into a monogram, the cross-bar of the second letter being added to the final upright stroke of the first, which is carried up above the line (Psalm XCI., etc.). But Æ, when it is a true diphthong, is, if at all, very rarely written as one character, in which case it appears to take the form of E with a cedilla, as in prẹteriit, Psalms LXXXVIII., XCIII, and Œ never occurs in combination. No other forms of unification of two or more letters appear to occur.

The orthography of some of the words forms a very interesting branch of the examination of the Manuscript. In addition to several mere clerical errors, many very remarkable instances of spelling, which indicate probably the pronunciation of the individual scribe, or of the district where the Psalter was written, are scattered throughout its pages. Among these may be instanced *prumptuaria* (Psalm CXLIII.); *Hismahelitae* (Psalm LXXXII.); *salmus*, for *psalmus* (Psalm LXXIX.); *inmensus* (*Fid. Cath.*); *inluminatio* (Psalm XXVI); *redemtor* (Psalm XVIII.); *inmaculati* (Psalm CXVIII.); *Diabpsalma* (Psalm IV.); *efuderit* (Psalm CI.); *sup*, for *sub* (Psalm XVII.); *liniretur*, for *leniretur* (Psalm XXVI.); *ós* always, and *a* sometimes have an accent over them (Psalms XXVI., CVI., CXLIII., *twice*, LXII., CXVIII., etc.); *áaron* is thus written in Psalms XCVIII., CV.; *oportuno* (Psalm XXXI.); *sterelem* for *sterilem* (Psalm CXI.); *faciae; gigans* (Psalm XVIII.); *orroris* (*Cant. Moy.*); *Babyllonis, habierunt, decim, eructuo, postola, decacordo, aurietis, oportunus, ymnis, orfanorum,* etc. Sir Thomas Hardy points out, in addition, other peculiarities, such as the occurrence of *adnuncio, adfligo, adsumsit, adpropero, adfero, adflicto, adtraxi, conpungar, conparatus, conlocavit, inrideant, inlustra, inmortalis, obprobrium, optenint, capud, reliquid, fulgora, subplantâ, harena, holera,* etc. The errors pointed out here seem to indicate that the scribe was not a Latin scholar, but was copying (perhaps from dictation), a language with which he had a very superficial acquaintance; but it must be borne in mind that Latin was, in the middle ages, for all who had any pretence of education, a living language, and, as such, subject to laws of mutation.[1]

The division of words is also a very necessary point to be observed. For while the general body of. the text has the words run together without breaks, yet a number of instances occur where a small space called *alinea*[2] has been left by the scribe, between two words, or even between parts of the same word. Sometimes a very harsh form of division of words occurs at the end of a line, such as *lunam et s|tellas,* (Psalm VIII.); *cons|tituisti,* (Psalm VIII.); *cons|-pectu* (Psalm 30); *omni|a,* (Psalm CXVIII., *lamech*); which evidently strengthen the opinion already expressed, that the writer had not much critical knowledge of the language which he was transcribing.

Erasures occasionally occur, such as *Exsurgat, Exsultate,* with the *s* in each case erased, (Psalm LXXII.); *Exsurge,* with *s* erased, (Psalm XLIII.); *Exspectans exspectavi,* altered into *Expectans expectavi,* (Psalm XXXIX.); a letter erased in *Eruct avit,* the first word of Psalm XLIV.; *ter* erased in *interfecta,* (Psalm CV.); etc.

[1] See Rêvue Critique, 2 April, 1870, on *L'Histoire des doctrines grammaticales au moyen âge,* by C. Thurot.   [2] See Hardy's Report, p. 14.

Inserted letters may be occasionally noticed, they having been omitted in the first preparation of the text ; these inserted letters are placed over line in the position they should properly occupy. For example, *ma^{g}na* for *magna*, (Psalm CVII.) ; *abs^{con}ditis* for *absconditis*, (Psalm XVI.) ; *fratre'mei* for *fratres mei*, (the Apocryphal Psalm) ; *et^{in}ira*, (Psalm XXXIV.). The first occurrence of the words *facti sunt*, originally written twice over, has been erased in Psalm LXXXII. At the " Canticum Moysi Prophetae," five concluding versicles, commencing " Ascenderunt populi," to " operatus es domine " have been omitted, and supplied on the lower margin of the leaf in a smaller Rustic handwriting of very weak and undefined form.

Many other peculiarities of the text in the way of abbreviations, contractions, erasures, insertions, and divisions of words might be pointed out, but a sufficient number of examples have been adduced to give the reader a correct idea of the nature of the transcript. The remaining point of interest, which it is necessary to mention, is the punctuation of the sentences. On examination of the text of the Psalter it will be found that as a rule each verse is commenced on a new line with an uncial letter at the beginning, occupying a position to the left of the body of the text in the page. But the number of paragraphs in the Utrecht Psalter does not in all cases coincide with the number of verses ascribed to other versions of the Psalms ; as, for example, the Utrecht Psalm XXVI., *Dominus inluminatio mea*, has twenty paragraphs, whereas the English

version has but fourteen verses. The increased
number is owing to the division of each of the
verses 1, 2, 3, 4, 5, 9, into two paragraphs respectively. In addition to this, occasionally a combination of parts of verses has been made, as may
be observed in the Psalm just mentioned, where the
tenth paragraph, " In petra exaltavit me ; et nunc
exaltavit caput meum super inimicos meos;" represents the latter part of the fifth and beginning of
the sixth verse of the English version, ". . . . he
shall set me up upon a rock. (6) And now shall my
head be lifted up above mine enemies round about
me :" . . . . Numbers of instances occur throughout the Psalter where a similar treatment has been
adopted.

The marks adopted throughout for punctuation
are the semicolon, and the inverted semicolon, the
former of these being used at the ends of the
versicles or paragraphs, the latter in a space left
for it intentionally at the rhythmic division of the
versicle in the middle, in the same manner, and,
generally speaking, in the same places where the
colon is used in the Prayer Book version of the
Psalms. There is nothing in the photographs to show
that these stops are not contemporaneous with the
text, for the colour of the ink is the same. And this
again has been instanced as an indication of late
age, for it is asserted that in ancient Manuscripts
there are usually either no stops, or simply the full
point. The full point does certainly occur in the
Psalter (*see* Psalm XXXIV. *Et adversum me*, etc.),
but it is very rare in comparison with the two forms

above described.   It is curious, too, to observe here that Mr. Bond considers that these two forms of semicolon "have every appearance of having been inserted, as was the common practice, by the reviser of the Manuscript."

The version of the Psalms which forms the text of the Utrecht Psalter has been shown by Sir Thomas Hardy, in his *Further Report*, Appendix III., to resemble so very closely the "Gallican Version," that the text of our Manuscript must be undoubtedly admitted to be Gallican.   In his collation of fifty-one Psalms there appear to be only three instances where the Utrecht text varies from readings exhibited by the established Gallican forms.   The term *Gallican*, we are told by Canon Swainson, is applied to this text "merely because it obtained a general currency in the first instance in countries north of the Alps, and was thus distinguished from an earlier recension by Jerome, which was retained for a time in the church of Rome and Italy."   "The Roman Psalter was gradually and steadily ousted by the Gallican.   The latter spread from Gaul and Germany to churches in the North of Italy, and was ultimately accepted by nearly all the churches in communion with the church of Rome."   On the other hand, Hardy says the Gallican Psalter is St. Jerome's more exact Latin translation, made in A.D. 389 from the Hexapla of Origen, or rather, perhaps from the Greek Septuagint, corrected from the Hebrew where the Greek was supposed to be faulty.

The headings and descriptive sentences attached

15

to the respective Psalms, are, with some omissions, practically the same as those found in the Vulgate version; but they present several curious readings, and occasionally are difficult of solution. For example: the Utrecht heading for Psalm XV. is "In finem pro adsumptione mationa psał dd," where the Vulgate reads "In finem pro susceptione matutina psalmus David;" and that for Psalm LIX. is "In finem his qui mutabuntur in tituli inscriptionem david in doctrinā cū succendit syriam et convertit ioab et percussit vallē salinarū xii mł," which the Vulgate gives thus: "In finem, Pro his qui immutabuntur, in tituli inscriptionem ipsi David in doctrinam, Cum succendit Mesopotamiam Syriæ, et Sobal, et convertit Joab, et percussit Idumæam in valle salinarum duodecim millia." The apocryphal Psalm "Pusillus eram," sometimes called the CLIst, placed in this Manuscript after the *Fides Catholica*, has an unintelligible heading, "Hic psał proprie scribitur dd et extra numerum cum pugnavit goliat hic psł in ebreis codicibus non habet sed ne a lxx interscriptib; edictus ē et idcirco repudad," for which an emendation[1] has been proposed thus, "Hic psalmus proprie scribitur David, et extra numerum, cum pugnayit Goliat. Hic psalmus in Ebreis codicibus non habet[ur] sed ne[que] a septuaginta interscript[or]ibus edictus est, et idcirco repud[i]and[us]."

It is natural to expect a very great amount of difference of opinion should exist with critical palæographers respecting the chief points of pecu-

---

[1] See *Athenæum*, No. 2438, p. 73, 18 July, 1874.

liarity which are exhibited by the text of the Psalter,
and this does exist in the principal treatises which
have been mentioned in the chapter devoted to the
Bibliography of the Manuscript. It is, however,
unnecessary in the present volume, which aims at
being descriptive rather than controversial, to say
more on the subject of these distinctions. The date
of the Manuscript of course depends in a great
measure on the peculiarities of its abbreviations,
orthography, and punctuation ; but when these
peculiarities cannot be assigned exclusively to any
one age, they lose that paramount importance which
the nature of the character employed for the text
alone can be said rightly to possess. Hence,—while
it must be admitted that the fewer the abbreviations,
the rarer the contractions, the less often the re-
currence of departures from classical orthography,
the simpler the punctuation, be found, by so much
the older the Manuscript itself must be—yet the
well known period of rise, flourishing, and decay of
pure Rustic texts, and of the same with uncial and
capital letters introduced, so far outweighs all other
evidence, that the ultimate verdict as to the date of
the Utrecht Psalter must be given in accordance
with these elements of greater importance.

CHAPTER V.

HAVING lingered thus long, but necessarily, upon the introductory topics which are raised by an examination of the Utrecht Psalter, it is time we should now look closely into the pictorial art which is exhibited by this remarkable and unique Manuscript. The present chapter, therefore, has been devoted to an almost page by page investigation of its contents. In it will be found an account of the principal illustrations with which its leaves are adorned, together with remarks relating to those peculiarities which appear to claim the interest or the attention of the reader as he turns over the plates of the *Autotype Facsimile*, which has done so much towards disseminating a knowledge of the volume since its reintroduction to English palæographers by the discernment of Professor Westwood.

On the folio (marked A) at the commencement of the book, and stained round the margins with the leather turnings-in of the original, or some ancient binding, are written at the top of the page the words

𝕮𝖑𝖆𝖚𝖉𝖎𝖚𝖘. 𝕮. 7.

in a rude Gothic or black letter, such as is seen in a great quantity of the Manuscripts among the Cottonian Collection in the British Museum. It is believed that this is the handwriting of the librarian who arranged the collection under the immediate supervision of Sir Robert Cotton. Below this is a small ticket, or label, of white paper, pasted on, and bearing this inscription in printed Roman characters, being the press mark of the Utrecht University Library :—

" Aevum medium.

Scriptores Ecclesiast.

No. 484."

On the outer margin, about one-fifth from the bottom, is the following manuscript note :—

" Bibliothecae urbis

Trajectinae

donavit

D. de Ridder."

apparently in a hand of the seventeenth or eighteenth century ; but it has not been determined whether this note is in the handwriting of the clerk or librarian of the University, or of " D. de Ridder," who presented the Manuscript to that institution.

The next folio (B) contains a short tabular list of the contents of the books written in an imitative character of the shape known as Gothic or black letter, such as we have already had occasion to notice on the previous leaf. The text of this is as follows :—

"𝔈𝔩𝔢𝔫𝔠𝔥𝔲𝔰 𝔠𝔬𝔫𝔱𝔢𝔫𝔱𝔬𝔯𝔲𝔪
in 𝔥𝔬𝔠 𝔠𝔬𝔡𝔦𝔠𝔢.

Psalterium, secundum septuaginta Interpretes ab Hier-onimo emendatum, sive.[1]

𝔓𝔰𝔞𝔩𝔪𝔦 𝔇𝔞𝔲𝔦𝔡𝔦𝔰, 𝔏𝔞𝔱𝔦𝔫𝔢 𝔠𝔲𝔪 𝔞𝔩𝔦𝔦𝔰[2] 𝔥𝔶𝔪𝔫𝔦𝔰 𝔢𝔱 𝔠𝔞𝔫𝔱𝔦𝔠𝔦𝔰 𝔖𝔞𝔠𝔯æ 𝔰𝔠𝔯𝔦𝔭𝔱𝔲𝔯𝔞𝔢 ~ ~ | 𝔬𝔯𝔞𝔱𝔦𝔬𝔫𝔢 𝔇𝔬𝔪𝔦𝔫𝔦𝔠𝔞, 𝔖𝔶𝔪𝔟𝔬𝔩𝔬 𝔄𝔭𝔬𝔰𝔱𝔬𝔩𝔬𝔯𝔲𝔪[3] 𝔢𝔱 𝔄𝔱𝔥𝔞𝔫𝔞𝔰𝔦𝔧. 𝔔𝔲æ 𝔬𝔪𝔫𝔦𝔞 𝔦𝔩𝔩𝔲𝔰𝔱𝔯𝔞𝔫𝔱𝔲𝔯 ~ | 𝔯𝔬𝔪𝔞𝔫𝔬 𝔥𝔞𝔟𝔦𝔱𝔲, 𝔣𝔦𝔤𝔲𝔯𝔦𝔰. 𝔢𝔱 𝔞𝔫𝔱𝔦𝔮𝔲𝔦𝔱𝔞𝔱𝔢 𝔦𝔪𝔭𝔢𝔯𝔞𝔱𝔬𝔯𝔦𝔰 𝔙𝔞𝔩𝔢𝔫𝔱𝔦𝔫𝔦𝔞𝔫𝔦 𝔱𝔢𝔪𝔭𝔬𝔯𝔞 𝔟𝔦𝔡𝔢𝔫𝔱𝔲𝔯 | 𝔞𝔱𝔱𝔦𝔫𝔤𝔢𝔯𝔢.

𝔉𝔯𝔞𝔤𝔪𝔢𝔫𝔱𝔲𝔪 𝔈𝔟𝔞𝔫𝔤𝔢𝔩𝔦𝔧 𝔖𝔢𝔠𝔲𝔫𝔡𝔲𝔪 𝔐𝔞𝔱𝔥𝔢𝔲𝔪 𝔡𝔢 𝔱𝔯𝔞𝔫𝔰𝔩𝔞𝔱𝔦𝔬𝔫𝔢. 𝔅. 𝔍𝔢𝔯𝔬𝔫𝔦𝔪𝔦 𝔠𝔲𝔪 𝔭𝔯𝔬= | 𝔩𝔬𝔤𝔬 𝔦𝔭𝔰𝔦𝔲𝔰 𝔞𝔡 𝔇𝔞𝔪𝔞𝔰𝔲𝔪 𝔓𝔞𝔭𝔞𝔪 𝔏𝔦𝔱𝔢𝔯𝔦𝔰 𝔏𝔬𝔪= 𝔟𝔞𝔯𝔡𝔦𝔠𝔦𝔰.

𝔠𝔞𝔯𝔱𝔞 𝔒𝔯𝔦𝔤𝔦𝔫𝔞𝔩𝔦𝔰 𝔏𝔦𝔱𝔢𝔯𝔦𝔰 𝔞𝔫𝔱𝔦𝔮𝔲𝔦𝔰𝔰𝔦𝔪𝔦𝔰 𝔥𝔩𝔬𝔱𝔥𝔞𝔯𝔦𝔦. 𝔯𝔢𝔤𝔦𝔰 𝔠𝔞𝔫𝔱𝔲𝔞𝔯𝔦𝔬𝔯𝔲𝔪 ~ ~ | 𝔟𝔢𝔯𝔠𝔲𝔞𝔩𝔬. 𝔢𝔱 𝔐𝔬𝔫𝔞𝔰𝔱𝔢𝔯𝔦𝔬 𝔰𝔲𝔬 𝔡𝔢 𝔱𝔢𝔯𝔯𝔦𝔰 𝔦𝔫 𝔚𝔢𝔰𝔱𝔞𝔫 𝔦𝔫 𝔗𝔢𝔫𝔢𝔬. 𝔠𝔬𝔫𝔰𝔢𝔫𝔰𝔲 𝔄𝔯𝔠𝔥𝔦𝔢𝔭𝔦: | 𝔱𝔥𝔢𝔬𝔡𝔬𝔯𝔦. 𝔄𝔫°. 𝔠𝔥𝔯𝔦𝔰𝔱𝔦. 679. 𝔦𝔫𝔡𝔦𝔠𝔱𝔦𝔬𝔫𝔢 𝔰𝔢𝔭𝔱𝔦𝔪𝔞."

This *carta* is no longer contained in the volume, but several pages have already been devoted to a consideration of its history, and the important light it throws upon the history of the whole volume.[4] We may pass on to the first folio proper (1 a) which contains on the upper right hand (outside) corner the well known signature of Sir Robert Cotton. Specimens of this signature may be examined in a great many of the Cottonian Manuscripts; for example, the reader may compare that

---

[1] This sentence in a hand closely resembling the donatory sentence on the preceding page.

[2] *Alliis* with the second *l* lined out.

[3] Apostoloru̅ with *m final* added in the late hand.

[4] Pp. 76, *et seqq.*

in the volume *Cleopatra C. VIII.*, which is almost
identical. Reversing the volume are some ancient
scribbles, as if the scribe had been trying his pens.
"m d o, d c, d d, d ds nr̄ & n o n u ɪ d b i t, d̄s a
autem, autē increm̄, increm̄tū dedit allā, . . . ipso."
These letters and words may be of an age almost
contemporary with the writing of the book, if they
are not indeed trials of pens by the actual writer of
the text. Turning the book back again to its
original position, and at the lower margin, are the
words "pennis valde fulgentibus refert . . . ."
" Stat sonipes," in a hand of the eleventh century;
and, finally, at the lowest edge of the page, in the
middle, is the stamp of the library at Utrecht, an
estoile of sixteen rays, those in cross and saltire
plain, those alternately placed between them, wavy,
charged with a shield of arms :—Party per bend—or,
as foreign heraldry would describe them, taillé d'ar-
gent et de gueules, with the inscription in ordinary
Roman capitals,

ACADEMIA RHENO TRAIECTINA.

On the *verso* or reverse side of this folio (1 b) is
the first of the wondrous specimens of pictorial
illustration that we shall have occasion to examine.
A whole page, indeed, is dedicated to the picture,
but a fairly wide margin of more than one inch is left
blank at the upper margin, and nearly three inches
have been left untouched at the lower margin. In
the foreground, on the right, we perceive a confused
heap of slain bodies; above them two winged
figures, each armed with a long trident, thrust their

weapons into prostrate forms which writhe under
the terrible punishment. To the left of these is
drawn a compact body of six or seven spearmen
looking towards the winged messengers of wrath ;
the foremost of the group has thrown down his spear,
and kneels on his right knee, while, with uplifted
arms and outstretched hands, he seems to implore in
vain some respite from his impending and inevitable
fate. In the centre of the foreground is a bearded
head in profile adorned with wings, and apparently
lying on the ground of the hillock which divides
from it the group of warriors. Further still to the
left, a solid, gnarled, and cable-like trunk of a tree
erects itself with a bushy head of fruit and foliage ;
the fruit being round, the leaves pip shaped, and
arranged in groups of three upon long stems. This
alludes to verse 3, "tamquam lignum quod plantatur
secus decursus aquarum." At the extreme left of
the foreground, at the head of a trench, here intended for a river, with a *hydria* or *prochoos*, without
handles, a vase of classical shape, at its source, is a
figure seated on the rising ground of the bank, and
draped and reclining with the knees bent slightly
upwards, and the head and shoulders resting against
a graceful reed-like tree. This part of the picture
appears to represent a vision, the sitting figure is in
a trance, the winged head represents his spirit and
looks towards the subject of his dream, the infliction
of Divine wrath upon those who have risen up in
rebellion against the living God.

In the back ground, on a peculiar wavy line of
ground, the middle of the picture is occupied by two

draped figures, turned almost back to back, but inclining their heads towards each other, and elevating their outer arms and hands, as if each strove to point out to each the group at either side of the page. That on the right hand shows us a king, seated in majesty, upon a chair-like throne with semi-circular back and rectangular footboard. The monarch holds in his right hand, by the hilt, a broad sword, the point downwards, resting on his right knee. At his right hand stands a group of warriors or armed figures, brandishing spears, and seemingly intent upon the words spoken by the king. The whole group is arranged under a pediment, and rudimentary tiled roof placed upon and supported by two plain columns on plinths, and with Corinthian capitals. The left hand group of the background consists of a circular temple of six columns of the kind already described, with a domed or arched roof terminating in the centre with a circular knob surmounted by a trefoil or fleur-de-lys. Beneath its shade, and seated on an altar-like throne with square footboard, but having no back, is a draped figure, perhaps intended to represent the divine Psalmist himself, intently gazing upon an open book which is placed upon a raised stand or lectern before him, in allusion to verse 2. Behind the throne stands a winged angel with outstretched arms, as it were, the personification of the heavenly inspiration by whose means the Psalms were conceived and written. Above these groups is a stratum of clouds; Sol, the full orbed sun, in human form personified, within a circle on the left; on the right, the crescent moon, attended by a train of stars, shines over the regal throng.

The whole of this picture is intended to portray, in literal fashion, the allegorical figures and tropes of poetical fancy contained within the verses of the first Psalm. For example, it may be that the circular temple with its occupant denotes the man whose " delight is in the law of the Lord ; and in his law doth he meditate day and night" (verse 2). The tree by the river in the foreground, called by Hardy the rose-bay, or oleander, alludes to the man who is " like a tree, planted by the rivers of water, that bringeth forth his fruit in his season ; his leaf also shall not wither " (verse 3). The destruction of the ungodly, alluded to in the sixth verse, is undoubtedly indicated by the angels bearing tridents and slaying the figures lying prostrate before them.

Folio 2 a contains the text of the first Psalm, commencing with the initial *B* of Beatus. The page also contains the opening verses of the second Psalm, ending in the middle of the seventh verse. The text is divided into short paragraphs, for the most part but not always corresponding with the present division into verses. For example, there are seven paragraphs in the first Utrecht Psalm for six verses English, verse 3 being divided into two in the leaf before us. In the centre of the page, running right across, and occupying about one-third of the entire space of the form, is a picture, the second in the book, and, like all throughout, an endeavour to illustrate and represent, in a literal way, the metaphorical diction of the Psalmist. In

the centre, on a lofty eminence, "the holy hill of
Zion" (verse 6), a draped figure, with a nimbus around
his head, breaks "a potter's vessel with a rod of
iron" (verse 9). On the right, a dense phalanx of the
heathen, and on the left, a similar, but smaller body,
each armed with spears, and some few among them
with ovate shields are taking "counsel together,
against the Lord, and against his anointed" (verse 2).
On the left, an engagement between five angels or
winged figures, armed with bow, battle-axe of
double edge, trident, shield, and spears, and a confused mass of figures upon the ground beneath,
striving vainly to ward off, or avoid if they may, the
missiles hurled down upon them from above. As
they "rage" (verse 1), He that sitteth in the heavens
laughs at them in derision (verse 4). From the clouds
on the upper right hand issues a right hand with the
two fingers and thumb in the act of benediction, but
not extended in so decidedly marked a manner as
was afterwards the custom in representations of the
hand of blessing. This is probably in allusion to
verse 2, "Blessed are all they that put their trust in
the Son."

Reuvens points out the value of this illustration as
showing in one and the same picture all the weapons
used by the draughtsman throughout his work. We
have the barbed javelin or spear, the two-edged
battle-axe with semi-circular lunetted blades, the
bows, arrows, and oval convex shields of the angels,
the trident, and the rod.

Folio 2 b contains the remainder of the second
and the whole of the third Psalm, at the head of

which is a picture representing in a pictorial and positive manner several of the images originally presented to the mind of the reader by the divine poet. The centre of the *tableau* is occupied with a long and straight bedstead with a rising scroll-shaped head-piece and cushions. Hardy[1] points to this " sella lectica " as an Eastern luxury not introduced into Rome until towards the end of the Republic, and by no means an Anglo-Saxon object. On this bed is David, contrite and characteristically of re-signed mind, rising from his slumbers at the invocation of an angel, in explanation of verse 5 : " I laid me down and slept; I awaked; for the Lord sustained me." The words " Non timebo milia populi circumdantis me " are illustrated by two groups of figures set out to the right and left of the central subject. That on the right hand bears branches of palm or willow, one in each man's hand. The left-hand group are armed with spears. Of this band, the foremost person is the subject of an attack made upon him by the winged figure, who, while he sustains the awakening sleeper with his left hand, strikes this rebellious leader upon the face with a long lance, in accordance with the text of verse 7 : " Thou hast smitten all mine enemies upon the cheek bone ; thou hast broken the teeth of the ungodly." Above the figure of the Psalmist, upon a lofty knoll, depicted in that wavy, swelling, and rolling manner which characterises the whole of these drawings, the Divine Form is seen, seated on a stool-shaped throne, with a projecting footrest,

[1] *Further Report*, p. 18.

a circular nimbus thrown around His head, and
stretching out towards the suppliant his right hand,
as it were, in vivid representation of the fourth verse.
"Voce mea ad dominum clamavi, et exaudivit me
de monte sancto suo," " and he heard me out of his
holy hill." The remainder of the accessories are a
hill with a house and a few trees, and at the extreme
limits of the picture two sturdy trees with decaying
trunks, lopped under branches, and peculiarly drawn
heads of foliage, probably intended to convey to the
eye some resemblance to the stately cedar[1] of
Mount Lebanon.

The lower margin of this same Manuscript page
is occupied with the illustration belonging to the
next Psalm. Here, on the right, is a basilica, or
rectangular temple, with plain door; a flight of four
steps; six windows in what may be called the clerestory, or the highest part of the side-wall beneath the
roof, which is represented by lines crossing at right
angles; a triangular pediment, and a circular knob
surmounting it at either end of the building. On the
right hand wall is an aisle, or lean-to addition, with
masoned side-walls; roof as already described; and
small doors, one at the side, the other at the front.
From each of these doors or openings a prostrate
figure, seen at half-length, is pointing outwards, and
probably represents the catechumens or congregation.
In the principal doorway is a priest, and in front of
him, on the steps, standing before an altar of Roman
shape with plain square shaft and plainly chamfered
or bevelled plinth and cap, is another priest, who is

[1] See Hardy's *Further Report*, p. 2, for remarks on the cedar.

officiating in front of the triple flame of fire which rises with its flickering, lambent tongues in anticipation of the sweet-smelling sacrifices of righteousness (verse 5), here put before the eye under the form of a sheep led to the slaughter by a votary who carries a round vessel in his right hand, and is followed by two others each bearing a barbed spear. The upper central portion of the view is occupied by a half length figure of the Almighty in the heavens. Beneath him, a most interesting group of "the sons of men." One man, armed with a spear and shield, leads two champing horses to the chase, while his two dogs grapple with a fierce animal which has been drawn so graphically, and yet indistinctly, that it is difficult to say whether it is intended to be a bear or a lion. Sir Thomas Hardy does not take notice of these creatures in his note concerning the animals found in the pictures. It may be, that this portion of the picture is the result of the artist's endeavour to translate the phrase "how long will ye love vanity," but the idea is very farfetched, and does not carry out the usual procedure of the draughtsman in most cases herein. There is nothing in the text of the Psalm which in any way would account for this rendering of the pleasures and vanities of the world but this sentence, and we must bear in mind that the excitement of the chase was one which was carried to an extent in the classical and middle ages which certainly places the indulgence of hunting in the category of vanities. Behind the hunter is a row or group of six persons; one holds a long lance or staff slightly curved, one is draped as a female with cincture, and fillet on the brows, others hold spears and a shield. Before them are two barrels and two *canthari*, or vases of classical goblet shape but without handles, in illustration of the seventh verse, "A fructu frumenti et vini et olei sui multiplicati sunt," which is translated in the English version in connection with the previous sentence, but here kept separate. Behind these again is a tall man standing in an oblong compartment, which resembles a box, with the lid partly open. He stretches out his hand towards the Almighty, and perhaps indicates the subject of the third, fourth, and eighth verses : " The Lord will hear me when I shall call unto him," " Stand in awe and sin not," " Thou, Lord, only makest me to dwell in safety." Cedar trees, the lily or reed, temples, one with a statue on the principal pediment, are drawn in shadowy outline to complete the *coup d'œil*.

The next page (folio 3 a) contains the whole of the fourth Psalm. The lower central part contains the picture belonging to the following Psalm, of which the text is given below the drawing, as far as verse 5. The scene here, as is most usual, is composed of two or more separate actions. In the middle of the foreground is one of those peculiar boxes, or coffins, with open lid, most probably alluding to verse 9 : " Their throat is an open sepulchre." On the left a tonsured priest ascends the steps of a temple, at the door of which is an altar. It is worthy of remark that the bald head refutes the statement, so frequently made, that there is an entire absence of mediæval religious forms, for here is a plain indication of the shaven crown distinguishing the cleric from the layman in the early ages of the church. Not that the occurrence of the shaven head helps at all to the approximation of a date, for the custom of cutting hair in a round is mentioned by St. Athanasius,[1] St. Jerome, and St. Ambrose, while on the other hand, St. Jerome and Optatus, in the fourth and fifth centuries, censured the practice as unbecoming spiritual persons; Casalius, too, explains that the tonsure betokens the priest's grief for his own sins and for those of his people. The walls of the building are lined to represent masonry, and it is drawn with upper windows, a tetrastyle arrangement of columns, triangular pediment, and roof of curved tiling (verse 7), "Introibo in domum tuam," etc. By its side stands a tree which may in some rough way be the representation of an olive tree. In the centre, above the open sepulchre, a winged man is making his way with rapid strides towards a group of several persons armed with spears; at the right hand corner three angels are destroying a seething mass of human forms in a pool of liquid fire fringed about its banks with a kind of short and scanty vegetation. This refers to verse 10, "Destroy thou them, O God." The background contains yet another image; a body of men, bearing palm branches, are turned towards an angel who is flying down from the upper heaven with a shield in the left, a crown in the right hand; while, from out the clouds on the extreme left of the view, the right hand of the Almighty Father stretches forth a second crown towards the adoring throng. This is the remarkable conception of the artist with

[1] Walcott, *Sacred Archæology*, p. 580.

reference to the concluding verse of the Psalm,
" Domine, ut scuto bone voluntatis coronasti nos."
" For thou, O Lord, wilt bless the righteous ; with
favour wilt thou compass him as with a shield."

The concluding verses of the fifth Psalm, and the
commencement of the sixth, are upon folio 3 b, which
also contains in its central part the illustration
adapted to the latter. Suspended in the heavens,
between two rugged hills, that on the left having
a small edifice with a cedar and wild olive tree, that
on the right similarly figured but with greater
elaboration and more space, is a half length figure of
the Almighty Father. Beneath him, in the valley, a
rectangular temple, of the peculiar classical kind
already described, and of most frequent occurrence
throughout the Manuscript, and two framed bedsteads each containing a half-reclining figure. These
may be taken to refer to the words of the 6th verse,
" Laboravi in gemitu meo? lavabo per singulas noctes
lectum meum? lacrimis meis stratum meum rigabo;"
" I am weary with my groaning ; all the night make
I my bed to swim ; I water my couch with my
tears." On the right, in the foreground, is a body of
men armed with spears, and departing from the presence of the suppliant. " Discedite a me omnes qui
operamini iniquitatem." " Depart from me all ye
workers of iniquity " (verse 8). In the foreground, on
the left, four angels, each armed with a long lance,
are standing on the bank of a pool, in which are
heaped up a confused mass of the impious who are
receiving their punishment from the celestials. " Eru-
bescant et conturbentur vehementer omnes inimici

16

mei." " Let all mine enemies be ashamed and sore vexed " (verse 10).

Folio 4 a is filled with the conclusion of the sixth, and beginning of the seventh Psalm. In the middle, and occupying about one third of the covered space, is the drawing which relates to this latter Psalm. This is one of the most beautifully conceived *tableaux* in the whole of the book, and for clearness, excellence of style and general effect may be compared with any of the illustrations that follow or precede it. Taking the subjects in the order of the text, we must begin with the extreme left, where, on a rising hillock, beneath a stunted cedar trunk a lion [1] is standing in solitary power and strength over the prostrate form of a human being. This undoubtedly points to verse 2, " Ne quando rapiat *ut leo* animam meam! du[m] non est qui redimat neque qui salvum faciat." " Lest he tear my soul like a lion, rending it in pieces, while there is none to deliver." A full length figure behind, and nearer to the centre, pours out his supplication contained in the following verses, and stands in graceful attitude gazing stedfastly, and withal with a kind of contented air, towards a small temple surrounded with trees of various growth, and towards the central subject of the whole picture, a representation of the Almighty King standing on a lofty rock, and armed with a bow and arrows in the one hand and a sword in the other. This refers to verses 12, 13, " Nisi conversi fueritis gladium suum vibrabit! arcum suum tetendit et paravit illum. Et in eo paravit vasa mortis! sagittas suas ardentibus effecit."

[1] See Hardy's remarks on the lion of the Utrecht Psalter, *Further Report*, p. 21.

" If he [the wicked] turn not, He will whet his sword;
He hath bent his bow and made it ready.   He hath
also prepared for him the instruments of death;
He ordaineth his arrows against the persecutors."
Grouped in a semicircle half round the figure of the
Father, at the base of the rock, stand thirteen persons armed with spears and clad in loose short
tunics, " Sinagoga populorum circumdabit te."   " So
shall the congregation of the people compass thee
round about " (verse 7).   An angel placed on a projecting corner of the rock extends his arms towards
the Creator.   In the foreground on the right is a
round pit or well with banked mouth and a few
sprigs of vegetation.   Into it is falling the wicked
Cush, the Benjamite, against whom this Psalm has
been specially directed, " He made a pit and digged
it; and is fallen into the ditch which he made."
" Lacum aperuit et affodit eum ? et incidit in foveam
quam fecit;" (verse 15).   The extreme right contains a woman lying on the ground and giving suck
to two infants, one being on each arm; this is the
literal rendering of the poet's metaphor, " Behold he
travaileth with iniquity, and hath conceived mischief,
and brought forth falsehood."   " Ecce parturit injus-
titiam ? concepit dolorem, et peperit iniquitatem;"
(verse 14).   The great beauty and inherent charm
of this picture is its simplicity, its well arranged
symmetry, and its carefully balanced subjects centring
upon the prominent figure of the heavenly Father.
The attitude of the subordinate beings are well
studied, and conceived with due regard to nature,
and the majesty of the suppliant, who makes his

18*

mute yet eloquent appeal to the Lord, is very strikingly made manifest. The lion with his human prey; the pitfall; the birth of the twins, mischief and falsehood; the "congregation;" the four armed men shooting and casting spears and darts against the suppliant, who is indeed none other than the Psalmist himself; all form so many little sketches complete in themselves, while at the same time they are harmoniously grouped together to form a whole of enticing interest, over which we may linger for a long time without exhausting all the details of the apparently simple composition. In this picture we may see faintly foreshadowed the dawn of that style which has rendered the spirit of Raffaelle immortal, because he did not despise the teachings of those who long before him had discovered the true principles of artistic representation, although to this he added the correction of faultless perspective and an improved depiction of relative proportions and backgrounds, combined with more equable distribution of detail.

Folio 4 b is occupied with the remainder of the seventh and the beginning of the eighth Psalm. The upper part of the lower half of the page bears the illustration which the draughtsman has prepared to represent the leading features of the latter Psalm, translating metaphor by tangible subjects, and grouping those points that best suit this most remarkable method of appealing to the eye to fix the poet's imagery more vividly upon the imagination of the reader. The upper part of this view, which has no background, or reduced vista of sight, is occupied with the Blessed Lord seated on a rainbow, and set within an oval line or frame which is supported by four angels, and of the shape so commonly adopted in all conventional representation of divine personages in glory, down to the very close of mediæval illustrative art. On each side three winged ministers of the divine will stretch forward attentively towards their Master, whose words they are, as it were, listening to with eagerness and joy. Each one of them bears a long staff, the upper end terminating in a cross. This refers to the opening sentences of the poem, "Domine, dominus noster? quam admirabile est nomen tuum in universa terra. Quoniam elevata est magnificentia tua? super caelos;" Beneath this heavenly host stand a group of "babes and sucklings" (verse 2) who are gazing upwards to their Father, while the "enemy and the avenger" are "stilled" by being thrust into a pit by an angel with a long lance and streamer of two pendants. One of these enemies has already fallen into the abyss, and three other companions are rapidly about to undergo the same manner of destruction. The right hand of the upper part contains the crescent moon and her attendant stars, "Lunam et stellas quae tu fundasti" (verse 3). Beneath these is a cedar tree with three birds on its branches, other three flying through the air, and in a pool fringed about with vegetation on its swelling banks, are a variety of fishes and aquatic birds. This group of natural life is balanced by a concerted subject on the left in the foreground. A rocky height with trees and houses, on its slope; at its base a group of horned sheep, goats, and oxen are disporting themselves at their will in their pastures.   These two subordinate divisions relate to the concluding strains of the song (verses 6-8), " Thou madest him to have dominion over the works of thy hands, thou hast put all things under his feet : all sheep and oxen, ... the fowl of the air, and the fish of the sea."   " Omnia subjecisti sub pedibus eius oves et boves universa/ insuper et pecora cåmpi; Volucres caeli et pisces maris/ qui perambulant semitas maris; "   The avenging angel, who stands on the right of the group of babes, is carefully set in balance by the erect figure of the Psalmist, who stands, with upturned face and hands extended forwards, composing his song of praise as he gazes upon the King of Heaven who inspires his theme.

The next page (5 a) is filled with the final portion of this Psalm, and a first portion of the following one; and folio 5 b contains the remainder of this the ninth Psalm and commencement of the tenth.   These two Psalms have not been separated in any way from each other, and it would seem that the illustration that is placed on folio 5 a at the head of the ninth Psalm has been intended by the artist to apply to passages contained in both these compositions.   On the left hand at the upper part of the picture is a representation of the Lord in an oval line of glory, attended by six angels, three on either side, bearing each one a staff or cross.   The Lord holds, in his left hand, an even balance, the emblem of justice, and the group may be taken to represent the words, " Paravit in judicio thronum suum/ et ipse judicabit

orbem terrae in aequitate? judicabit populos in jus-
titia;" (verse 8).   There are four groups in the foreground of the picture.   On the extreme left a cedar
tree overshadows a kind of walled polygonal enclosure
wherein a small knot of suppliants stand taking
"refuge in times of trouble;" on the principal buttress
or column over the doorway stands a solitary figure
with hand upraised in adoration.   In front of the
walls a man with uplifted sword, and two comrades
with spears, are falling upon the enemies of the
Lord.   Beyond these, a hill with trees scattered over
it bears a warrior with spear and shield, addressing
the image of the Father, as if he spoke in the words
of verse 19, " Exurge domine non confortetur homo?
judicentur gentes in conspectu tuo;"   The hill leads
us to one of the two central groups; hell, a low,
rectangular, masoned building vomiting flames.   This
is undoubtedly the hell of verse 17, a representation
of the infernal pit, as unlike the gaping jaws of hell
of later mediæval conventionalism as can possibly be.
Into this structure are being driven the wicked "and
all the nations that forget God," "omnes gentes
quae obliviscuntur Deum."   A winged angel with
a long rod hovers over the heads of the hurrying
throng and hastens their destruction.   One of the
crowd turning slightly backwards seems to implore
in vain a respite from the horrors of the punishment.
Broken walls, and a group of armed men, "destroyed
cities," lead us on to a peculiar tent of four upright
standards supporting a convex, swelling, sail-like
roof, beneath which, on a wide throne sit three
figures; the one on the right holds a fourth figure

by the hand and a long scroll or waving device of uncertain meaning. This group probably refers to verse 4, "sedisti super thronum qui judicas justitiam," "thou satest in the throne judging right." On the extreme right hand of the picture a temple on the hills, with a triangular pediment; four figures in animated attitudes, and four more below these, shut off a small group of four persons gazing with dismay upon a man fallen supine on his back from off a square pedestal which is falling from its base and seems to threaten to overwhelm him, "Dixit enim in corde suo non movebor." "He hath said in his heart I shall not be moved" (verse 6). The last portion of this fertile drawing is a small but clear figure of a lion, crouching secretly in his den "to catch" the poor. This is placed in the central part of the foreground, and is so small that it is almost sure to be overlooked at first sight, but careful search will show the subject of verses 9, 10 of the tenth Psalm, English Version, here forming paragraphs 32-34 of the ninth Utrecht Psalm, "Insidiatur in abscondita quasi leo in spelunca sua; Insidiatur ut rapiat pauperem?" etc.

The next picture is placed before the tenth Psalm on folio 6 a, the upper part of the leaf containing the remainder of the foregoing Psalm, the lower part the whole of the tenth Psalm except the last paragraph. The subjects which this illustration takes in hand to depict are varied, yet when we contemplate the whole as it is set forth on the leaf before us, we cannot fail to admire the exceeding beauty, naturalness, and congruity of the whole allegory, so harmoniously has

the grouping and balancing of the component parts
been effected. It is, indeed, a question whether any
better arrangement of the details could be carried
out. Verse 1 is literally shown by the bird fleeing
to the mountain, "in montem sicut passer." Verse
2, "the wicked bend their bow," etc., supplies two
figures, one with bow bent pointing at the "upright
in heart," three venerable men in conversation, seated
on the brow of the mountain; while the other makes
ready his "arrow upon the string." The next verse,
"quae perfecisti destruxerunt," gives rise to a motley
group of destroyers, who, armed with long instruments
resembling the modern adze, surround a square
building and throw down one of its sides. The walls
of the house are masoned in square blocks, in front
is a triangular pediment, the roof being of slightly
convex tiles laid as is now the custom in long ridges,
and the two upper corners of the roof are finished off
with small cup-like crockets or finials. This is the
shape and style of building which is frequently met
with throughout the series of drawings in the Manuscript, but some examples are elaborated with
pilasters, and other enrichments, as will be observed
hereafter. The crowd of destroyers do not, however,
perform their work unhindered, the denunciations
contained in verse 6 are come upon them, "Pluit
super peccatores laqueos? ignis . et sulphur et
sp[iritu]s procellarum pars calicis eorum;" The
"fire and brimstone" falls on them in an incessant
shower, the "laqueos" or snares are already at their
throats, one man falls backwards half strangled,
while others vainly struggle to free themselves from

the fatal coils of the heaven-sent halters. The left
hand side of this realistic *tableau* balances in most
exact proportion with the groups described. Opposite the shower of fiery sleet sits " the Lord in his
holy temple," serenely poised in mid-air upon an
orb, at the entrance of a rectangular temple with
masoned sides, enriched with three pillars, and an
imbricated roof adorned with ball-shaped finials.
The stricken crowd of destroyers is counterpoised in
turn by a number of men with uplifted hands,
looking towards one who holds an even balance, and
turns his gaze towards the Lord in His Majesty
overhead. This group relates to verse 5, "The Lord
trieth the righteous," etc., " Dominus interrogat jus-
tum et impium?" or better perhaps to the concluding
words of the Psalm, " aequitatem vidit vultus ejus."

· Not the least interesting point that this picture
raises is the question of the shape and material of
the temples and ecclesiastical buildings. Sir Thomas
Hardy[1] enters at length into a very interesting
examination of their peculiarities, and shows their
dissimilarity from anything like Anglo-Saxon art,
pointing out that the early churches in England were
made of wood and thatched with reeds, or at least
with lead, yet in the Manuscript there is not a single
instance of an ecclesiastical building being covered
either with thatch or lead, they are all roofed with
stone of a particular nature, described by Pliny as a
substitute for tiles and of common use for the purpose by being cut up into thin slabs. It is, however,
difficult to imagine that in this particular illustration

[1] *Further Report*, p. 19.

the two buildings are roofed with slabs of this stone, because there is a decided convexity about the lines which can only be reasonably and naturally explained by the well known shapes ' of Roman tiles, but still some of the drawings appear to show a flat roofing material which may perhaps be composed of this stone slab work.

Folio 6 b contains the eleventh Psalm with a pictorial interpretation which occupies fully half the page. This illustration has obtained a large amount of notice at the hands of critical palæographers. At the right hand corner in front stand the " speakers of vanity," whose reprobate deeds are mentioned in verses 2-4. The poor of the 5th verse, halt and maimed, are crawling about over broken and rugged ground, stretching forth imploring hands to the Lord, who, with cruciform nimbus, and attended by a band of angels, steps down from his universal seat, and hands a long spear, with a cross bar near the head, to an avenging spirit. This is probably St. Michael, the Archangel, who, with buckler girt on his left arm, and wings erect, and loose flowing robe trailing behind in the vivid haste of his eagerness to obey the divine will, shows rapidity, agility, and power, in every detail of his attitude, " Now will I arise, saith the Lord." " Propter miseriam inopum et gemitum pauperum / nunc exsurgam dicit dominus ; " Verse 6, " The words of the Lord are pure words : as silver tried in a furnace of earth, purified seven times," is indicated here most skilfully by a furnace or smith's forge, a flaring fire, two workmen

---

' See S. Birch, *History of Ancient Pottery*, p. 469, 2nd Edit., 1873.

beside it, one blowing (the bellows) behind the hearth, the other with hammer and pincers turning round as if to demonstrate the success of his assay, which is trickling down the front of the fireplace in a wavy stream. Near this group a suppliant with an inscribed scroll probably indicates the words of the Lord already alluded to. There are three faintly drawn figures of seated men in the left hand corner of this picture, but the forms do not appear to have been finished, and have a similar outline to three sitting figures just above them.

The most remarkable groups, however, are for the realisation of the concluding verse, " The wicked walk on every side," or as the Utrecht Version renders it, " In circuitu impii ambulant." There are two separate renderings of this image. In the centre of the foreground an upright standard is surmounted with a cross-shaped turnstile which is driven round by four stalwart operators, at a rapid rate. This is apparently the literal rendering by the artist of *circuitus*, and to this Professor Westwood alludes as a kind of circular treadmill or roundabout pushed round by four men. Messrs. Cahier and Martin, he states, mention a similar subject in the Paris MS. Suppl. Latin, 1194, the connection of which to the Utrecht Psalter has been already referred to.[1] In addition to this realistic rendering another pictorial translation of the phrase has been placed in juxtaposition to it. A broad ring, or disk, around which are ten figures in a variety of attitudes turning it upon itself in a kind of rotary motion, is drawn with

[1] See page 121.

a spirited expression which is quite remarkable for its lifelike force.

The picture which responds to this illustration in the Harley Psalter 603, the relation of which to the Utrecht Psalter has been already indicated, points out how faithfully the artist of this later Manuscript has adhered to the archetypal teaching of the older codex. A few variations, however, may be noticed. The roof slabs of the forge are filled in with a small spot in each square; the stream of pure silver running from the fire, which is thin and hardly noticeable in the Utrecht picture, is clear and large in the Harley copy, and appropriately depicted in a bright blue colour. The general tone of the drawing is free and noble; the nimbus of the Lord is more decidedly detailed; the roundabout ring is plain, and the scroll also held by the figure in the background is devoid of the marking which the corresponding scroll in the Utrecht picture has. It is curious to notice that a shield, lying on the ground in the foreground of the Utrecht picture, has been sketched in here to correspond, but in finishing his work the Harley artist omitted to notice it and yet has left to this day the preliminary plummet or pencil lines of its sketching faintly shown in the vellum, but not painted in with the coloured lines which are employed throughout the finished art work of the volume.

A comparison of the corresponding picture in the Eadwine Psalter at Cambridge, a positive photograph of which is contained in the MS. already described, Brit. Mus., Add. 29273, f. 7, shows that the limner of this later picture has faithfully adhered to the

Utrecht prototype. There are, however, two or three additions of less ancient style, such as the masonry at the front of forge, of which also the slabs of the roof are embellished with *annulets*, an improvement by the artist on the *spots* of the Harley picture. The disk, or *circuitus*, is made more prominent and its rim appositely inscribed with the legend " In circuitu impii ābulāt." The perspective is just as peculiar and defective; the hummocky waves of ground are hard, and poorly conceived, whereas the Utrecht model has rapid sketchy lines of original thought. These three pictures, originating, without the slightest doubt in the fertile imagination of one man, show as it were three successive stages of development, and point out how different, with all their verisimilitude, the results of transcription really are. The simplicity of one detail alone, the roofing of the melting house or smithy, irresistibly claims for the Utrecht Psalter, were every other means of proof wanting, the oldest stage of the idea; the depiction of the same with a slight yet well defined embellishing of spots or dots evinces how the artist of the Harley picture, copying what to him must have been an old picture, strove to modernise its details where he could without offence; the elaboration of the spots into rings or annulets seems to show that the Canterbury monk Eadwine was cognizant of the Harley as well as of the Utrecht Psalter, and derived his teaching from the later as well as from the earlier codex. These drawings so forcibly illustrate the fact that the artistic results shown in this Manuscript were in their own age and in ages immediately succeeding them, considered notable examples of draughtsman's art, that they have been chosen for reproduction in the present place.

Folio 7 a is occupied for about two thirds of its space with a picture placed in front of the twelfth Psalm. This, although it thus occupies a large space, contains only one subject of most interesting execution. Beneath a finely designed and branching tree, whose well pruned trunk and sparse wiry head, instinctively point to the cedar, sits a large figure of the Royal Psalmist draped in a long dress down to his bare ankles. With uplifted hands and head turned upwards, he gazes in ecstacy upon the Lord, who from out the clouds beyond the mountain range on the extreme left stretches forth in his right hand an object somewhat resembling a horn or cornucopia,[1] whence proceeds a wavy line of holy anointing oil, or perhaps of spiritual fire, and some direct rays which reach down and touch the eyes of the king, who sings, " Lighten mine eyes lest I sleep the sleep of death." " Inlumina oculos meos ne unquam obdormiam in morte." The anxious profile of the heavenly Father, his flowing vestments, the book-like object held in his left hand, the nimbus around his head, complete this part of the picture. Below the Psalmist, and in the middle of the foreground, is a box-like coffin or bed with half-opened lid ; and on the left a group of eleven warriors armed with barbed

---

[1] See a similar object in an Anglo-Saxon picture of very beautiful execution, MS. Cotton, Tiberius, C. VI., folio 10. David, King and Psalmist seated on his throne, with his harp in his hand is being anointed with "the holy oil," from the horn-shaped object in the clouds. A horn of just the same shape is held by Saul, in a picture in the same Manuscript (folio 7 b) representing him in the act of anointing the youthful David.

and crossed spears, and ovate bucklers, are led by a foeman, who stretches out his right hand to his companions while his left holding a bow points in the direction of the principal figure. The clothing of this bowman appears to consist of two parts, a tight fitting under garment barely reaching to the waist, and an ample cloak fastened up over the right shoulder with a circular knob or fibula.[1]

Folio 7 b gives us the whole of the 13th Psalm except one line which is on the following page. It also contains a picture in the upper half of the space. The Lord looks down from heaven upon the children of men to see if there are any that understand and seek God. "Dominus de caelo prospexit super filios hominum! ut videat si est intelligens aut requirens Deum;" (verse 2). His form is clothed to the feet, and he wears a cruciform nimbus, as he sits on an orb or mound within an ogival vesica, with three winged ministers on either side his seat, each one bearing a long standard with wavy streamers and bending forward to hear the voice of his master. The earthly scene below in the foreground is varied and animated. On a hummocky hill bearing a tree of the conventional type herein used for the cedar, stands a man with spear and shield probably intended for the *insipiens*, or "fool" of verse 1, who saith in his heart, "There is no God." Before him is a crowd of men, women and children, and three mounted warriors with pennoned spears. These are probably intended for those pointed out by the

---

[1] Reuvens describes this dress as: "Een kort hembd zonder mantel, en dan een puntig schortje."

Psalmist in verses 3-5. The phrase "Sepulcrum patens est guttur eorum" is shown by a rectangular chest with half opened lid, used frequently throughout the Manuscript to represent a bed or the grave. In the foreground on the left are three small groups; in one of them two men are disputing for a captive woman (in allusion to the final verse) who is held by one hand by each, while they hold over her head a long javelin or lance; in the second group one figure is wrestling with another who thrusts a broad sword into his stomach; in the last group a soldier is spearing a fallen foe, and a third man also armed with a spear is on the point of wounding with it the slayer of the fallen one. "Veloces pedes eorum ad effundendum sanguinem." In the background at the left is a very interesting drawing. In the centre of a circular temple with dome-shaped roofing composed of convex tiles and capped with a low flat finial boss, supported by seven slender pillars of plain stone with narrow capitals sustaining arches of the simplest curve, sits a man enthroned, with a sword in his hands. Before him on the one side are two swordsmen, holding each a decapitated head, on the other side a group of suppliants, a prostrate figure of a man, and a tall figure standing on the rock, pointing with the right to the throne, with the left to the three horsemen already described. Two serpents, to complete the picture, are coiling their lithy folds around the pillars of the temple, in memorial of the phrase, "venenum aspidum sub labris eorum" (verse 3).

Folio 8a is occupied by the whole of the 14th

Psalm, which takes up the middle third of the page between two pictures the upper one of which relates to this Psalm, the lower to the following one. In the picture referring to the 15th Psalm we may notice the curious book on its rest or table; the curtained temple with its altar, before which the episode alluded to in verse 4 is vividly depicted; and the gnarled tree with lanceolate leaves, attributed by Sir Thomas Hardy to the rose-bay or oleander.

The lower picture, rightly attached to the 16th Psalm, the text of which is given on the following page, is composed of no less than six subordinate groups. On the right hand at the top of the drawing half length figures of the Lord, with cruciformed nimbus, and rolled book in hand, attended by winged ministers. Below this a compact body of men in eager conversation (alluding to verses 3, 4). Below these again, at the right hand corner of the foreground, three bedsteads with scroll-heads and full cushions, on which recline as many figures, in reference to verses 7, 9, "Insuper et caro mea requiescet in spe." The central group demands an all absorbing interest. It is described by Westwood as the visit of the three Maries to the tomb, which is represented as a small square building with a circular domed tower, built at the side of a rock. The angel is seated on a fallen slab in front of the sepulchre, addressing the three sorrowful forms who appear to approach with fear and trembling, keeping closely together as they come nearer to the tomb. In an opening at the side of the sepulchre is seen the head and upper half of the body of the Saviour, the remainder being hidden by the projection of the rock. "There can be no doubt," says Westwood, "as to the artist having in this unusual treatment intended simply to delineate the napkin which had enveloped the head of the Saviour lying apart. This is apparently an illustration of the latter part of the 1st verse of the 15th Psalm at the head of which it is placed." Professor Westwood's interesting remarks regarding the picture are worthy of notice, but he has fallen into a curious error in the concluding part of the passage quoted above, for the picture is not placed at the head of the 15th Psalm English Version, which has two divisions in its 1st verse, "Domine quis habitabet in tabernaculo tuo? aut quis requiescet in monte sancto tuo? but at the head of the 15th Vulgate or Utrecht Psalm, answering to the 16th English, of which the 1st verse Vulgate is only composed of one member, "Conserva me domine quoniam speravi in te," the Utrecht taking in the 2nd verse, "Dixi domino Deus meus es tu quoniam bonorum non eges," to form a paragraph which, too, cannot be said to have any connection with the picture of the holy sepulchre. The picture, on the contrary, undoubtedly refers to verse 10, "non dabis sanctum tuum videre corruptionem." "Neither wilt thou suffer thine holy one to see corruption."

There are yet two other groups to be examined. On the brow of a hill to the left stands a man holding in the one hand a vessel with ample hands, and of the form of an ancient Greek *Kantharos*,[1] in the other a coil of rope which passes also two or three times

---

[1] See S. Birch's *Ancient Pottery*, p. 396, 2nd Edit.

17*

round his waist and rolls down to the ground in front of him. This is a literal realisation of the 5th and 6th verses, " The Lord is the portion of mine inheritance and of my *cup* . . . . the *lines* are fallen unto me in pleasant places," or as the Latin is rendered, "Dominus pars hereditatis meae et *calicis* mei . . . . *funes* ceciderunt mihi in praeclaris." The other episode, which is drawn in the left hand corner of the foreground, shows us the Saviour with cruciform nimbus standing on the prostrate form of a woman, and drawing out from the hell of the 10th verse two figures each of whom he holds tenderly by the hand, "quoniam non derelinques animam meam in inferno."

The next page (8 b) contains the text of the 15th Psalm, the picture for which has just been described. The lower half of the page holds the illustration intended for the 16th Psalm, which follows it on the succeeding folio. It would be impossible, in the space here at command, to attempt to describe this pictorial representation of the Psalm so minutely as might be done, but notice must be made of three subordinate parts. The latter half of verse 2, "Oculi tui videant *aequitates*;" " let thine eyes behold the *things that are equal*," is realised by a figure of a man on a dome-shaped building holding *two equal balances* in his hand. The metaphors of the 12th verse, " the lion that is greedy of his prey," and the " young lion lurking in secret places," " leo paratus ad praedam et catulus leonis habitans in abditis;" are drawn in a very clever manner. The phrase of the 14th verse, " Saturati sunt filiis et dimiserunt reliquias suas parvulis suis," which has been translated by the words " They are full of children, and leave the rest of their substance to their babes," is depicted by two long tables at which are feeding the naked children of the quotation.

Folio 9 a, in addition to the whole of the text of the 16th Psalm, has a picture on the lower third part of its space, in reference to the long Psalm, XVII., of which the text is given on the two succeeding pages, 9 b and 10 a, and part of 10 b. This picture is far too complicated to describe at length, but some curious pieces of it may be indicated. Verse 5, " The sorrows of hell compassed me about," supplies the monstrous but human features of the hell of mediæval fiction, with gaping jaws swallowing a doomed man. Verse 10, " Et ascendit super cherubim et volavit ⁄ volavit super pennas ventorum;" "And he rode upon a cherub and did fly: yea, he did fly upon the wings of the wind," is a charming part of the illustration, the breathing heads for the personified winds, the winged heads of the cherubims, the Lord being supported in a *vesica* between them, are marvellous specimens of the art of the drawings. Verse 33, " He maketh my feet like hinds' feet," gives us three horned deer upon a mountain on the right. The sentence " Quoniam tu inluminas lucernam meam domine?" is realised by a lamp lighted, and set upon a tall candelabrum upon a tripod foot, similar to those classical specimens which are now deposited among the antiquities of the British Museum. The metaphors contained in verses 34-40 are centred in a figure of imposing attitude àrmed with the " bow of steel," and the " shield of salvation," while the enemy is fallen under his feet, and on his head he wears a helmet of peculiar form, resembling the Phrygian helmet, and specially noticed by Reuvens, Westwood, Hardy, and others.

The next picture is that on folio 10 b, and refers to the 18th Psalm of which the text is placed on the following page. This most beautiful composition of words is appropriately delineated in the Utrecht Psalter, but we may not linger too long over its beauties. The 1st verse, " Caeli enarrant gloriam Dei? et opera manuum ejus adnunciat firmamentum;" introduces to us two suns, set in juxtaposition, full orbed, and with the bust of a king wearing an antique or rayed crown in each circle, and two moons, also at the full and near to each other, containing a female bust with a crescent on her head. Verses 2, 3 are represented by a thronging multitude of eighteen persons in excited and animated discourse, for " there is no speech nor language where their voice is not heard." The " bridegroom coming out of his chamber " here takes the likeness of the Saviour, with the usual distinguishing nimbus, passing down the steps of a small curtained temple, and accompanied by two angels with wings erect. The " strong man " running a race, " ut gigans ad currendum viam," carries a sword and shield, and is clad only in some airy cloths about his loins, and he hurries along the way bending forward with rapid strides, outstretched arms, and eager aspect. The phrase, " In sole posuit tabernaculum suum," translated by " In them hath he set a tabernacle for the sun," is also carefully and literally treated. To the left of the tabernacle, in the background, is a demi-figure wearing an antique crown and holding in his hand a blazing torch. It is difficult to say to what particular passage of the Psalm this figure is alluding unless it be the 5th verse, "in sole posuit tabernaculum suum," and so the figure would be a repetition of the half length figure seen in the sun's orb already mentioned.

Folio 11 a contains, in addition to the 18th Psalm text, a picture on its lower margin which accords, as indeed it is intended to do, not inaptly with the 19th Psalm, the text of which follows it on the succeeding page. This Psalm consists of nine verses in the Vulgate Version, and of ten paragraphs in the Utrecht Manuscript, the 6th verse of the former forming two divisions in the latter arrangement; and in this verse is the word xpm̄ which is contracted for Christum according to later Manuscripts. This picture is as useful for contemplation as those which have already been examined, but we may not dilate much in the description. The "holocaustum pingue" of verse 3 is represented by an ox and two sheep before an altar, beside which stands a suppliant priest who has come from a temple which is of its kind a handsome specimen of ecclesiastical edifice, with its clerestory, imbricated roof, crestings and trifurcated finials, its curtains, its doorway, and its masoned aisle walls. Verse 7, "Hi in curribus et hi in equis," is well and spiritedly shown by two mounted riders falling off their stumbling chargers, a third knight already fallen bites the dust as he falls upon a shattered shield and broken spear. While the chariot of two wheels and as many horses lies a perfect heap of wreck to point the reality of the metaphor. A fourth rider is just being disabled by his horse rolling over him with hoofs erect in the air. "Ipsi obligati sunt et ceciderunt." The concluding verse, "Domine, salvum fac regem?" is depicted in this realistic table by a shirted figure holding in his hands a vase and napkin, and wearing on his head a peculiar crown of three fleurs-de-lys, or a crown fleury, affected by the monarchs of France in very late mediæval times, as well as by King Louis I. early in the ninth century.

Folio 11 b comprises the text of the Psalm of which the picture has already been described; and on its lower half a representation referring to the following or 20th Psalm. Of this picture, the Lord, in a nimbus and vesica, with three attendants on either side of him; cedar trees on the extreme sides of the margins; and a remarkable figure placing a crown of three points fleurées upon the king, in allusion to verse 3, "posuisti in capite ejus coronam de lapide pretioso;" are the principal subjects.

Folio 12 a indicates the text of Psalm XX. and the picture for Psalm XXI., a long poem of thirty-one verses, or thirty-two paragraphs, which are given in the following page and part of folio 13 a. Naturally this picture is crowded and complex. "Circumdederunt me vituli multi," etc. (verse 12), is given in a way we should expect, and so also are the "canes multi" of verse 16. A curious candlestick set upon a tripod is worthy of notice, and among the many metaphorical expressions with which this prophetic Psalm is filled the parting of the garments (verse 18) and the dried potsherd, "aruit tamquam testa virtus mea" (verse 15), are most graphically set forth. In the centre of the picture is a plain cross, on the arms are hanging a crown of thorns and the scourge of two thongs, and by its side are set the spear, and the sponge upon a long staff. The spear has an indistinct object, which seems intended either for a phial of vinegar or perhaps a lizard, nearly half way up the shaft, but it is impossible to determine what this small and uncertain shape is put to signify. Westwood draws especial attention to the details of the subject, and points out what appears to him to be a monogram of the letters P. V. with a straight cross bar, attached to the cross at the place where the feet of the crucified Saviour would be drawn. The photographic facsimile certainly indicates an apparent letter or combination of letters in the place alluded to, but there are many letters into which with equal probability the monogram, if indeed it be a monogram, may be resolved. This peculiar grouping of the instruments of the divine passion is well worthy of examination, for in after ages the group was collected into a heraldic device, entitled the "shield of the passion," or "the arms of Jesus Christ," by the early designers of religious heraldry, and its eager and universal adoption as an adornment of churches, and church furniture, manifests the high favour with which the emblematic form was received during the middle ages. Mr. H. S. Cuming has figured several typical forms of the shield of passion emblems in a paper contributed to the *Journal of the British Archæological Association*, Vol. XXXI. p. 92, embracing specimens from painted windows, stone carvings, and encaustic tiles, of various dates and from various localities.

Folio 13 a contains in its middle third part the illustration of Psalm XXII., of which the text in *nine paragraphs*, corresponding to *six verses* of the Vulgate, is given below. The "green pastures" of verse 2 are shown by browsing herds and flocks, the "still waters," "aquam refectionis," of the same verse, by a stream of water welling from a hole in the rock and coursing along by the side of the pastured cattle. Behind the Psalmist, a winged angel holds in one hand the rod and staff on which David leans, in the other an anointing horn (in reference to verse 5, "inpinguasti in oleo caput meum"), with which he anoints the poet's head. Before him is the table mentioned in the same verse, which has three serpentine legs or trusses, and is spread with many dishes; and the phrase "calix meus inebrians quam praeclarus est," "my cup runneth over," is depicted by a two-handled *kantharos* which the Psalmist holds in his left hand. In the background on the left is a very good example of the temple structures drawn throughout the Manuscript. It is of rectangular plan with a side aisle entered by a semicircular arch in front; the walls are lined to represent large blocks of stone, the roof to represent convex tiles laid in parallel ridges; there are three square windows in the upper part of the principal wall of the nave and in that of the aisle; and the two triangular pediments are adorned each with a spherical finial surmounted by a plain cross. In the principal doorway is a Roman altar with a swinging lamp above it, between two ample curtains, drawn aside to show the interior of the building. From out the clouds overhead issues a hand with four fingers extended in the act of benediction. This temple has been introduced into the picture in relation to the concluding verse, "ut inhabitem in domo domini," " I will dwell in the house of the Lord." [1]

Folio 13 b presents to us the 23rd Psalm, the text being on the lower half, the picture on the upper half of the page. The " king of glory " (verses 7-10), with cruciform nimbus and long spear with a cross-piece near the point, is approaching a city, followed by a faithful train of soldiers armed with spears and shields, clad in tunics, stockings in wrinkled folds, (reminding us of the Anglo-Saxon forms of this portion of dress, as shown in English Manuscripts of the tenth and following centuries), and peculiarly shaped helmets with a winglike crest or ridge along the back and over the top of the head. This helmet is referred to by Westwood and other writers as of Phrygian form. In front of the Saviour stands a draped figure with a helmet as described, and with a broad sword of classical form, pointing towards the arched doorway of a town wall, which is flanked on either side with a round tower of masonry

---

[1] For full descriptions of the imagery of this and the previous Psalm, see two works by the Rev. John Stevenson, *Christ on the Cross*, London, 1844; and *The Lord our Shepherd*, 1853.—S. Bagster and Sons.

surmounted by two tiers of windows.   In the space
inclosed by the polygonal wall is a compact group of
worshippers, while in the doorway stands a single
figure watching the approach of the king, and over
the arch another almost similar figure seems to look
down eagerly and intently upon the coming host.
This scene evidently is intended to realize the concluding portion of the Psalm, "Attollite portas
principes vestras? et elevamini portae aeternales et
introibit rex gloriae;" etc.   Above the Saviour, in
the background overhead, are five angels and a
hand issuing from the clouds, with two fingers bent,
and two extended in the act of pronouncing a blessing, "Hic accipiet benedictionem a dómino."

With regard to the nimbus which occurs so
markedly in this and other examples of art throughout the Utrecht Psalter, a great deal has been
advanced with the object of proving the general
lateness of its adoption as an attribute of the Deity
or of Divine personages.   It will be well therefore to
bear in mind that Sir Thomas Hardy [1] adduces the
opinion of Martigny, as expressed in his *Dictionnaire
des Antiquités Chrétiennes*, that the nimbus was first
applied to the Saviour, and this at a period long
anterior to Constantine; and the opinion of Padre
Garacci that in the fifth century Christian artists
either used or omitted this symbol indifferently, but
that after that time its use became universal.
Didron [2] attributes the origin of the nimbus to the

[1] *First Report*, p. 27, 28.

[2] See *Observations on the Nimbus*, from Didron's *Iconographie*, by Thomas Wright, *Journal of the British Archæological Association*, Vol. I., p. 121; *Observations*, etc., by G. J. French, *ibid.*, X. 332; and by H. S. Cuming, *ibid.*, XI. 84.

fire-worshippers of the East, and to the intention of expressing by fire or flame the emanation of the Divine power and intelligence. Examples certainly exist in the Roman catacombs which are attributed to the sixth century, and it has been asserted that the Gnostics employed the nimbus on their mystical rings; but it is evident that from the μηνίσκος or metal disk employed to protect Greek statues when exposed to the air and weather, and from the disk-shaped nimbi of Roman paganism seen on the heads of Apollo and Diana, engraved by Montfaucon, of Jupiter and Circe, in paintings at Pompeii, and on a large number of Roman coins, Christian artists derived the luminous circle with which they invested the heads of the personages of the Holy Trinity, and, in later ages, the portraits of saints and other members of the Church. Cuming considers the cruciform or cruciferous nimbus not to have been employed before the ninth century, as a rule, but he cites D'Agincourt's *History of Art by its Monuments* for a fourth century ivory tablet in Greek style, where the Almighty Father is adorned with cruciferous nimbus, as well as a mosaic of the fifth century at Ravenna, in the church of St. Agatha Maggiore, in which the Lord is depicted with a similar object, and a third example furnished by the same author from a fresco in the catacombs of St. Ponziano's church, Rome, of an age between the sixth and eighth centuries, where a nimbus with decorated edge and cross is placed on the head of Jesus Christ. Cuming also points out the image of the Saviour with cruci-form nimbus on the coins of the Byzantine Emperor

Justinianus Rhinometus, A.D. 685-711. We cannot therefore, with these facts before us, assign to the employment of the nimbus, as constantly seen in the illustrations of the Utrecht Psalter, an important position in the category of those details which have by some been pointed out as important indications of the late date of the Manuscript.

The next folio presents to our view the picture placed at the head of Psalm XXIV., and the text as far as the twelfth paragraph. The two principal points of interest in this are the quiver, or case for arrows, from which a soldier is withdrawing an arrow at the entreaty of two bowmen who stand before him; and a large vase, or vessel of cup-like form, before which stands a female holding a closed roll or volume in one hand, while she extends her other hand towards a group of three children, in reference to the passage, " Delicta juventutis meae? et ignorantias meas ne memineris?" or perhaps to ："Innocentes et recti a[d]haeserunt mihi?"

Turning to the next page, the final portion of Psalm XXIV. is followed by a picture and the beginning of the next Psalm; and in this page some remarkable drawings are contained. A curious group consisting of a naked man held by an iron ring round the left ankle, a staple having been driven into the ground, with two men scourging him; a temple, of the form already described, on the left hand, and two others on the right hand in the background, one of which is embellished by the addition of a round tower with a domed roof; the Almighty with his attendant angels; and in the centre of the picture a drawing which plainly indicates the essentially classical origin of the set of illustrations in this Manuscript. This drawing is in reference to verse 6, "Lavabo inter innocentes manus meas?" "I will wash mine hands in innocency;" and presents to us an aqueduct of ten simple semicircular arches sustained on plain columns, conveying the water in an oblique course from a distant mountain, the surplus water at the head of the stream forming a river which streams along to the right of the picture. The aqueduct terminates in a figure of a lion sejant, from out of its mouth the water is discharged with a jet into a broad basin, around which are the innocents to whom the Psalmist alludes in the quotation. This method of conveying water is of very ancient origin, and ruined remains of similar works executed by the Romans are to be found not only in Italy but generally throughout the Roman Empire, although it would be difficult perhaps to point to any in Britain.

The illustration to the 26th Psalm is contained on folio 15 a, the principal part of the picture being devoted to a very spirited realisation of the 2nd and 3rd verses. The host encamped, "si consistant adversum me castra? . . . . si exsurgat adversum me proelium?" gives rise to the introduction of two groups of peculiarly shaped tents, formed apparently by a long sheet of canvas thrown over a cross bar, the ends of which jut out slightly beyond a short projecting part of the cloth. It would be interesting to identify the peculiar shapes of these tents with those of any known nation. They neither resemble

Roman, Egyptian, Syrian, or Anglo-Saxon, and Mr.
H. Payn has not claimed for them any weight in his
essay on the Eastern origin of these illustrations.
In the background of the picture is a fine example of
temple with domed round tower, apse, transept or
porch, and chapels, sacristies, or added rooms grouped
between the apse and the porch. The weapons, such
as the bow and arrows, spiked shields, and barbed
spears carried by the enemies and the host are of the
usual kind which have been before noticed, and the
groupings of the battle, fallen horses, and overthrown
riders, are well conceived and artistically portrayed.

Folio 15 b gives the picture applied to Psalm
XXVII. They "that go down into the pit" are
shown to us in a seething pit into which winged
figures armed with trident are driving the "workers
of iniquity." In the background on the left hand, in
front of a temple overshadowed by the Lord and his
angels, stands the Jewish king with crown of fleurs-
de-lys on his head, and hands upraised towards the
sanctuary, attended by an angel holding up over the
royal head an umbrella, and followed by a band of
servants. This refers to verse 2, "Exaudi domine
vocem deprecationis meae dum oro . ad te ! dum
extollo manus meas ad templum sanctum tuum ; "
. To this drawing of the umbrella Sir Thomas Hardy
refers with great stress as a positive proof that the
drawings are not the composition of an Anglo-Saxon
artist. The umbrella, as a symbol of sovereignty,
had been probably used by the Jews from the time
of Alexander the Great and his successors, when the
Jewish territory became the prey of Egyptians and

Syrians, and when the Jews affected either from fear or degeneracy the customs of their conquerors, introducing among other things the umbrella, originally a Bacchic implement, into their religious ceremonies, probably at the Feast of Tabernacles, in remembrance of divine protection given to the Israelites in the desert. He mentions also the occurrence of this object on coins of Agrippa the Elder, and refers to the work of Paciaudi, *De Umbrellæ Gestatione*, published at Rome in 1752.

The 28th Psalm, of which the illustration is represented on the following page (16 a), contains a graphic poem descriptive of the majesty and power of "the voice of the Lord" (verse 4). This is vividly realised by the Lord enthroned in glory, as usually drawn throughout the Manuscript, while from beneath his feet three heads, the personification of storm winds, pour forth their blasts "upon the waters," break "the cedars of Lebanon," and shake the wilderness (verses 3, 5, 8).

On folio 16 b the pictorial application of Psalm XXIX. is shown. The pit or "lacus" is apparently a favourite theme with the artist, who draws drowning human forms, and savage tormentors armed with tridents, and having for their hair snakes and fiery serpents, with a vivid force which shows a kind of acquaintance with the gladiatorial exhibitions of the Roman empire. The tree on the right hand, with lopped branches, twisted trunk and sparse lanceolate leaves is identified by Sir T. Hardy with the sycamore.

On the next page we have the illustration selected by the artist for the 30th Psalm, the text of which occupies the lower half of this page and all the next. In this we see the "net privily laid," the "dead man out of mind," the "broken vessel," the "pavilion" or "tabernaculum," the "strong city," and many other images of the poet's mind treated in that practical manner which characterises the whole of these drawings. The occurrence of the phrase, "commorantium in circuitu," suggests to the artist a crowd of persons arranged in a semicircle witnessing a man playing upon the double pipes, while another dances before him to the music, and keeps time with his hands, which seem to hold clappers or castanets, κρόταλον, of well known classical use. This group may perhaps have reference also to the "vanitates supervacue" of the 6th verse or seventh paragraph. Another vanity is that of a bear held by a leash in the hand of its master, and apparently about to stand upon its head. This scene is described by Westwood, and has been noticed by Thomas Wright in his *Domestic Manners*, a work which draws largely from the Harley Psalter already so frequently alluded to.

Folio 18 a contains the text and drawing of Psalm XXXI. In this we may take notice of the "spina" and the "multa flagella peccatoris," the translations of which seem to be obscure in the English Version ; the horse and the mule "which have no understanding," and "the floods of great waters," which here occupy the foreground, and are full of a large kind of fish, perhaps intended for the tunny of south European seas.

The 32nd Psalm commences on the next page,

and has a special illustration, of which certain
appearances of a different touch and style of execution would appear to suggest, either that the single
draughtsman of the series of drawings had acquired
a new method in his art or affected a variable
treatment, or else that the whole illustration is the
work of another hand. Westwood, in his description
of these drawings, indeed, states that " it seems
evident that there were different hands employed,
the figures in some of the compositions being small
and very neat, whilst in others they are much larger
and ruder," and indeed all critics seem to be agreed
on this point, but it is difficult to say whether he
refers particularly to the hand which in designing
and drawing this picture has entered into a more
indistinct and broken kind of pencilling than the
preceding pictures exhibit, or whether he alludes to
some coarse and large styles which we shall presently observe in future folios. In this realisation of
the Psalm the most prominent group is that of the
water in allusion to the words " Congregans sicut in
utre aquas maris?" (verse 7), where a classical treatment has been adopted, and he that " gathereth the
waters of the sea together as an heap" appears to be
seated as a water-god upon a sea-dragon, or marine
creature with convoluted tail and recurved beak, and
to be holding in his hand an inverted vessel, which
has been alluded to in the quotation.

The 33rd Psalm has its picture principally devoted
to the illustration of the words " Multe tribulationes
justorum? et de omnibus his liberabit eos dominus;"
" Many are the afflictions of the righteous: but the

18*

Lord delivereth him out of them all." Crucifixion with the head downwards, decollation by an executioner armed with a sword in either hand, roasting to death over a grating or a rack, are pourtrayed in a most graphic manner; and close at hand, beside each martyr, stands or hovers an angelic minister with a cloth in his hand ready to receive the departing soul and convey it purified and unspotted into the presence of its Maker. Mr. Howard Payn very naturally sees[1] in these instruments of torture and martyrdom a reference to the persecutions of the Diocletian era, A.D. 284.

We have now carefully reviewed and described the illustrations of the first thirty-three Psalms, and the remainder, being cast in the same moulds, and evolved from the thoughts and feelings of the same artist or school of artists by whom the first were produced, hardly require so much special examination, but it will be well to note prominent peculiarities and beauties as we turn over the remaining pages of the Psalter. The picture applied to the 34th Psalm has in the foreground a peculiar net, held up by three upright poles, " Quoniam gratis absconderunt mihi interitum laquei sui," etc. In the 35th Psalm the phrases " Filii autem hominum in tegmine alarum tuarum sperabunt; Inebriabuntur ab ubertate domus tuae? et torrente voluptatis tuae potabis eos; " are rendered by two bands of the sons of men receiving in chalices the " torrentes " which flow in powerful streams from the mouths of two birds; it would be difficult to say whether they

[1] Sir T. Hardy's *Further Report,* p. 15.

be doves or eagles, set upon poles within hollow quatrefoiled columns on either side a portal over which sits the Lord with His attendant angels, drawn in the conventional manner employed throughout the Psalter. Westwood points out the spirited group of horses and oxen in this picture. The 36th Psalm introduces to us the broadsword drawn forth from its scabbard; the sun personified in a circle, with an antique crown of six rays upon his human head; ploughing, measuring out seed, sowing, and reaping with the scythe; one of the mowers holding and sharpening his scythe with a stone exactly in the manner practised at the present day. These scenes are in allusion to verses 11 and 29. At the extreme left are two figures thrusting swords into their own bowels, "Gladius eorum intret in corda ipsorum." These forms of the implements of agriculture, when compared with drawings of the same objects and the same scenes in the Saxon Calendar, MS. Cotton, Julius, A VI. in the British Museum, clearly point to an older age and one of feebler mechanical ingenuity. Westwood and Reuvens draw especial attention to the incidents selected here by the draughtsman for illustration. In this picture also is a fine example of oleander. The next Psalm (XXXVII.) has a coarse and rough illustration. The verse, "Quoniam lumbi mei impleti sunt inlusionibus! et non est sanitas in carue mea;" is treated in a memorable way by three winged illusionary forms issuing from the clothing that covers the loins of the figure of the Psalmist. Psalm XXXVIII. shows a peculiar

crown on the head of a king, not unlike the crown
of later continental and English use, seen on coins
and seals of the eleventh and twelfth centuries.
The horses of this illustration are charmingly
grouped and evidently the conception of a truly
artistic mind.   Psalm XXXIX. has a representation
of two greyhounds or hunting dogs with collars
round their necks.   The open temple, filled with
worshippers, the goats for sacrifice, and the " volume
of the book " (verse 7), are all worthy of examination
by reason of their remarkable treatment.

The following folio (24 a) contains for the 40th
Psalm a temple or ecclesiastical structure of a class
very unlike that usually affected by the conventionalism of the painter; it has a circular tower
topped by a dome and cross, a pointed roof, and
a semicircular apse, and no windows or roofing lines,
in any part, but three small orifices in the upper
part of the tower.   The phrase, " universum stratum
ejus *versasti* in infirmitate ejus; " " thou wilt make
(turn, *Heb.*) all his bed in his sickness," is translated
pictorially by a sofa-shaped bedstead overturned
and falling forwards.   The round table with the
vase and cakes is of the kind already described
in foregoing Psalms.   There is another example of
the same in the next Psalm, XLI., where the
beautifully natural simile of the first verse, " As
the hart panteth after the water brooks, so panteth
my soul after thee, O God," " Quemadmodum desiderat cervus ad fontes aquarum? ita desiderat
anima mea ad te Deus; " enables the draughtsman to show his exquisite skill in a group of two

greyhounds in a leash chasing a hart towards a watercourse which leaps down from a mountain into a lake, and overflowing this passes on towards the extreme limits of the foreground. The sun and the moon peer down upon the hunt from opposite corners of the sky, each orb containing the head of the personified Sol and Luna with appropriate crowns, the radiated, and the crescent-shaped.

Folio 25 a contains two pictures; that for Psalm XLII. a short poem of five verses or six paragraphs, the fifth paragraph being composed of parts of verses 4 and 5. The chief point of interest here is the "harp" or "cithara," which is formed of a long stem terminating in a triple leaf, and a vase-shaped base or shell, altogether being an object very unlike the classical lyre or harp as seen in the ancient statues of Apollo and other deities. The tents or tabernacles of this picture resemble those already described where they occur in a former Psalm.

The lower picture in this page is to be attributed to the 43rd Psalm, "Exurge quare dormis domine? exurge." "Awake, why sleepest thou, O Lord? arise," gives us the sleeping Lord reclining on a bed, and not conventionally set in a vesical frame, but still attended by three watchful ministers on either side of His heavenly couch, that he may hear "the voice of many angels round about the throne." Spread before him is a city wall of polygonal form, with bays of masonry in square blocks alternately set, and with squared buttresses

each capped with a flat stone and with peculiarly
shaped hooks or bent iron cramps upon the upper
row of the stone work in the bays. The gateway
is of an elaborate style of architecture, with its
arched portal and square towers of three stages on
either side. The quiver, sword, and horn in the
centre of the picture are also to be compared with
the earliest mediæval forms of corresponding relics.
Psalm XLIV. shows us two excellent groups of
the "king's daughter" and "the virgins her companions;" and the "raiment of needlework" (fim-
briis aureis) is depicted here by a dress covered
with small circular ornaments or golden spangles,
each enclosing a dot or spot. The crowns which
occur so frequently in this picture are of the nature
of a band or fillet encircling the head, and with
one, two, or more projecting trefoil-shaped additions
on the upper margin. This picture has also a good
specimen of the tree with triple heart-shaped leaf,
which has been alluded to before more than once.
The illustration of the 45th Psalm is selected from
verse 2, "Transferentur montes in cor maris;"
"Though the mountains be carried into the midst
of the sea," where we perceive a range of mountains
set in the foreground of the sea, each hill being
occupied by a seated figure. The wall of the city
is of polygonal faces, or bastions, with towers at
short and regular distances, and it runs quite across
the page, enclosing a temple and many spirited
groups of men, while above is the Lord in glory;
and from out of the clouds on either side of him
are issuing two angels, blowing upon long horns

or trumpets slightly curved, "Dedit vocem suam mota est terra;" "He uttered his voice, the earth melted."

The following folio (27 a) contains the picture of the 46th Psalm, which has a city wall, portal or gateway, groups of figures holding palm branches, and crowned with the fleury coronet already described. In this, too, the forms of the harps, some of which are of the true classical lyre-shape, while one is of the kind apparently termed the *cythara*, or the *triangular psalterium*. Of these the lyre is found in illuminated Manuscripts preserving its classical form, down to the eleventh century, but the latter shape is not so well attributed to any particular period.[1] The vesica containing the Saviour is not only attended as usual by six angels, but is borne up by four other winged servants, two of whom are blowing trumpets, in allusion to the 5th verse, "God is gone up with a shout, the Lord with the sound of a trumpet." "Ascendit Deus in jubilo? dominus in voce tubae." The 47th Psalm is of interest for its picture of two ships riding in the sea, "in spiritu vehementi conteres naves Tharsis;" "Thou breakest the ships of Tarshish with an east wind." These vessels have the low free-board, the broad beam, the rising swan-like poop and prow, with beaked ends, the single mast and swelling mainsail of lateen, with its ropes fluttering loosely in the east wind, or "spiritus vehemens," of two winged heads blowing fiercely from the left

---

[1] See "On the Musical Instruments of the Middle Ages," in *Journal of the British Archæological Association*, I., 291; and II., 221, by E. de Coussemaker.

hand corner of the foreground.   There is little here in common with the recognised form of the ancient galley so universally depicted on coins and other Roman and Greek remains, for the absence of oars or other appliances for directing transit, the shortness and rotundity of the whole shape seems on the other hand to point more to the coasting boat or mercantile vessel, which must not only have been employed throughout the European coasts long before the extension of Roman influence, but have survived also for a long time after the decline of that imperial power.   The picture of the 48th Psalm contains instances of the crown fleurée, the triangular musical instrument ("aperiam in *psalterio* propositionem meam"), the box-like grave or bed, the rectangular tabernacle or temple, the balance, and the cedar and oleander trees, one of which as usual stands on the one margin of the picture, to balance the other which has been planted on the opposite edge.   Psalm XLIX. has some very spirited drawings of goats, and bullocks (verse 9), and the "fowls of the mountains" are shown by three birds in a cedar tree on the right hand.   The waving pennons or banners on the spears in the hands of the angels near the Lord, and the classical treatment of the orbs of heaven, personified as usual with antique crowns and flaming torches, are well worthy of careful notice.

The illustration which has been prefixed to the 50th Psalm contains a most charmingly and naturally conceived group of a shepherd and his flock.   The background of the picture has a drawing of the "walls of Jerusalem," unlike the masoned walls of edifices hitherto described. The wall here is without marks of masonry, but adorned with a string-course, and a bevelled or pent capping along the top. Sir Thomas Hardy points out the details relating to the story of Bathsheba, Uriah, and Nathan.

Folio 30 a holds the picture and the text of Psalm LI. This picture is of a large and coarse style of drawing, very unlike those that have preceded it. The treatment of the details is in very great contrast with that of the previous pictures, and there can be no doubt that we either see here the finished work of another artist, or, if it be of the same hand as those already described, it must have been executed under altered conditions and have resulted from the imitation of an original picture not belonging to the same series which has hitherto supplied the details of the illustrations in the Psalter. The work is, however, certainly contemporary with the previous work. The same kinds of lines of waving form indicate the rising and sinking of the ground. The stunted olive tree is seen here and in other places with almost similar form, " Ego autem sicut oliva fructifera." The Lord, seated on the sphere, and within an oval vesica, is supported on either side by four seated figures in flowing robes, who are conversing eagerly together, thereby constituting grouped designs very different to the three winged angels seen on either hand of the Lord in previous pictures. The temple, in which sits the subject of the opening verses of

the Psalm, " Quid gloriaris in malitia ? qui poteus
es iniquitate," etc., is also designed and elaborated
in a style quite at variance with what has gone
before.   Here we see columns with plain shafts
resting on plinths of two grades, and adorned with
foliated capitals somewhat resembling the Corinthian
architecture ; a triangular pediment enriched with
a fleur-de-lys or other flowering ornament in the
entablature ; and a roof apparently composed of
stone slabs, alluded to by Sir T. Hardy, and discussed in the present description of the 10th Psalm.
Westwood remarks of this picture that it is similarly
represented in one of the few illuminations in the
small purple Psalter of the Douce Collection in
the Bodleian Library, Oxford, as well as in the
Psalter of Count Henry which is preserved in the
Cathedral Library at Troyes, and published by
Gaussen.   Reuvens draws attention to the cap-like
crown worn by the principal seated figure in the
centre of the vestibule of the temple, which bears
strong contrast with the preceding crowns of three
points which have already noticed and hitherto
been alone observed.

The illustration of the 52nd Psalm contains,
among other. groups, a circular temple, sustaining
on four columns a domed roof covered with curved
tiles and finished at the top with a spherical boss.
The next picture, for the following Psalm, contains
principally two subjects.   The sacrifice alluded to
in the words " Voluntariae sacrificabo tibi ?" gives
us a temple, a priest, two altars, and a sheep with
a long tail reaching to the ground.   The scope of

the whole Psalm, the cry of the Psalmist for deliverance from his enemies, has suggested to the draughtsman a picture of many riders, armed with spears and a battleaxe, most of whom are fallen to the ground and crushed beneath their overthrown horses. The 54th Psalm also affords an opportunity for a picture of a combat in front of a city wall. The phrase, "Et dixi quis dabit mihi pennas sicut columbae? et volabo et requiescam." "And I said, Oh that I had wings like a dove," etc., introduces the dove flying away to the solitary tree upon a mountain. The sun is here again personified with radiated crown, but the moon and stars are treated naturally. These details have been introduced in reference to verse 10, "Day and night they go about [the city]." In the centre of the picture is a round table on three carved legs, and on the right hand of it a warrior with three spears held up erect in his left hand; on his head is a helmet of peculiar shape, being drawn without the cresting noticed in foregoing pictures as of Phrygian origin, a fine example of which is to be observed in the picture prefixed to the 17th Psalm.

The 55th Psalm is interesting for the weapons held by those who are alluded to in verse 1. These are the battleaxe with two semicircular edges or blades, the trident, the spear, and the sling, or perhaps, large stone. There is also a good example of the standard or staff with a short flag of two waving streamers and a cross piece, held by the Divine Protector. This figure appears to have been originally drawn to a somewhat smaller scale and in advance of the position it now occupies; but the drawing has been carefully erased (although the photograph clearly shows the remains of the drawing) before the final place and size of the figure were determined upon. Psalm LVI. has for the central group of its realistic illustration, a picture of the poet king, holding a harp or lyre, and sustained by a winged angel near the side of a large bed, which is flanked on the right side by a lion, on the left by a lioness, in allusion to verses 4, 8, "Eripuit animam meam de medio catulorum leonum ? dormivi conturbatus; .... Exsurge psalterium et cythara ?" "My soul is among lions, and I lie even among them that are set on fire .... Awake, psaltery and harp."

In the following illustration, that appertaining to the 57th Psalm, a great quantity of the metaphorical expressions of the text have been inserted, and we may notice the serpent (verse 4); the breaking out the great teeth of the young lions (verse 6); the deaf adder that stoppeth her ear (verse 4); the snail which melteth, "caera quae fluit" (verse 8); the candelabrum, probably also referring to *caera;* and the water god with inverted vessel, "tanquam aqua decurrens" (verse 7). This introduction of a natural representation of a snail in the foreground at the corner on the left hand suggests to the careful enquirer a very important fact; namely, the possibility that the whole series of pictures, in its first state, was produced to accompany the Hebrew text, which in this Psalm, for example, contains the expression relating to the snail; transformed in the

Vulgate and Gallican versions (which are derived
from the Greek Septuagint) into the word *caera* or
wax.' If this be so, a very strong argument is
brought to bear upon the point already in some
measure discussed,' that these drawings which we
have before us in the Utrecht (Gallican and Sep-
tuagintal) Psalter have been copied into it from an
illustrated exemplar of a Hebraic version; just as
in the Harley Psalter, as we have already seen, the
Utrecht drawings have been affixed to a transcript of
the Roman version.

In the same picture, in the upper part of the
background, are four angels, each armed with a
weapon, and one of these is a long sword without
either cross piece or pointed end, but of one uniform
width throughout its length. This unusual shape
of sword is pointed out by Reuvens as worthy of
comparison with other forms of the same weapon.
The next picture, that of Psalm LVIII., should
be remarked for the rendering of verses 6 and 14,
where the enemies " make a noise like a dog and
go round about the city," are shown by two hounds
within and as many without a city wall drawn as
a rectangular enclosure with masoned walls and
corner turrets. Another group shows us the Psalmist
rescued by the Almighty from the impending sword

' The confusion between the snail, שַׁבְּלוּל, *shablul*, of the Hebrew Version, and the
κηρός, caera (wax), of the Septuagint and Vulgate Versions respectively, does not
appear to arise in this case from a mis-reading of the Hebrew points, a fertile source
of so many variations in the translations of Holy Writ. We should, therefore, here
perhaps conceive the difference to arise from an intention of the translator of the
Hebrew into the Septuagint, not without parallel examples in other passages, to
substitute the more natural and obvious metaphor of the melting of wax for the
melting of a snail, supposed, but erroneously, " to consume away and die by reason
of its constantly emitting slime as it crawls along." *Chaldee Paraphrase.*

' See p. 117.

of the enemy; another, a number of persons seated round a circular table; and a third detail in the illustration is a very freely drawn rank of four angels up in the clouds, armed with many and various weapons, with which they are waging a successful war upon the "workers of iniquity," and "the bloody men." "Eripe me de operantibus iniquitatem / et de viris sanguinum salva me."

Psalm 59 has its illustration selected from verse 9, "Who will bring me into the strong city?" "Quis deducet me in civitatem munitam /" and presents to our inspection a polygonal enclosure, within and without which a desperate encounter is taking place between men armed with spears and shields. And in another group of combatants on the left, the broad Roman or Saxon sword is of conspicuous size. The next Psalm (LX.) has in its drawing much that should be noted, especially the three storied column or tower, "turris fortitudinis a facie inimici;" the tabernacle with its arcading, and roof tiled and crested according to previous models; the second allusion to the tabernacle in the form of a pyramidal tent, pegged out on the ground and upheld by a central standard surmounted by a ball and cross; and the half length figure of the Lord in the clouds, holding a wreath of victory towards the suppliant who is just come forth from the tent, or towards the kneeling king who adores him from the entrance of the tabernacle.

The same page contains the drawing that is applied to the 61st Psalm. The most interesting group is that which points to verses 2 and 6, "He only is my rock and my salvation." The Lord, with nimbus, shield and spear, stands erect and divine between the six usual attendants upon his voice. On the next page, in the drawing of Psalm LXII., is a very spirited olive tree set beside a temple, the outline of which, like most in the series, is deficient in perspective. "When I remember thee upon my bed," gives us a view of the box-like couch already described, and the "portion for foxes" is a mass of human beings stricken down by the spears of their opponents and devoured by foxes.

One of the most striking groups in the Manuscript is that afforded by the picture designed for the sixty-third Psalm, verse 3, "Quia exacuerunt ut gladium linguas suas? intenderunt arcum rem amaram." "Who whet their tongue like a sword," etc. In the centre is a grindstone set up between two posts and turned by a man who is working at the handle, while another man applies the edge of his sword to the revolving surface of the stone. Above this is the group of two men bending "their bows to shoot arrows;" and on the left in the foreground is a man seated astride upon a bench, and apparently sharpening or fabricating a sword. This latter group is probably a secondary realisation of the same metaphor as that to which the grindstone alludes, for we have seen occasionally in foregoing pictures two separate depictions of the same verbal imagery treated in different ways.[1]

The 64th Psalm[2] has its picture set in a different

---

[1] The corresponding picture in the *Eadwine Psalter* has been facsimiled in Westwood's *Palæographia Sacra*, pl. 43.

[2] Here also called lxiii., see page 161.

way to all that have preceded it; for, while those are drawn to occupy the whole breadth of the page of the Manuscript, this is enclosed within a circular line of exactly four inches diameter. The picture itself is very similar in detailed conception to those already described. But the vine laden with grapes and trained upon a frame or trellis is of great interest, and has not as yet been met with in the drawings. The circular line which contains the picture is inscribed in another fainter line less than a quarter of an inch larger in its span. The narrow band which is enclosed thus between the two circles contains the symbols of the Zodiac, alluded to in verse 8, "a signis tuis," signa here having reference to the "signa caelorum," the starry constellations of heaven, the "lights in the firmament" which are set "for signs and for seasons, and for days and for years" (Gen. i. 14). In the upper part of the picture, outside this zodiacal belt, are two small circles, with rims shaded to stand out prominently, containing the one a half length figure of the sun, the other of the moon, with radiated crown and crescent horns. These two refer to the phrase, "exitus matutini et vespere delectabis," verse 8. A question naturally suggests itself here to enquire the reason of the artist's departure from the usual arrangement of the pictures across the width of the page, in favour of a circular empanelling of his conceptions. But the reply is not, we may take it, difficult to be made. It is evidently the result of a deeply affected understanding of the text, which is here recording the universal power of the Lord throughout the world, "Visitasti terram et inebriasti eam?" And hence the Psalm has allured the artist into endeavouring, by the orbicular arrangement of the picture, the border of zodiacal signs, the sun and moon, and the cartographical nature of the details, to represent a map of the world, the *orbis terrarum*, such as his acquaintance with the diagrams of the early geographers of Western schools would allow him to reproduce without altogether discarding the realistic interpretation of mystical elements which his series of illustrations takes upon itself throughout.

The 65th Psalm has a picture which affords excellent examples of the flagella or short handled whips with doubled thongs, "posuisti tribulationes in dorso nostro," "thou laidst affliction upon our loins," (verse 11). Verse 6. "Qui convertit mare in aridam? in flumine pertransibunt pede?" "they went through the flood on foot," is indicated by a stream of water, welling from a globose jar over-turned, at the right hand corner of the picture, and flowing in a direct line along the foreground. Two figures are fording the stream with naked feet, and with garments gathered up in a bunch held in the right hand. Psalm LXVI. (here erroneously numbered LXXI., the second X being a mistake of the copyist for a V) has an illustrative design of very simple conception, the most interesting parts of which are the half length figure of the Lord, with nimbus on his head, and balanced scales in his hand, "Thou shalt judge the people righteously," "judicas populos in aequitate;" and the earth

yielding her increase, "terra dedit fructum suum,"
in the forms of a cedar tree, two vines laden with
their fruit, trained upon poles in a waving scroll-like
manner, and a variety of smaller plants and bushes.
The next Psalm has also, by a slip of the writer's
pen, been numbered LXXII. for LXVII. The
designs of the artist here are very well conceived
and grouped together, but there is only space to
notice the angel "bringing out those which are
bound with chains;" "the chariots of God are
twenty thousand, even thousands of angels," here
taking the form of a classical quadriga[1] with four
prancing horses shown rising out from the clouds
at half length, and directed by a winged angel of
wrath with a whip in his hand; another angel
"wounding the head of the enemy;" the tongue
of the dogs "dipped in the blood of the same"
(verse 23); "the players on instruments" with a
lyre and a triangular harp; and a damsel playing
with a timbrel, "in medio juvencula tympanistria-
rum" (verse 25), a musical object that here acquires
the form of a cylinder with incurved or depressed
surface, and covered with skin at the ends, which
are struck with the hands after the manner of the
modern Indian hand drum. The bulls and calves,
the kings with presents, the bodies in their beds
or graves, the people feasting at a round table set
with vessels, are all so many groups which combine
to form a very instructive picture.

The illustration prefixed to the 68th Psalm strikes

[1] This may be in allusion to verse 33 of the Hebrew Version, "him that rideth on
the heaven of heavens." See page 247.

us principally on account of the scene in reference
to the opening verses, "intraverunt aquae usque ad
animam meam; Infixus sum in limo profundi?"
etc. In the foreground, riding upon the deep waters,
are three vessels with beaked prows and curved,
bowl-like shape, two of them having rudders of the
classical and conventional form. In the central ship
is a human figure falling from the stern into "the
deep mire," where the floods are ready to overflow
him, as he raises his hand to the Lord and seems to
speak in the words of verses 14, 15. The waters
round about are filled with aquatic birds and fishes.
On the right hand is a round table, on which are
placed several vessels of various shapes, some of
which appear to have been overturned (verse 22).
The 69th Psalm has, in its picture, the Lord hasten-
ing to send help to the Psalmist, who stretches forth
his hands to the winged messenger on the hill : while
above, out of the clouds, a half length figure of the
Lord looks down benignantly upon him. In the
foreground on the left is a group of those who are
"turned back for a reward of their shame," "Aver-
tantur s·tim erubescentes," a passage in which
the Utrecht Psalter has a curious correction of a
clerical error rather than a contraction in the word
statim.

The details of the illustration prefixed to the 70th
Psalm are principally to be noticed for the group
of three persons holding snakes and bifurcated forks
with barbed points, and the temple with its hanging
lamps and curtains; but above all for the three
musical instruments which are drawn in allusion to

the phrase, "psallam tibi in cythara." These are, a lyre of three chords; a guitar-like object, the long stem held upon the shoulder of the musician, and an organ with nine pipes of graduated heights set up upon a square frame which contains the apparatus for producing and directing the wind. The simple form of this organ may well be contrasted with the more complicated forms which will be noticed lower down. Psalm LXXI. introduces to our observation ships, trees, and many details that have been already observed; and, among others, three kings adoring the Lord, and wearing the plain flat cap-like crown which has been contrasted with the crown fleury in a former place. The Lord, with cruciform nimbus, and within an oval frame, sits upon the sphere of the universe, with a prostrate figure beneath his feet; while, on either side, is a winged angel, a crown of branches overhead, and two other winged figures, the right hand one carrying in his hands a small circular plaque in which is drawn a human bust, probably referred to the sun, "Et permanebit cum sole," or, "ante solem permanet nomen ejus?" "His name shall be continued as long as the sun," verse 17.

The 72nd Psalm (here numbered by error LXXVII.) has a very spirited representation of a mare and her foal; a body of armed men; a party at a table feasting; graves or couches; a group of naked children; a walled city; a fine and noble figure of the Almighty casting arrows or darts at a mass of the wicked, that is surging and writhing in the flames of a pit (verses 18, 19). In the centre of the foreground is a pillar raised upon

a plinth of three orders, and sustaining a statue
of a warrior with a shield and a long spear. Mr.
H. Payn sees in this a representation of the column
of Diocletian at Alexandria, now popularly called
Pompey's pillar. In the next picture we may notice
the classical depiction of the sun and the moon,
"Tuus est dies et tua est nox?" The destruction
of the sanctuary with fire and axes (verse 5-8) gives
the artist an opportunity of introducing a very
beautifully drawn group of destroyers armed with
adzes, and hewing at the "carved work," while
one among them lifts up to the roof a wisp of
lighted material, or a long torch. The lions, the
bears, the serpents or dragons, and the sheep, are
all of good design, and grouped in a manner such
as we have already noticed as peculiar to this series
of illustrations. Psalm LXXIV. (by inadvertence
of the scribe called LXXIII.) presents to us the
realisation of verse 3, " The earth and all the in-
habitants thereof are dissolved: I bear up the pillars
of it." The earth is seen as a liquid mass with
floating fragments and a few bird-like figures in it;
ten pillars or columns set at equal distances all
along the length of the picture, sustain a piece of
the land on which is a numerous body of warriors,
armed and habited, as usual, with the tunic, the
wrinkled hose, the barbed spear, and the spiked
shield: at their feet are a number of the slain. The
foremost soldier holds in his hands the skull of a
stag with branching antlers; and on a rock overhead
is a figure holding a similar skull, and breaking with
a long staff the skull that is held by the soldier.

This relates to the last verse, "Omnia cornua peccatorum confringam, et exaltabuntur cornua justi." The "calix in manu domini" is held by a winged angel, who is passing down from heaven towards the armed host.

The 75th Psalm has well drawn figures of three horses, with horsemen, into each of whom is entering a small spirit, in reference to verse 6, "Dormitaverunt qui ascenderunt equos." Some vessels of elegant outline are drawn in the right hand corner of the foreground, near two beds with sleeping figures, into whom also are entering other small naked spirits in allusion to the 5th verse, "They have slept their sleep," etc.

The next picture, that prefixed to Psalm LXXVI., has a full length figure of the Almighty standing in a vesical frame; and a boat or vessel, of the shape already described, holding four persons, and floating in water filled with fishes and marine animals. On the banks are groups of the redeemed people, (verse 15); and towards the boat a man stretches out a long pole, in reference to verse 16, "Viderunt te aquae Deus." Folio 44 b containing the final portion of this Psalm, is left blank with the exception of seven lines of writing at the top, but the extreme translucency of the vellum allows several of the words to appear through, and the photograph reproduces these with remarkable clearness. In the upper part a later hand has essayed to draw a female head with cap or headdress and short curling hair. The 77th Psalm, which contains seventy-two verses, principally relating to the history of the Israelites, their

journeyings, their disobediences, and their divine
punishments, is illustrated with a long and mul-
titudinous procession of persons, old and young,
men and women, nearly encompassing a central
group of a king, with diademed crown having a
boss or knop of a shape somewhat resembling a
fleur-de-lys, and spear, standing before the figure
of an old man, who with a large open book resting
upon a carved stand or lectern, and inspired by a
hand of blessing issuing from the clouds above the
curious chair-like throne which he has just vacated,
is opening " his mouth in a parable," and uttering
" dark sayings of old " (verse 2). The 78th Psalm
(here in error also numbered LXXVII.) shows us
outside the walls of the city the dead bodies of the
servants of God " given to be meat unto the fowls of
the heaven, the flesh of saints unto the beasts of the
earth " (verse 2); where lions, hyenas, and vultures
are feasting upon the dead whose blood is " shed
like water round about Jerusalem."

The 79th Psalm shows a beautiful drawing of the
wild boar out of the wood wasting the vine brought
out of Egypt, while they " which pass by the
way do pluck her."   Of this design Sir Thomas
Hardy speaks at length, and very justly claims
it as the conception of an artist who had a perfect
knowledge of the vines of Palestine; and by no
means likely to be the work of an Anglo-Saxon artist.

Among the ensuing illustrations we may notice
the mounted horsemen in a well drilled rank, the
psaltery, lyre, and horses; and the " hands delivered
from the pots," of Psalm LXXX.; the figure of

Atlas sustaining the "foundations of the earth"
(alluded to with praise by Professor Westwood);
and a repetition of the statue on the column of the
81st Psalm; the tumult of enemies, on horse and on
foot, with spears and shields, horns, pennons, with
triangular tents and all the pomp of war, persecuted
with the tempest, and made afraid "with the storm
of the Lord," in the 82nd Psalm; and the crowned
king, the city walls, the tents and the trees of Psalm
LXXXIII.

Psalm LXXXIV. has an interesting representation
of ploughing and reaping, and a most practical
depiction of covering the sin of the people, in the
form of a group of men over whom two angels
are drawing a large cloth. In the 85th Psalm is
another example of a statue upon a carved monument of three stages; and a royal figure with single
crested crown. The picture prefixed to the 86th
Psalm is full of elaborate architecture, and has a
central group of the birth of Jesus Christ. The
Virgin lying on a bed of irregular shape, and four
attendants dipping the nimbed infant into a large
bowl-shaped vessel; this group refers to verse 5,
"Homo natús est in ea." The next picture has
a number of dead bodies in boxes or graves, in
allusion to verses 4-6, and a central figure among
them holding up his hands in supplication to the
Lord. In this the sun and moon appear under the
forms already pointed out. Psalm LXXXVIII. may
be examined for its pictures of ships; its crowned
figures; its architectural buildings; the sun and the
moon; and a crucified figure between two execu-

tioners, with a circular line drawn over all the design
in the centre. Psalm LXXXIX. (here also numbered LXXXVIII. by mistake of the copyist) for
its polygonal wall and temple; its groups of warriors;
and its "grass which groweth up." The next picture shows us Sol and Luna as before expressed; a
fine group of the Lord and His angels; a stag hunt;
and a Medusa-like face in the clouds which probably
relates to the 6th verse, "demonio meridiano."

On the following folio (54 a) is a specimen of the
triangular harp; and on the next, for the 92nd
Psalm, ships,' a temple with curved roof within a
circle which seems to have no special application,
but held up by two strong men; two seated figures
blowing long horns; and in the middle a throne
or chair with carved legs, crossed bars, "established
of old" for the Lord who is descending in a vesica to
occupy it. Among the most noticeable parts of the
following picture is a king seated with cap-like crown
and spear, a figure holding a palm branch, and a
battle-axe, and angels chastising the heathen by
casting down burning torches from heaven upon
them. Psalm XCIV. realises the scenes of Moses
striking the rock, and the images set up and wor-
shipped by the Israelites in the wilderness, in
allusion to the "forty years," "quadraginta annis
offensus fui," of verse 10. The 95th Psalm shows
good examples of walls; two suns with antique
radiated crowns; and a temple set in an oval
medallion, having separate scenery in the front
of the picture, after the manner we have seen

' In this picture Mr. H. Payn recognises the inundation of the river Nile.

employed in the 92nd Psalm. The confusion of those
"that serve graven images" (Psalm XCVI., ver. 7)
introduces a group adoring two statues standing
upon an architectural monument of three stages,
which is toppling over to destruction, while in the
foreground the "multitude of the isles" suggests
to the artist the idea of three islands in a sea, each
with a few figures standing in it. In the text of
this Psalm the word *confundantur* is written *con-
fundant*[2], with a good example of the obliquely placed
(2), which stands occasionally in this Manuscript as
the contraction for the termination *ur*.

The same page gives the drawing for Psalm XCVII.
And it has been selected by Dean Stanley as one
of the illustrations appended to the *Reports*, because
it gives the various forms of the contraction mark,
and the above mentioned abbreviation, and also
because "the drawing exhibits the jagged outlines
of the draperies referred to in some of the *Reports*
as characteristic of English work of the tenth and
eleventh centuries,' and the classical origin of the
design in the river god." The *cithara*, the *tubæ
ductiles*, and the *tuba cornea* (verses 5, 6) are here
introduced, as well as the realistic balance, in reference to the *aequitas*, or *equity* of the judgment of
the Lord mentioned in the last verse. The sea
roars, and the fulness thereof, in the guise of sea
serpents; and, sheltered by a rocky cave, a horned
sea god holds a branch in his hands and reclines
upon the back of a dragon, or monster with coiled

---

[1] For a criticism upon this statement, see Sir T. D. Hardy's note on page 18 of
the *Further Report*.

folds of body and equine head. In the centre is a medallion in a nearly perfect circle, containing a number of persons, old and young, who are singing unto the Lord "a new song" (verse 1). Psalm XCVIII. has in its drawing "the cloudy pillar," a true column with plinths, shaft and capital, surmounted by a smoking fire or cloud. In the centre the Lord "sitteth between the cherubims," one of whom is placed on each side of the conventional representation of the Almighty. There are some capital groups of horsemen, and in the foreground, in the middle, the phrase "moveatur terra," "let the earth be moved," verse 1, introduces a sturdy figure of Atlas, drawn as a monster with human face in his middle, who struggles to uphold the weight of the earth, the *scabellum* or footstool of our God (verse 5).

The next folio (57 b) has a drawing of walls, horned sheep or goats, and groups of men, for Psalm XCIX.; and for the 100th Psalm, some interesting figures holding books, and outside a city wall the early destruction of the wicked (verse 8). The next Psalm, the 101st, gives an illustration of the "pelican of the wilderness," the "nicticorax in domicilio," or "owl of the desert," and the "passer solitarius in tecto." In the foreground is a large figure of a female, surrounded by her children and holding a cornu copiæ, in allusion probably to the final verse. Three angels with hammers and chisels are "building up Zion" (verse 16), and "taking pleasure in her stones" (verse 14). It is interesting to note that the concluding words of the rubric or heading to this Psalm, not capable of being contained in one head line, have been written in a lower line on the right hand column, in a Rustic hand of weaker and later character than that of the body of the text; but as we cannot suppose that a very great interval of time elapsed between the transcribing of the text and that of the rubrics, these Rustic words must either have been written in by the reviser some considerable time after the completion of the work, unless we accept the writing as that of one whose power of writing this character was even less firm than his who transcribed the body of the book. A long insertion, apparently in this same style of character, will be adverted to presently.

Psalm CII. has the usual sun and moon, as Osiris and Isis, within circular medallions; and the principal accessories for noting here are the cedar tree; the trident; the long crosses with wavy streamers held by angels; the crown of victory; and the human jaws of hell which are engulphing a body of miserable wretches thrust down by demons with serpentine hair. Professor Westwood specially points out this latter group as a grand representation of the mouth of the infernal regions. The next Psalm is principally to be examined for its vessels; its sea birds, marine animals, and a huge water dragon; various birds and animals; the "wild asses" or "onagri;" the "volucres caeli;" the wild goats, conies, and lions devouring a human prey, and seeking "their meat from God." There is also an interesting scene of ploughing with a most simple plough, and another of a man feasting at a long table while an attendant places a crown on his head. Psalm CIV. has for the subject of its illustration David relating the story of God's providence over the Israelites and their chosen leaders, to a crowd of worshippers eagerly hanging upon his words, and the Deity in the clouds overhead holds out a scroll towards the inspired narrator.

Folio 61 b contains the picture of the 105th Psalm, one group of which is drawn in reference to the passage of the Red Sea, and the waters are covering the enemies, " Et operuit aqua tribulantes eos ! unus ex eis non remansit." (verse 11); while the chosen people are led in safety through the depths, " et deduxit eos in habyssis" (verse 9). The illustrative design prefixed to Psalm CVI. has been chosen by the Dean of Westminster for one of those appended to the *Reports*. It is full of interesting and important details, oxen at the primitive plough ; a man in the stocks ; others pruning vines and planting vineyards" (verse 37); or going down to the sea in ships, of the shape already pointed out ; others preparing a city for habitation ; and two chair-like thrones in allusion to the phrase, " et in cathedra seniorum laudent eum." (verse 32).

The 107th Psalm has in its drawing fine examples of the " psalterium et cythara ; " an hexagonal enclosure with walls and gateway, with the washpot or " lebes," and the " calciamentu[m] meum " takes the form of a pair of sandals with long straps cast over the wall by a king adorned with a very fine specimen of the crown with three fleurs-de-lys. Over a temple on the left the early sun shoots down his rays upon the Psalmist who appears to be ejaculating " Exsurgam duluculo ?" " I myself will awake early." Psalm CVIII. has a most spirited group of the " diabolus " or " Satan " (verse 6), with wings of different form to those of the angels over-head, thrusting his knee into the back of the wicked man ; and the fatherless children grouped beside the widow (verse 9), who is reclining beneath a tree, upon a mound, tearing her hair and rending her garments, form a very remarkable detail in the picture. The 109th Psalm has in its medallion the depiction of the opening verse, " The Lord said unto my Lord, Sit thou at my right hand," etc. The Lord seated on a bench, and with cruciform nimbus, sits beside " My Lord," who is adorned with a plain nimbus and seated on a sphere ; be-neath their feet the " scabellum pedum " of two prostrate enemies is placed. Verse 6, " He shall wound the heads over many countries," gives rise to an angelic figure discharging darts against a body of armed men, the foremost of whom, a crowned king, is pierced in the head and falling backwards. On one side is a group with lighted torches, on the other a youth with a Phrygian helmet, and with shield and spear stands upon a dead foeman, and appears to collect in a bowl some water from a stream welling down a rock. For " he shall drink of the brook in the way," " de torrente in via bibet ?"

Psalm CX. gives a group to illustrate the verse, " He hath given meat unto them that fear Him :" an angel flying down with a dish of food towards a square table on which are set three vessels of meat ;

and a temple closely resembling those that have been already recorded.

The next folio (65 b) has a picture full of edifices of various forms, the central one having a circular apse, in which, under a domed roof, sits the good man whose horn is exalted in the form of the head and antlers of a deer which crowns the summit of the tiled roof over his head. His house contains three hanging lamps, probably in reference to verse 3. In the foreground are classical vases, a group armed with tridents and javelins, and another group of the poor, to whom a female is handing a mass of bread. The illustration of the 112th Psalm (here by error numbered CXI., as the preceding Psalm), if we may judge by the photographic aspect, does not appear to have been finished, the lines being in some places very faint and almost imperceptible. The picture is very evenly balanced, the Lord with his six angels; a vacant seat flanked on either side by a long couch, upon which sit the princes of the people (verse 8); below these, two groups of the "servants of the Lord" engaged in a song of praise (verse 1); and in the foreground, in the centre, the barren woman, "sterelem," who is made a joyful mother of children (verse 9). He that "raiseth up the poor out of the dust" is on the left of the seat, helping a clinging figure to raise himself from the ground. The 113th Psalm (which corresponds to the 114th and 115th of the English version) shows us the sanctuary of Judah, a chest slung on a pole and carried by two bearers; this chest is depicted with greater elaboration in the corresponding place in the Eadwine Psalter. The Jordan driven back here curls its eddying waters away from the staff of the Jewish leader, but in the later treatment of the Eadwine Psalter two large fishes appear to take the place of the curved waves. The water flowing from the stricken rock; the dead bodies in their graves, who "praise not the Lord;" the skipping rams; the houses of Jacob, of Aaron, and of Israel, are graphically drawn: and on two ladders reared against a tower are two men striving for the possession of a bird which is eluding their grasp, while others are falling headlong down the ladder, and "go down into silence," "descendunt in infernum." The next Psalm, the 114th (corresponding to CXVI., verses 1 to 10 of the Vulgate), has a very large figure in a rocky cave (in allusion to verse 3), stretching forth its monstrous hands, the personification of the sorrows of death, the pains of hell, towards the escaping Psalmist. The 115th Psalm (forming the second portion of the Vulgate 116th) shows us the death of the saints, and pre-eminently the crucifixion of the Lord, which Professor Westwood points out for especial notice because of the short-sleeved garment which clothes the body of Jesus to the feet; a representation, the conventionalism of which is claimed by him for a later period than that to which others are willing to ascribe it.

The short 116th Psalm of two verses, has an illustrative design of all the nations praising the Lord. This picture is useful because it shows how the original designs have been adapted to the exigencies of this particular Manuscript; for the third column, not containing so much text at the end of the preceding Psalm as the first and second columns, only admits of one angel on the right hand of the Deity against the usual three on the opposite side. The 117th Psalm, in reference to the 4th verse, "They compassed me about like bees," "Circumdederunt me sicut apes?" shows us a warrior attacked by a swarm of these insects; and another group in the same drawing demonstrates how "the stone which the builders refused is become the head stone of the corner," where three masons are busied about their building the angle of a wall. The lengthy Psalm which follows this, the 118th, has a fine specimen of a temple, and kings seated with warriors on a long couch, over which a battle-axe is poised, in allusion to the 23rd verse. The names of the Hebrew letters which are prefixed to the subdivisions of this Psalm are translated into St. Jerome's Latin equivalents (not in all cases correct) in the following manner:—

Beth	Domus.[1]		Mem	Ex ipsis.
Gimel	Plenitudo.		Nun	Sempiternum.
Deleth	Tabulam.		Samech	Adjutorium.
He	Ista.		Ain	Fons, sive ocul[us].
Vav	Et.		Fe	Os, non ab osse.
Zai	Haec.		Sade	Justitia.
Eth	Vita.		Coph	Vocans.
Teth	Bonum.		Res	Capitis.
Ioth	Principium.		Sen	Dentium.
Caph	Manus.		Tav	Signa.
Lamech	Disciplina.			

[1] See *Opera S. Eusebii Hieronymi*, in Migne, *Patrol. Cursus*, vol. 23, p. 1306.

The 119th Psalm has a coarse picture, with the tents of that peculiar shape adverted to in the description of the 26th Psalm. This drawing has been, like its fellows, much altered in the Eadwine Psalter, which, however, adheres in the idea to the Utrecht, whereas, as has before been pointed out, the Harley Psalter gives new designs after the 113th Psalm.

The next folio is very instructive, because it contains two pictures, the first in the coarse style, the latter in a very neat and beautifully fine style of drawing, on the same page. In the former of these, the natural figure of the waning moon may well be contrasted with the half-length personifications so constantly met with throughout. The pavonaceous heading to the scroll of the bed (verse 3), and the crowned figure of the king, should also be noticed. In the latter the mention of the tribes going up into the " compact city " of Jerusalem affords the artist an opportunity of displaying an unsurpassed specimen of his wonted skill in architectural buildings and dense bodies of men

There are two pictures on each of the next three folios (72 b-73 b); and in these six samples of the art of the illustrator, which yield to none in merit or in interest throughout the volume, may be noticed the same striving after a realistic effect as a means of impressing vividly upon the mind of the reader, the metaphorical scenes which pass before his eyes as he consults the accompanying verses. Here may be seen the varied weapons, bows and arrows, broad swords, and javelins; a man holding a curious snare for birds which flee from his half-revealed body sitting in a bush; the fording of a torrent; temples of various styles, several with altars, curtains, and lamps; embattled city walls with watch towers at their angles; prostrate bodies fastened to the ground by fetters; the "virga peccatorum" in form of stout switches held by two who are about to inflict a punishment upon them; the "sowing in tears" that fall in thick showers from a body of men on one side of a picture which on the other contains the sheaves which have been reaped in joy; snake-like streams of water; tables having carved trusses with lions' heads, and loaded with viands in vases of various form; the "bread of sorrows," "panem doloris," which appears to be in the shape of round flat cakes, marked with three curved lines in a simple triangular pattern; reaping with sickles; gathering grapes from espalier vines into spherical baskets and treading out the wine in a vat; the olive plants, "novella olivarum;" and the fruitful vine, "vitis habundans," in the shade of which, crowned and seated at a feast with his children and his wife, is the man "that feareth the Lord, that walketh in his ways."

The 128th Psalm exhibits the grass upon the house-tops, mowers with scythes of a shape very similar to the present style, and men gathering sheaves. Verse 4, "Dominus justus concidit cervices peccatorum," "he hath cut asunder the cords of the wicked," shows us a shower of battle-axes and spears, and in the words of the poet, an

> "Iron sleet of arrowy shower
> Hurtles in the darken'd air,"

cast down from the heights of heaven by an angelic

host, one of whom is receiving from the hands of the Almighty a sword, the type of destruction. One of the battle-axes has cut through the neck of a man who is falling forward. A curious group here is that of a forge with a blazing fire about which are three men armed with hammers, probably in allusion to verse 3. The shape of this forge is that of a rectangular box, with curved back to the fire-place, and in the front of the fire is a square object which may either represent an anvil or some portion of the apparatus to produce the wind.

The next Psalm, " De profundis," introduces to our notice another rare example of those large figures, so completely out of proportion to the size of the surrounding beings, and to the general shapes of the persons seen throughout the series. It is a draped body, three quarters length, holding up a scroll, and crying out of the depths unto the Lord. The occurrence of the phrase, " A custodia matutina usque ad noctem?" explains the personifications of the sun and moon, with lighted torches and appropriate crowns, which have already received the attention of the reader. The 130th Psalm has a well drawn example of an olive tree, and an interesting group of the " child that is weaned of his mother," or " ablactatus."

Psalm CXXXI. has a picture of a city wall with arched portals and bodies of men marching out; a temple with a procession of torch-bearing priests accompanying four shrine-carriers, approaching it; the " horn of David;" the wreath of victory; and lamp for the anointed one, " paravi lucernam xp̄o

meo," in the form of a bird, set upon a tall candelabrum with tripod foot and beaded stem. The architecture of the tabernacle which contains the bed
(verse 3) is of a very different order to the "habitation for the mighty God of Jacob." The roof is
semicircular, and the sides of open arching, with
curtains stretched from pillar to pillar. Psalm
CXXXII. finds its principal group in the anointing
of Aaron (verse 2), who stands in the centre of a
congregation while a winged figure, issuing from
the clouds overhead, pours from a horn the precious
ointment, "that went down to the skirts of his
garments," for "there the Lord commanded the
blessing," "Quoniam illic mandavit dominus benedictionem," and His hand is drawn over the head of
the throng. The mountains of Sion show us a
wandering stream leaping down from a hill on which
are two statues upon short columns, a lion, a wild
boar, a bear, and four deer, and in the air the visible
dew of Hermon falling upon the trees. The
133rd Psalm naturally seems to require that
he who would take upon himself to pictorialise the
verses of the text should represent the "domus
domini," the "atria domus dei nostri." Hence we
have a drawing of heaven and earth; the former
realised by a crescent moon and attendant stars,
the latter by a broad belt of verdant banks and
water, wherein are disporting swans and other
aquatic birds, and fishes. The centre of the picture
is occupied with a very elaborate structure intended
to represent the temple. It has a curved roof
covered with convex tiling, a dome surmounted with

ball and cross and supported by two columns with
foliated capitals; small apertures in the clerestories
over lean-to aisles which have their slanting roofs
covered in with slabs, the numerous fastenings or
pegs of which project very prominently, and their
sides composed of open arcading of four columns
sustaining semicircular arches.   The approach is
by a broad flight of steps, perhaps in allusion to
the object of this Psalm, which is entitled, a " Canticum graduum," or " Of degrees."   Three swinging
lamps hang beneath the dome; and the steps and
aisles are occupied with a throng of worshippers.

The next Psalm has a smaller temple (in reference
to verse 2), set within a walled city and between two
groups with harps; the personified sun and moon;
the "lightnings for the rain" (verse 7); "the idols
of the heathen," "simulacra gentium," set within
small walled enclosures; the smiting of great nations,
the slaying of mighty kings, and the death of the
"primogenita Aegypti ab homine usque ad pecus;"
a ship; and the sphere, on which the Lord is seated,
upheld by two large heads of cherubim.

The 135th Psalm, the verses of which throughout
ring to the refrain of "quoniam in aeternum misericordia ejus;" "for his mercy endureth for ever;"
offers many pictures to the facile pen of the artist,
who seems to have found his art more easy of
expression as he passes on to the completion of
his work, and so he introduces many more individual
groups into the same amount of space which holds
so few in the earlier pictures of the series. In this
instance, just as the text of this and the preceding

Psalm resemble each other in no slight degree, and just as the scope of the two is of a similar nature, so also the picture of this Psalm has very much in common with that which precedes it. The statues, the ship, the winged throwers of the lightning, the city fortifications, the sun and moon, all occupy similar positions with those in the previous illustration. Among minor points of interest are the hinges and ornamental iron work of the valved doors in the wall, and the overthrown riders. The 136th Psalm in its picture renders the " flumina Babylonis " by a winding river, on the borders of which are the " salices " or willows on which hang the " organa " of the captive Jews, here rendered into harps of the conventional *cithara* shape, and thus more closely translating the Hebrew (and English) version than that of the Vulgate. " We hanged our harps upon the willows," " In salicibus suspendimus organa nostra."

Kings of the earth are praising the Lord and worshipping towards His holy temple in the next picture ; and the phrase, " in medio tribulationis " (verse 7), appears to be rendered by a hollowed site in the foreground wherein are two men seated, each with one foot set in the stocks, and two other prisoners held down to the earth by chains or cords round the neck, one being also confined by a ring round the ankles. Psalm CXXXVIII. affords another of those rare examples of figures of large size, in this place intended to represent the personification of the *facies*, or the *spiritus* of the Lord (verse 7), but not without reference also to the *infernum* of verse 8. The head and arm alone of this large figure are shown in the left hand corner of the foreground, about to engulf a human being, while another is thrust towards him for a similar fate by one armed with a trident. The 139th Psalm is principally to be noted for the two "aspides" or "adders," referred to in the 3rd verse; the "laqueus" or "funes," the "snare for me, and cords," which here takes the form of a net held by warriors armed with spears and cuirasses or breastplates of armour, with a short plaited petticoat below them. On the right of the picture burning coals fall upon the wicked and they are cast into the fire (verse 10). Psalm CXL. has a monstrous head in the left hand corner of the foreground, and a very large trawl-net in the centre of the picture, in allusion to verse 10. "Cadent in reciaculo ejus peccatores?" "Let the wicked fall into their own nets." The animals in this page are the work of a good designer.

The two pictures for the next Psalms on the following folio (79 b) are of coarse workmanship. In the former we must observe the net, or snare, privily laid at the foot of a flight of steps; in the latter a gigantic half length figure of the sun; the dead dwelling in darkness shown by coffins piled up in a cavern; demon forms with snakes about their bodies and heads, and armed with tridents spears and a hook, attacking one rising from the grave and leading two captives with their hands fettered. Psalm CXLIII. has an illustration of the Lord teaching the hands of David to war, by handing to an armoured figure a shield and a broadsword with its scabbard and baldric, from the heavens. The groups of sheep and oxen; the fighting-men armed with battle-axes, spears, sword, and triangular breastplate; the "novella[e] plantationes," or plants grown up in their youth, and the "promptuaria plena," or garners full of all manner of store, must be noticed in this plate.

The 144th Psalm has several well executed figures of animals, in reference to verse 16, "imples omne animal benedictione;" a group of trident-bearers destroying the wicked (verse 20); the raising up of one that is "bowed down," "erigit omnes elisos;" and a winding river which springs from the right hand and passes along the whole length of the foreground to the left hand corner. Of a very different style is the broad water with fishes and birds in the picture of Psalm CXLV., which also contains a very elaborate throne, with carved ornaments at the back and side arms, and with a sloping foot-rest ornamented with three arches in front. Psalm CXLVI. has its illustration in the same folio, but this is of that coarse style which characterises several of the drawings which have already been adverted to. In this may be noticed city walls, musical instruments, and the weapons of the class already examined, spears, axes, standards and shields; the moon and the "number of the stars;" the casting down of the wicked; the rain (verse 8); the beasts, and the young ravens, one of which is perched upon a stump on the extreme right of the foreground; the horse and the rider overthrown, in allusion to verse 10.

Folio 82 a contains the picture prefixed to the 147th Psalm. The most conspicuous group is that in reference to verse 2 (or 13 of the Vulgate version, which combines the 146th and 147th Utrecht Psalms), "quoniam confortavit seras portarum tuarum?" "for He hath strengthened the bars of thy gates." Two angels are holding thick bars in the staples of the folding doors of a city gate. The wheat, (frumen-·tum), the snow like wool, the hoarfrost like ashes (nebulam sicut cinerem), the ice like morsels (cristallum sicut buccellas), and the flowing waters, are all depicted with a realistic force that we have seen employed already in former places. Two angels are coming down from heaven, one bearing an open book (verse 15), the other a personification of the "facies frigoris" (verse 17), in the shape of a monstrous head. The band of warriors who have piled their spears in a sheaf beside them, and placed their shields on the ground before them, while with palm branches in their hands they raise their thanksgiving to the Lord, forms a very interesting group. Psalm CXLVIII. has a picture of very beautifully balanced proportions. The artist has evidently striven to introduce a drawing of all the material works of the divine creation which are invoked by the Psalmist in this hymn of universal praise. The most prominent groups that claim our notice are the broad belt of stars beneath the heavenly throne, and the quaint representations of the sun and moon in medallions as before, but held in the hands of gigantic half length figures, a most unusual, and almost unique form of these celestial bodies. The hosts, the earth, the dragons, the deeps, the fruitful trees, the creeping things, the flying fowl, kings, princes, judges, young men and maidens, old men and children, are inserted in well set groups; and the beasts are represented by pairs of oxen, stags, bears, lions, and wild boars, among the trees on the banks of the water.

Of the 149th Psalm the most instructive parts are the women with the *psalterium*, the *tympanum*, or hand-drum, and a harp of ovoid shape which appears to occur here for the first time; and the allusion to verse 8; "To bind their kings with chains, and their nobles with fetters of iron," where we may see two kings set in the stocks, and other two led, chained at the hands, by a divine messenger towards a temple on the right hand. The concluding Psalm has also its picture on this folio (83 a). The eight instruments of music mentioned in the text, namely tuba, psalterium, cythara, timpanum, chorus, cordæ, organum, and cymbala, are variously represented. The *tuba*, trumpet or cornet, is large and slightly curved; the *psalterium* triangular; the *cythara* of three shapes already described where they occur; the *timpanum* or timbrel is a cylindrical hand-drum with recessed centre; the word *chorus* may perhaps signify *dance* (English Version) or *pipe*, as in the marginal note (of the same version), in which case it is shown by the same shape as the *tuba* already alluded to. The *corda* must be taken as equivalent to the *psalterium* and *cytharæ;* and the *cymbala* are double plates of metal rattled together and tossed into the air, held by two thongs in the hand of the performer. The *organ* is of very intense interest on account of the great amount of detail it exhibits.[1]   Westwood says of this object that it agrees exactly with that given by Strutt from the Eadwine Psalter, copied by T. Wright in his *Domestic Manners.*

Much controversy has arisen among the principal writers upon this Psalter with regard to the organ, which is played upon by two performers by means of a manual arrangement or finger board, the wind being driven through the pipes by bellows worked with two levers on either side of the instrument, each lever being held by an assistant.   Some consider that this form of musical instrument does not appear to have been in use (at any rate, north of the Alps) before the time of Charlemagne; Dr. Vermuelen states that the construction does not admit a date so far back as the sixth century: but, on the other hand, Sir Thomas Hardy records a reference to organs worked by bellows in St. Augustine's treatise on music, and also mentions an excellent representation of an organ, not very unlike that one here depicted, carved on an early catacomb stone in Rome.[2]   Hence all that can be gleaned from the evidence of the organ here and in other places is, that the date of the drawings is not in any way affected by the introduction of these objects.

It now remains to examine the pictures prefixed to the appended canticles and pieces.   The first is the " Canticum Isaie Prophetae," commencing " Confitebor tibi domine quoniam iratus es mihi/" being

---

[1] Compare the simpler *organ* in Psalm 70, folio 40 a.   [2] *Report,* p. 26.

the 12th chapter of the book of Isaiah. The principal points of interest in the drawing are the figures with water-vessels of various ancient forms, and in the centre a quatrefoil-shaped well or fountain with stone mouth, over which the water of salvation is flowing down to the gate of a city wall, where the stream divides and runs towards either corner of the foreground. " With joy shall ye draw water out of the wells of salvation ; " Aurietis aquas in gaudio de fontibus salvatoris ? "

The next piece is another " Canticum Isaie Prophetae," " Ego dixi in dimidio dierum meorum ? " being the 38th chapter of Isaiah, verses 11-20. Here we see the lions (verse 13), the birds of verse 14, the shepherds (verse 12), and the gates of the grave, held open by an angel (verse 10). The mournful plaint of the prophet, " I have cut off like a weaver my life : he will cut me off (from the thrum) with pining sickness ; " Praecisa e[s]t velut a texente vita mea ? dum adhuc ordirer succidit me ? " (verse 12), has suggested to the pen of the artist an exceedingly delicate and excellently grouped representation, which Professor Westwood points out for especial notice. The treatment of the idea is certainly very ancient and classical, and is none less than a group of the Fates employed in weaving the web of human destiny, one of them with a pair of shears cutting off the shortened span of life alluded to in the quotation.[1]

The third " Canticum " of Isaiah, rightly shown

---

[1] See a very rude copy of this group from the Eadwine Psalter in T. Wright's *Domestic Manners*, p. 108.

by Sir T. D. Hardy to be that of *Anna* (*i.e.*, Hannah, the mother of Samuel), "Exsultavit cor meum in domino?" is from 1 Samuel ii. 1-10. There is in this picture a small circular medallion, after the style noticed in some of the later Psalms. In the lower part of this are the broken bows alluded to in the phrase, "Arcus fortium superatus est?" in the upper part a female accompanied with nine crowned figures, in reference to the words, "ut sedeat cum principibus," etc.

Then follows the "Canticum Moysi Prophetae," commencing, "Cantemus domino," Exodus xv. 1-13, 17-20. The four verses (14-17) have been added on the lower margin of the page in a handwriting of Rustic capitals of a weak, imperfect, and uncertain style. It would be interesting to determine whether the insertion is to be considered in the light of a rectification of a clerical error, or whether the abridged form of the Canticle was ever employed in the early ages of the church. If this later addition be not an insertion to complete the original form of the Canticle, but rather the effect of a newer liturgical arrangement which can be attributed to a period within which the writing of the Psalter can be shown to have been current, much will have been done towards a solution of the true date of the Manuscript. But this is one of those questions which as yet the paucity of research affords no well grounded means of answering.

The "Canticum Abacuc Prophetae," commencing "Domine audivi" (Habakkuk iii. 2-19), has a picture containing many most interesting groups, the "tentoria Aethiopiae" of the form described under the 26th Psalm; the rivers and seas, the chariot, the "gurges aquarum," the "abyssus," the "altitudo," or "deep," that "lifted up his hands on high," the "pedes cervorum," and the fig-tree or "ficus" of verse 17. But above all in interest are two groups, one of the scourging, the other of the crucifixion of the Lord, the latter being designated by Professor Westwood as one of the earliest representations of the three crosses. Beside the Saviour stand two figures, one with a spear, the other with a sponge on a reed, in accordance with the details of the Gospel narratives.

This is followed by the "Canticum Moysi ad filiis Israhel," from Deuteronomy xxxii. 1-43, commencing with the words, "Audite caeli quae loquor?" The picture here is one of those specimens of even balancing of groups pointed out in several former instances. The central figure is Moses, the lawgiver, standing on a hill, holding a book of the law, and reciting his song to two bodies of men. On either edge of the picture is a cedar tree, and in the branches an eagle stirring up her nest (verse 11), "aquila provocans ad volandum pupillos suos? et super eos volitans." In the clouds is the Saviour with sword and arrows in his hands, and surrounded by animals, the lion, and the wolf, in allusion to verses 23, 24. In the foreground is a well drawn scene of milking goats and kine into large chalices, and a man churning with a cylindrical vessel not far unlike the form of the modern churn.

In the following Canticle, that entitled "Bene-

dictio trium puerorum," and commencing, " Bene-
dicite omnia opera domini domino.'" (from the
Apocrypha). The three children are seen in the
fiery furnace ' placed on arches in the centre of a
picture containing a number of groups, carefully
balanced, and intended to, represent " all the works
of the Lord." The corners of the foreground contain two very elaborate examples of " whales and all
that move in the waters ; " " Coetae et omnia quae
moventur in aquis." Professor Westwood especially
points out the classical representation of water in
this illustration.

The " Hymnum ad matutinis," better known as
the " Te Deum " from its first words, follows next in
order. This composition is attributed to St. Ambrose,
Bishop of Milan ; and a hymn with the same commencing words is noticed by Hardy as mentioned in
The Rule of St. Benedict. But Canon Swainson's
Report states that the older. versions of the " Te
Deum " vary considerably from each other and from
the text in the Utrecht Psalter, which later text
was not fixed before the time of Charlemagne.
Yet the Canon speaks of the *old* phrase, " Su-
scepisti hominem " being altered into " Suscepturus "
at the suggestion of Abbo of Fleury ; the Utrecht
version retaining the former phrase would seem
therefore, by this kind of reasoning, to be prior to
both Charlemagne and Abbo. Sir T. Hardy points
out another old variation, *munerari* for *numerari*, in a
succeeding verse of the Utrecht text. The picture
has a temple, and groups of the principal characters

' Compare a similar form in the illustration prefixed to Psalm 65.

invoking the praise of their God. The Canon's translation of the title as "*daily* at matins" appears unreasonable, and the argument founded upon this redundancy of translation, namely, that as the daily use of the hymn commenced in the ninth century, the Psalter cannot be earlier, must necessarily be rejected. The word scāe, in the phrase, "Te ergo scāe quesumus tuis familis subveni;" "We therefore pray thee," etc., is styled "unintelligible" by Canon Swainson, but there can scarcely be any difficulty in reading it as a contraction for sancte, in the vocative; *e* being occasionally in this Manuscript thus strangely written, as may be seen in the words *voluntariae* (p. 244), *caera* (p. 246), *coetae* for *cete* (p. 282), fili *unigenitae* in the "Gloria in excelsis," *virginae* in the Apostles Creed.

The next poem is that entitled "Canticū Zacharie Prophete ad matutinum," or "Benedictus," (Luke i. 68-79). This picture has a group of the Nativity, with the Child being washed in a large vessel, as we have already seen depicted in Psalm LXXXVI. The Blessed Virgin reclines upon a bed placed at the door of a circular edifice with a domed roof, over which shines the "dayspring," or "oriens ex alto;" and the horn of salvation, held in the hands of the Almighty, sheds visible rays "to give light to them that sit in darkness," under a cave in the foreground. Here, too, the fig-tree and the cedar balance each other on the margins of the drawing.

The "Canticum sanctae Mariae," or "Magnificat," (Luke i. 46-55), shows us, in addition to the interesting groups of realistic expressions derived from the images of the text, a very unique representation of the Blessed Virgin, standing before the hand of the Lord, which is blessing her from the clouds; and in front of her, and as it were held up by her hands, her spirit, in the form of a small child stretching out its hands toward the sky, "exsultavit *spiritus* meus;" "my spirit hath rejoiced" (verse 47). · That this is really intended for a figure of her spirit, and not for the child Jesus, is plainly manifest from examples already pointed out in the illustration to Psalm LXXV., where a similar metaphor occurs.

The "Canticum Simeonis ad completorium," or "Nunc dimittis," (Luke ii. 29-32), on folio 89 b, has a charming group of the Virgin offering the Child to the high priest at the entrance of a temple, with an attendant standing behind her and holding two doves in a cloth. According to Sir Thomas Hardy, St. Benedict's writings do not mention this Canticle, so that it would appear to be an introduction into the liturgy of later date than A.D. 530, but this is opposed to Prebendary Walcott's opinion.[1]

The same page contains the "Gloria in excelsis," without any rubric or heading. The picture prefixed to this very ancient angelical hymn is of simple but harmonious construction. By the side of the Almighty Father is the "Lamb of God," and in the foreground groups of worshippers, and an angelic figure offering two palm branches to the leaders of the song.

[1] *Sacred Archæology*, p. 112.

The "Oratio Dominica secundum Matheum," (Matt. vi. 9-13), is written without the doxology. Its picture represents the Saviour in the midst of the twelve disciples, elevating their hands in prayer: and from out of the heavens overhead the right hand of the Lord is extended in the act of benediction. The same folio (90.a) contains the Apostle's Creed, with the rubric "Incipit Symbolu[m] Apostolorum." The picture prefixed to this composition is of very great interest. It contains, and we should naturally expect that it would so contain, a number of groups illustrative of the various events in the life of Christ which form the principal subjects of the text. Hence we may see the arraignment of Jesus before Pontius Pilate; the crucifixion in the presence of the three Maries; the holy sepulchre; the descent "ad inferna;" the angel at the tomb; the ascension, treated in a very original manner, the rising figure of the Saviour being led up into heaven by the Divine hand of God, while the assembled disciples gaze fondly after their Lord, whose entire form is yet in their sight, and not, as in pictures of later conventionalism, half hidden in the skies; the "Holy Ghost" as a dove with a branch; the Church; the resurrection of the body, and other groups. Not the least interesting is the group of the Almighty Father, seated in the heavens in majesty, on his right hand the Blessed Virgin, also seated, and holding the Infant Saviour, with cruciform nimbus, in her arms, while the Holy Spirit in form of a dove hovers overhead. With regard to the text of this creed, Sir Thomas Hardy, in his first *Report*,' treats in a lengthy and exhaustive manner the objections that have been by some urged with regard to the employment of the phrase, " descendit ad inferna *!* " which they allege to have been introduced not before the latter end of the eighth or beginning of the ninth century ; and he instances its use in several symbols or creeds, the earliest cited being that of Aquileia in the beginning of the fifth century.

On folio 90 b is the Athanasian Creed, or " Qui-cu[n]que vult," with the faulty rubric " Incipit Fides Catholicam." The picture is one that de-mands great attention, for, while throughout the volume we have observed every picture endeavours to represent in some way, more or less natural and realistic, a rendering of the imagery of the diction and the metaphors or incidents of the texts, here, for the first time, a departure is made, and the illustra-tion fails to give as we should expect, a group or series of groups illustrative of the Divine nature and attributes of the personages of the Holy Trinity. The picture, on the other hand, contains a repre-sentation of a synod or council of ecclesiastics, seventy-eight in number, seated on benches and cushions in a complete circle. The interior space is occupied with a full length personage, intended for a pope or archbishop, who is being invested with a pallium or stole by two attendants. On each side of this figure is a square upright desk of thick frame-work, and sloping top supporting a large open volume, a scribe seated writing in a roll, and beyond

' Pp. 29-32.

these two other scribes seated between a bowl of ink and dipping into it their pens to write on scrolls held before them. The picture is evidently intended to show a view of the Council of Nicea, or some synod in which the Fides Catholica was accepted for the church at large; and from the similarity of its artistic work with the other pictures in the volume, must be taken as of contemporary execution. If, therefore, any evidence could be acquired respecting the date of the admission of this Creed into the liturgical formula of the Church, that same date would in all probability give us also the time of the execution of the illustrations in this Manuscript; for on account of the unique departure which we witness here, viz. from realistic rendering of metaphors to a historical cartoon representing an event of great importance in church history, there is no doubt that the artist is pourtraying a scene at which he probably was present, or which at least was of coeval occurrence. But unfortunately no means appear to be available for the solution of this question, the actual date of the admission of the creed into the Church being undetermined; and hence we are debarred from deducing any theories of the date of execution of the art shown here, from the theological point of view.

The text of this creed will be found in the next chapter. It is followed by the Psalm termed the Apocryphal Psalm by general acceptance. The Rubric has been already pointed out[1] as an illustration of the imperfect and arbitrary nature of the abbreviations, which cannot be here said to be of

---

[1] See page 186.

regular use, and seem to weaken the theory of after revision by a Latin scholar of the text prepared by a mere scribe. The Rubric as it stands in the Manuscript is not easily explained without the aid of supposed contractions, which seem to shew that the scribe was ignorant of the language he was writing and took no notice of marks over lines in the book from which he was copying.

This is the last of the pictures, and a portion of it is reproduced by Professor Westwood in his great work. There are four groups:—the angel appearing to David feeding his father's sheep; a figure seated playing an organ, "Manus meae fecerunt organum? et digiti mei aptaverunt psalterium;" the organ here being very similar to that in the picture described at page 278, with two wind boxes, a double row of pipes, and a carved ornamental frame along the sides and upper part; the death and decollation of the "alienigena" Goliath; and on the right hand of the picture Saul, the king of Israel, seated in majesty upon a throne, crowned, holding a sword and sceptre terminating with a carved effigy wearing a helmet, and surrounded by a group of warlike attendants.

The next folio (92 a) was originally left blank, but a few words have been scribbled on it of the time of the eleventh century, an eagle's head and some other scratches of the artist's and the scribe's pens. On the other side of the leaf are, " m^i vivere xp̄c est - vere - sp̄c," a study of a bust with spear and sword, a female head roughly drawn, and the commencement of one of those beautifully intricate lacertine letters or winding ornaments, composed of stalks, leaves, heads, wings, etc., which abound in many books of the tenth and eleventh centuries. Then follow a number of leaves, which have been added by Sir Robert to the original volume of the Psalter, for the only reason, apparently, that in size they coincided with each other, a practice which has been shown to have been frequently made use of by that collector. Of these, two leaves contain the epistle of Hieronymus to Pope Damasus, generally prefixed to the Vulgate version of the Old Testament, in fine uncial writing of the end of the seventh century, written in two columns of thirty lines to a column. The final letters of lines are occasionally united into monograms, or a curve (~) over the line indicates an omitted *m*. Among the combined letters may be noticed NT, EN, ES, US, OR, UR. Towards the end of the line the letters are sometimes very much reduced in size in order to get in a certain number of letters, and there are many corrections and erasures. A middle comma is used for the terminative *-us*, in *-bus*, or *-ue*, in *que*, or it is used as a stop. The text begins, " Incipit prologus. Beato Papae Damaso Hieronymus. Novum opus facere me cogis, etc.," and ends, "vel vicina dicerunt," with a colophon in Rustic writing: " Opto ut in xp̃o valeas et memineris mei papa beatissime. Explicit."

The next leaf contains, from the same Bible, the ending of the " Prologus secundum Mattheum quattuor evangeliorum," a complete copy of which may be read in the British Museum, Additional MS., 11849, a very fine Manuscript of an early date. The text of the fragment commences with the words, "qui

negant xp̄m in carne venisse," and ends with "vivis
ᵉˢˢᵉcanendas."   The Royal MS., I. B. vii., in the
British Museum, may be examined for prefatory
material very much the same as is shown by these
fragments.

Then follows the *Praefatio Matthei*: "Mattheus in
Judaea sicut in ordine," etc., complete, to which is
subjoined the abstract entitled "Capitula lectionis
secundum Mattheum," in eighty-eight sections, comprised in four leaves or eight pages altogether, ending
thus: "in finem saeculi praesentiam pollicetur, Explicit."

Folio 100 contains the general title to the Gospels,
"Incip̄ | in nomine dn̄ī | n̄ī ihū xp̄ī euange|lia numero
IIII. | Sec̄ mattheum | Sec̄ marcum | Sec̄ lucan' |
Sec̄ iohannem |," in most beautifully formed uncial
letters of the height of a quarter of an inch, arranged
within a circle of five and a half inches diameter
concentric with an outer circle of seven and a half
inches diameter, coloured blue about an eighth of an
inch wide; the belt thus formed is filled with thirteen
semicircular escallops or festoons of the same colour
interlaced, over and under, with the same number of
large, and twice the number of smaller semicircular
ornaments coloured pink.   Each of the lozenge
shaped spaces of the field between the intersecting
curves has one letter of the following line :—

+ ΑΓΙΑ ΜΑΡΙΑ ΒΟΗΘΗCΟΝ ΤΩ ΓΡΑΨΑΝΤΙ.

"Holy Mary, help the writer."

The next six pages contain the gospel of St.

---

[1] The form of this word has been attributed to great antiquity.

Matthew in very fine and bold uncial writing of the seventh century, in two columns of about twenty-eight lines to a page, with numerical canons on the margins; the lines being of unequal length, and the words in many cases run together, but with an evident leaning towards division, the space between the words in a great number of instances being very distinctly shown. The text is consecutive from chapter i. 1, " LIBER ' generationis," to chapter iii. 4, "de pilis camelorum." The last folio (104) has the beginning of the gospel of St. John in the same handwriting, from " In principio," chapter i. 1, to " et dixit non sum," chapter i. 21.

And here we close the *Utrecht Psalter*, having examined carefully, and, as minutely as the space at command has allowed, described every point of interest raised by the contemplation of the art, whether of the writing or pictures, which this book affords; a book standing alone, *sui generis*, in the library of ancient literary relics, for its manifold peculiarities; and, like the Sphinx of old, offering to our researches complicated paradoxes, to which, as yet, the combined knowledge of those best competent to decide has failed to propose unanimous responses. In the concluding chapter some of the causes of this divergence of skilled opinion will be brought under discussion.

The necessity of acquiring more evidence of a collateral and comparative nature, with which to contrast the many peculiarities which this Manuscript possesses, is indeed very great. But, until

---

' This word in large plain gold capitals.

this be acquired, we must be content to accept the qualified decision of those whose opinion has been formed by the examination of existing palæographical materials; and in the following pages these opinions of skilled writers will be found to have been tabulated and placed in apposition, and their teachings considered, and, where possible, accepted.

CHAPTER VI.

IN this, the concluding division of the work, it is proposed to give the correct text of the Athanasian Creed from the Utrecht Psalter, with some account of the theological points raised in connection with the palæography, and the means for accounting for them ; a table of the expressed opinions of many writers of acknowledged authority concerning the date of the Manuscript, notices of some specially conflicting points selected from the great number of such difficulties, remarks as to the probable date of the work, its place of origin, its object, and its actual use, and, finally, the aspect of future solutions likely to be offered, obtained, and received, and the general conclusions derived from the examination of the book.

The text of the Athanasian Creed does not appear to have ever been printed directly and *verbatim* from the Utrecht Psalter, excepting only the transcript, with separated words and extended contractions, in Sir Thomas Hardy's privately printed *Report*. No apology is therefore needed for recording it here line for line, with contractions and other peculiarities, exactly as it is written in the Manuscript itself. The large letters of the first two lines are in the uncial character, as are also the first letters of the paragraphs which stand to the left of the text. The whole of the body of the text is written in the Rustic letters described in a former place.

INCIPITFIDESCATHO *LICAM*
Q *UICŪQUEUULT*
SALUUSESSEANTEOMNIA
OPUSESTUTTENEATCATHO
LICAMFIDEM;
Q UAMNISIQUISQUEINTE
GRAMINUIOLATAMQUE
SERUAUERITABSQUEDU
BIOINAETERNUMPERIBIT;
F IDESAUTEMCATHOLICA.
HAECESTUTUNUMDMIN
TRINITATE.'ETTRINITA
TEMINUNITATEUENERE
MUR;
N EQUECONFUNDENTES
PERSONASNEQUESUBSTAN
TIAMSEPARANTES;
A LIAESTENIMPERSONA
PATRISALIAFILIIALIA
SPSSCI;
S EDPATRISETFILIIETSPSSCI
Col. 2.] UNAESTDIVINITASAE
QUALISGLORIACOAET
NAMAIESTAS;
Q UALISPATERTALISFILIUS

TALISETSPIRITUSSC̄S.

I|NCREATUSPATERINCRE
ATUSFILIUS.'INCREATUS
ETSPIRITUSSC̄S;

I|NMENSUSPATERINMEN
SUSFILIUS.'INMENSUS
ETSPIRITUSSC̄S;

A|ETERNUSPATERAETER
NUSFILIUSAETERNUS
ETSPIRITUSSC̄S;

E|TTAMENNONTRESAETN̄I.'
SEDUNUSAETERNUS;

S|ICUTNONTRESINCREATI
NECTRESINMENSI.'SEDU
NUSINCREATUSETUNUS
INMENSUS;

Col. 3.] *S*|IMILITEROMNIPOTENS
PATER.'OMNIPOTENSFI
LIUSOMNIPOTENSETSP̄SSC̄S;

E|TTAMENNONTRESOMNI
POTENTESSEDUNUSOMP̄S;

I|TAD̄SPATERD̄SFILIUS
D̄SETSPIRITUSSC̄S;

E|TTAMENNONTRESDII
SEDUNUSESTD̄S;

I|TAD̄NSPATER.'D̄NSFILIUS
D̄NSETSPIRITUSSC̄S;

E|TTAMENNONTRESDN̄I.'
SEDUNUSESTD̄NS;

Q|UIASICUTSINGILLATIM
UNAMQUAMQUEPERSONĀ
D̄METD̄N̄MCONFITERIXP̄IA
NAUERITATECONPELLIMUR;

I|TATRESDEOSAUTTRES
DOMINOSDICERE.'CATHO

LICARELIGIONEPROHIBE

MUR;[1]

Col. 4.] P|ATERANULLOESTFACTUS.'

NECCREATUSNECGENITUS

F|ILIUSAPATRESOLOEST.'

NONFACTUS.'NECCREATUS.'

SEDGENITUS;

S|P̄SS̄C̄SPATREETFILIONON

FACTUSNECCREATUSNECGE

NITUSSEDPROCEDENS;

U|NUSERGOPATERNONTRES

PATRESUNUSFILIUSNON

TRESFILIIUNUSP̄SS̄C̄S

NONTRESSP̄SS̄C̄I;

E|TINHACTRINITATENIHIL

PRIUSAUTPOSTERIUS.'NI

HILMAIUSAUTMINUS;

S|EDTOTETRESPERSONAECO

////[2]AETERNAESIBISUNT . ET

COAEQUALES;

I|TAUT̄PEROMNIASICUTIĀ

SUPRADICTUMESTETTRI

NITASINUNITATE.'ETU

NITASINTRINITATEUE

NERANDASIT;

Q|UIUULTERGOSALUUS

ESSE.'ITADETRINITATE

SENTIAT;

S|EDNECESSARIUMEST

ADAETERNAMSALUTE.'

UTĪNCARNATIONEM

QUOQUEDN̄INOSTRI

IH̄UX̄P̄IFIDELITERCRE

---

[1] Originally *prohĭbem^r*, but *m^r* erased and *mur* added below the line.

[2] *Co* here erased, but very evident traces remain.

Col. 5.]

E DAT
STERGOFIDESRECTAUTCRE
DAMUSETCONFITEAMUR.
QUIADN̄SNOSTERIH̄SXP̄S
DIFILIUS.D̄SETHOMOEST;

D S̄ESTEXSUBSTANTIAPATRIS.
ANTESAECULAGENITUS.
ETHOMOESTEXSUBSTAN
TIAMATRISINSAECULO
NATUS;

P ERFECTUSDS̄PERFECTUSHO
MOEXANIMARATIONALI.
ETHUMANACARNESUB
SISTENS;

A EQUALISPATRISECUN
DUMDIVINITATEM.
MINORPATRISECUNDŪ
HUMANITATEM;

Q UILICETD̄SSITETHOMO
NONDUOTAMENSEDU
NUSESTXP̄S;

U NUSAUTEMNONCONUER
SIONEDIVINITATISIN
CARNE.SEDADSUMPTIO
NEHUMANITATISINDŌ;

U NUSOMNINONONCON
FUSIONESUBSTANTIAE
SEDUNITATEPERSONAE;

N AMSICUTANIMARATIO
NALIS.ETCAROUNUSESTHO
MO.ITAD̄SETHOMOUNUS

Col. 6.]

ESTXP̄S
Q UIPASSUSESTPROSALUTA
NOSTRADESCENDITADIN
FEROSTERTIADIERESUR

A | REXITAMORTUIS;
SCENDITADCAELOSSEDIT
ADDEXTERAMDĪPATRIS
OMNIPOTENTIS;

I | NDEUENTURUSIUDICARE
UIUOSETMORTUOS;

A | DCUIUSADUENTUMOM
NESHOMINESRESURGERE
HABENTCUMCORPORIBUS
SUIS;

E | TREDDITURISUNTDEFAC
TISPROPRIISRATIONEM

E | TQUIBONAEGERUNT
IBUNTINUITAMAETERNĀ?
ETQUIMALAINIGNEM
AETERNUM;

H | AECESTFIDESCATHOLICA
QUAMNISIQUISQUEFIDE
LITERFIRMITERQUECREDI
DERITSALUUSESSENONPO
TERIT;

The Latin text of the same Creed, with Anglo-Saxon gloss from the ancient Manuscript Vespasian A. 1, fo. 155, which has been so often alluded to in the preceding pages, is worthy of a place here for comparison with the Utrecht text.

INCIPIT FIDES CATHOLICA.

swa hwa swa wȳle hal wesan beforan eallum
QUICUMQUE UULT SALUUS ESSE . ANTE OMNIA

þearf is ꝥ he nime þæne fulfredan geleafan .
OPUS EST . UT TENEAT catholicam fidem .

þonne nymþe hwylc anwealhne and unwemne
Quam nisi quisq: integram inuiolatamq:

gehealde buton tweon on ecnysse he forwyrð.
seruauerit. absque dubio in aeternum peribit.

geleafa soðlice fulfremed þes is þ anne god
Fides autem catholica haec est. ut unum dm̄

on þrynnysse 7 þrynnysse on annysse we arweorþien.
in trinitate. & trinitatem in unitate venerem͛.

7 na gemyncende hadas 7 na swede
Neque confundentes psonas neque substantiam

syndriende. sum is soðlice had fæderes.
separantes. Alia est enī persona patris.

sum suna ac fæderes 7 suna 7
alia filii alia spc scī. Sed patris & filii &

gastes haliges an is godcundnys gelic
sps̄ scī una est diuinitas aequalis

wuldor efen ece mægen þrym. swylc fæder swylc
gloria coaeterna maiestas. Qualis pater talis

sunu. þæslic 7 gast halig ungesceapen fæder
filius. talis & spc̄ scs̄. Increatus pater.

ungesceapen sunu ungesceapen 7 gast halig.
increatus filius. increatus & spc̄ scs̄.

únámetenlic fæder unametenlic sunu unameten-
Inmensus pater. inmensus filius. inmen-

lic 7 gast halig. ece fæder ece
sus & spc̄ scs̄. Aeternus pater. aeternus

sunu ece 7 gast halig. 7 þeah na
filius. aeternus & spc̄ scs̄. Et tamen non

þrý   ece   ac   an   ece   swa swa   na
tres aeterni: sed unus aeternus . Sicut   non

þrý ungesceapene ne þry unametegude ac   an
tres   increati: · nec tres   inmensi . sed unus

ungesceapen   7   an   unametegod   gelic
increatus   &   unus   inmensus . Similiter

ælmihtig   fæder   ælmihtig   sunu   ælmihtig
omnipotens   pater . omnipotens filius . omnipotens

7   gast halig   7   þeah   na   þrý   ælmihtige
&   spc̄   scs . Et   tamen   non   tres   omnipotentes

ac   an   ælmihtig   swa   fæder   sunu
sed unus omnipotens . Ita ds̄ pater . ds̄ filius .

7   gast   7   þeah   na   þrý   godas   ac
ds̄   &   spc̄   scs . Et tamen non tres   dii . sed

an   is   swa   fæder   sunu   7
unus est ds̄ . Ita dn̄s pater . dn̄s filius : dn̄s &

gast   halig   7   þeah   drihtnes
spc̄   scs . Et tamen non tres   dn̄ı   . sed

is   forþon swa swa synderlice   anne
unus est dn̄s . Quia   sicut   singillatim   unam-

gehwýlcne   had   7   drihten   andettan
·quamq: personam dm̄   &   dn̄m   confiteri

cristenre   soðfæstnýsse we beoð genýd   swa   þrý
xpīana   ueritate   compellimur . Ita   tres

godas oððe drihtnas cweþan of cýriclicre æfestnýsse
deos   aut dominos dicere: catholica   religione

we beoð forboden   fæder   of   nanum   is   geworden
prohibemur . Pater   a   nullo   est   factus .

ne gesceapen ne acenned sunu frā fæder
nec creatus . nec genitus . Filius a patre

anum is na geworden na gesceapen ac
solo est . non factus . nec creatus sed

acenned gast halig frā fæder 7 suna na
genitus . Spc̄ scs̄ a patre & filio non

geworden ne gesceapen ne acenned ac
factus nec creatus . nec genitus sed

forðgewitende an eornostlic fæder na þrӯ
Ꝑcedens . Unus ergo pater non tres

fæderas an sunu na þrӯ suna an gast
patres . unus filius non tres filii . unus spc̄

halig na þrӯ gast halig 7 on þӯsse þrӯnnesse
scs̄ . non tres spc̄ sci̅ . Et in hac trinitate

nanðingc ær oððe æfter nanþing mare
nihil · prius aut posterius . nihil maius

oððe læsse . ac ealle þrӯ hadas efenece
aut minus . Sed tota[e] tres ꝑsonę coaeternę

him sӯnt 7 efenlíce swa ꝥ þurh ealle
sibi sunt . & coaequalès . Ita ut ꝑ omnia

swa swa nu ío bufan gecweden is 7 þrӯnnӯs on
sicut iam supradictum est & trinitas in

annӯsse 7 annӯs on þrӯnnӯsse to arwyrþienne
unitate . & unitas in trinitate ueneranda

sӯ se þe wӯle eornostlice hal wesan swa be
sit . Qui uult ergo saluus esse . ita de

þære þrӯnnӯsse an gӯte ac nӯdbehefe is to
trinitate sentiat . Sed necessarium est ad

þære ecan hælo þ̄ þe flæscnẏsse ƿitodlice
eternā salutem ut incarnationem quoq:

drihtnes ures anragehƿẏlc getrẏƿlice
dm̄ nr̄ ı̄ʜᴜ xp̄ı . unusquisque fideliter

he hihte is eornostlice geleafa riht þ̄
credat . Est ergo fides recta ut

ƿe gelẏfan 7 ƿe andettan . þ̄te drihten hælend
credamus et confiteamur . quia dn̄s n̄r ı̄ʜᴄ

crist godes sunu god samod 7 mann is god
xp̄ᴄ dei filius d̄s pariter¹ & homo est . D̄s

is of sƿede fæderes ær ƿoruldum acenned
est ex substantia patris ante sęcula genitus

7 mann is of sƿede modor on ƿorulda
& homo est ex substantia matris in secula

acenned . fullfremed god . mann of
natus . Perfectus d̄s̄ . p̄fectus homo . ex

saula gesceadƿisre 7 menniscum flæsce ƿuni-
anima rationali & humana carne sub-

gende efenlic fæder æfter godcundnẏsse
sistens . Aequalis patri secundum diuinitatem .

læssa þam fæder æfter menniscnesse se þeah god
minor patre ²ˈ scd̄m humanitatem Qui lic& d̄s

he sẏ 7 mann na þa tu þeahhƿæþere ac an
sit & homo . non duo tamen sed unus

is. crist an soðlice na of gecẏrrednẏsse
est xp̄ᴄ . Unus autem non conuersione

godcundnesse on flæsce ac of afangennẏsse
diuinitatis in carne . sed adsumptione

¹ *Pariter*, omitted, *Utr.*   ² *Patri, Utr.*

mennisclicnesse on gode · an eallunga na of
humanitatis in deo . Unus omnino non con-

ge //// nesse swede · ac of annẏsse hades
fusione substantiae . sed unitate psone .

witodlice swa swa saul gesceadwislic 7 flæsc
Nam sicut anima rationalis & caro

an is mann swa god 7 mann an is crist
unus est homo . Ita ds̄ & homo unus est xp̄c .

se þrowude for hælo urra he adune astah
Qui passus est pro salute[1] nr̄a . descendit

to helwarum þe þriddan dæge he aras fram
ad inferos tertia die resurrexit a

deaþum he astah to heofenum he gesit to
mortuis . Ascendit ad caelos . sed& ad

þære swẏþran god fæderes ælmihtiges þanon
dexteram dei patris omnipotentis inde

he toweard is deman cwice 7 deade to
uenturus est[2] iudicare uiuos & mortuos . Ad

þæs to cẏme ealle menn arisað habbað
cuius aduentum omnes homines resurgere habent

mid limgesiþum his 7 to agẏldenne sẏnt of
cum corporibus suis⫽ & reddituri sunt de

weorcum agenum gescead . 7 þa þe god dẏdan
factis propriis rationem . & qui bona egerunt

hẏ gað on lif ece 7 þa þe soðlice ẏflu
ibunt in uitam aeternam . //// qui uero mala[3]

on fyr ece þis is geleafa cyriclic
in ignem aeternum . Haec est fides catholica

[1] Saluta, Utr.   [2] Est, omitted, Utr.   [3] Et qui mala, Utr.

þonne nẏmðe hwẏlc getrẏwlice 7 trumlice   gelẏfe
quam   nisi   quisque fideliter firmiterque crediderit

  hal   beon   na   he mæg
saluus esse non poterit.

One of the great values of this text, which may be fairly dated along with other additions to the MS. about A.D. 1050, is to show with how few and unimportant variations the ancient Latin form of the Creed, as given by the Utrecht Psalter, has been adhered to in this later copy.

It has already been pointed out that the theological aspect, which the Utrecht Psalter possesses with regard to the occurrence of the Athanasian Creed in its text, is subordinate to the palæographical consideration of the Manuscript. The probable date of the Creed of St. Athanasius, called "the Confession of Faith," "Fides Catholica," and "Symbolum Sancti Athanasii," has been for a long period, and is likely long to remain, a fruitful source of controversy. St. Athanasius, reputed by many to be the author of the Creed, was elected Bishop of Alexandria in A.D. 326, and died in A.D. 373, having spent a great part of his life, and acquired a large share of his reputation, in successfully opposing Arius, or, as he is sometimes called, Arrius, the leader of a sect which denied the divinity of Jesus Christ (A.D. 315-336). By those who thus ascribe the authorship of the Creed to the Saint, it is referred to about the year 340. This controversy between Athanasius and Arius was warmly espoused by the Emperor Constantine, who himself presided at the first General Council of Nicæa or Nice in 'Bithynia, 19th June to 25th August, A.D. 325, wherein the consideration was on the consubstantiality of the Son of God, against the teaching of Arius.   In this Council the Arians were condemned, but their doctrine prevailed in some parts of the East for a time, and found an imperial votary in Constantius II., the third son of the great Constantine, who ruled from A.D. 337 to 361.   Other theologians, however, believe the Creed to be the compilation of Vigilius Tapsensis, an African bishop who flourished in the fifth century, Paulinus of Aquileia,' Pope Anastasius, Hilary of Arles,² Eusebius of Vercelli, or Victricius of Rouen,³ and their principal argument against the authorship of Athanasius rests on the undoubted fact that hitherto no copy of the Creed has been met with in the Manuscripts of the *Opera S. Athanasii*.   Venantius Fortunatus, the well known literary Bishop of Poictiers, is considered to have written the first commentary on the text, in A.D. 570.   The date of the first appearance of the Creed⁴ has been variously fixed from A.D. 336, the middle of the fourth century, to as late as A.D. 642, the beginning or middle of the seventh, and so rare are early copies of it that if it could be shown on palæographical evidence that the Utrecht Psalter belongs to the sixth century, then the text of the Athanasian Creed contained herein would be, as it is by many believed to be, the earliest example of the Creed extant.   To attempt to enter into a history of the Creed would be un-

---

¹ Ffoulkes.   ² Waterland.   ³ Walcott, *Sacred Archæology*, p. 47.
⁴ "Waterland himself preferred a date between A.D. 426 and 430."—Hardy.

necessary here, for many plainly evident reasons, and principally because all that has been adduced in the foregoing pages points irresistibly against the adoption of this extremely early date for the Utrecht Manuscript, and so removes from it the theological importance bestowed upon it by those who would carry back its art and its palæography to so distant a period. Even to enumerate the writers upon the Creed would be impossible, for in one part alone of the Catalogue of the British Museum Library there are two hundred and fifty works upon the sainted Bishop and his Creed. However, among the more prominent writers who have handled the subject mention may be made of Daniel Waterland, whose *Critical History*, first published in 1723, and lately reprinted in 1870 by the Rev. J. R. King, recapitulates the opinion of thirty-two distinguished scholars, from the time of Voss in 1642, to that of Oudin in 1722. And in more recent times the names of Ffoulkes, Hardy, Ommanney, Brewer, and Swainson stand out pre-eminently in the mass of literature to which the controversies which beat around the Athanasian Creed have given rise.

Before we dismiss the subject of the Creed, attention may not inaptly here be directed to an important Manuscript in the British Museum (Add. MS., 24,902), formerly in the library of Baron de Warenghien, and purchased at the sale of his books after his death, in 1855, by M. Claudin. It was purchased for the British Museum in June 1862. This fine Manuscript, of the tenth century, contains at folio 71 a tract, attributed by some, but apparently without proof, except that it is combined with known works of that writer, to St. Augustine. The opening sentence of the treatise has a very interesting bearing on the age of the Athanasian Creed, and is in these words :—

"INCIPIT EXPOSITIO FIDEI CATHOLICAE; Traditur quod a beatissimo ATHANASIO alexandrinę ęcclesię antistite istud fidei opusculum siṭ editum *sicut etiam in veteribus codicibus invenitur pretitulatum.* Quod idcirco tam plano et brevi sermone tunc traditum fuisse cognoscitur ut omnibus catholicis etiam minus eruditis tutamentum defensionis prestaret adversus illam tempestatem quam ventus contrarius hoc est diabolus excitavit per Arrium."

Now the value of the expression *in veteribus codicibus* will be variable in accordance with the opinion that St. Augustine of Hippo, who died in A.D. 430, is the author of this Exposition ; if so, we can hardly imagine a writer of the fourth and fifth centuries would apply such a term to a Manuscript younger than the third or fourth, and this would decide at once the date of the creed, which no one seeks to make older than A.D. 340. If, on the other hand, as is more likely, this "Exposition" is the work of an unknown theological writer who flourished in a century intermediate between the date of Augustine's death (A.D. 430) and of the Manuscript itself wherein it occurs, viz., the tenth century, then we must shift the conversion of the above Latin phrase from *fourth* to sixth, seventh, or eighth century, and so gradually lessen the important value of the quotation.

It may be frankly admitted that the Utrecht Psalter affords little or no clue to the date of the Athanasian Creed. And we yet have to find from palæographical evidences data on which to found a correct and unassailable opinion concerning the true epoch of one of the most important tests of the Christian belief.

During the progress of the enquiry into the history and art of the Utrecht Psalter, many points of detail have been remarked wherein the opinions of the learned appear to converge, and to admit of combination. Such as, for example, the unique forms of the Rustic letters; the antiquity of the tri-columnar arrangement of the text, of the non-division of words, of the punctuation, and of the general appearance of the Manuscript; the early conventionalism of the pictorial art; the great beauty exhibited by the designs; and the high artistic excellence of the conceptions. Again, points have been instanced where, on the other hand, great divergence of skilled opinion has been made manifest. Perhaps in no case has there been more severe literary conflict than in what has been written respecting the initial letter B in the word *Beatus* at the beginning of the first Psalm. Sir Thomas Hardy calls it an Irish letter commonly found in Irish Manuscripts from the sixth to the ninth century,[1] and emphatically rejects its alleged Anglo-Saxon origin, adducing some very powerful arguments in support of this opinion. Mr. Bond, however, considers this letter a strong and decisive proof of a later age, and that it has been erroneously

---

[1] *Report,* p. 21.

stated to be of Irish execution and of early date.
The form of the pattern used in the ornament is
derived from ancient Irish work,[1] "but the whole
design of the letter and colouring, including the
outer edging in red to the gold ground, is unmistakeably of a different, probably the Anglo-Frankish,
school."[2] Mr. Thompson reports that the letter
" belongs to the class which is found in Carlovingian
Manuscripts of the ninth century though rather
simpler in form." In reply to these opinions Sir
Thomas Hardy[3] insists upon the well known practice
of inserting initials, and other embellishments, long
after the completion of Manuscript texts; and
demurs to the employment of the term Anglo-
Frankish, although it would naturally seem to allude
to the intercourse between England and the Franks,
when various persons skilled in arts connected with
the production of Manuscripts passed from one
region to the other, especially as we know that the
illustrious Englishman Alchuine[4] was the tutor of
the children of Charlemagne, *circ.* A.D. 782. If this
great light of theological and literary learning
gathered around him at Tours a circle of English
students,[5] these would possibly form the Anglo-
Frankish school alluded to by Mr. Bond. Professor
Westwood appears to refer the letter under consideration to the Anglo-Saxon style. But unless it
can be shown that the form of the letter requires

---

[1] "It was from Ireland that the Anglo-Saxons learned the art of illumination."
Hill's *English Monasticism*, p. 290.

[2] *Report*, p. 3.   [3] *Further Report*, pp. 25, 26.

[4] Born about A.D. 735 at York; died at Tours in 804.

[5] See Hardy's *Catalogue*, Vol. I., p. 503.

imperatively to be attributed to an earlier date than the eighth or ninth century, a fact as yet by no means satisfactorily proved, the value of its evidence with regard to the age of the text is practically of no account.

It will be interesting to notice the principal opinions, concerning the date of the Manuscript, that have been placed on record by the foremost writers and describers of its contents.

The writer of the *elenchus* contained in the first leaf of the Psalter, as given above at page 190, considers that it appears to attain in antiquity to the times of the Emperor Valentinian.[1] There were three emperors of this name, who ruled from A.D. 364 to 375; 375 to 392; and 425 to 455, and it is not easy to say to which the reference relates.

Archbishop Ussher considers it to belong to the age of Pope Gregory the Great,[2] who occupied the See of Rome from A.D. 590 to 604.

Waterland appears to endorse Ussher's opinion.[3]

Gustave Haenel, whose knowledge of ancient Manuscripts has been always considered very extensive, assigns it to the sixth century,[4] in his *Catalogi*, published in 1829.

Baron Van Westreenen van Tiellandt, in his *Naspeuringen* of 1833, says, "All the representations . . . . are evidently derived from the times of the Low Roman Empire, in which not a shadow of the Gothic[5] occurs." He says, with regard to the

---

[1] See page 140.　　　[2] See pages 130, 133.　　　[3] See page 133.

[4] See pages 126, 130, 133.

[5] Cf. "They are in fact Gothic in their style." Mr. Bond's *Report*, p. 3.

writing, that "everything concurs to justify the estimation of Haenel, who places it in the sixth century, as an intermediate epoch." "The Psalter may date just as much from the end of the fifth or the beginning of the seventh, as from the sixth century . . . . The writing seems to be of somewhat later date."

Professor H. J. Royaards concurs in the opinion expressed by Baron Van Westreenen van Tiellandt in 1833, as already mentioned.[1]

Professor Westwood, in his *Archæological Notes* of 1859, considers that "a date not more recent than the sixth or seventh century[2] ought to be assigned to the Manuscript," but under certain circumstances he would "have no difficulty in referring the text to the fifth or sixth century," yet the initial letter of the first Psalm "would bring it to the seventh or eighth[3] at the earliest."

The notice of the facsimiles acquired by A. D. Schinkel,[4] and sold at the Hague in 1864, attributes the drawings to the seventh century.

Professor Westwood's great work of *Facsimiles*, in 1868, appears, from the uncertain expression upon the plate, to waver between assigning the date of the Psalter to the sixth or the ninth century.[5]

P. J. Vermuelen, in his report of 1872 to the University of Utrecht, has "always assigned it to the eighth or ninth century,[6] A.D. 750-850."

Sir Thomas Hardy, in his *First Report*,[7] of 1872,

[1] See page 125. [2] See page 134.
[3] See page 135, and Sir Thomas Hardy's *Report*, p. 35 note, where the ninth century is even mentioned.
[4] See page 123. [5] See pages 136, 137. [6] See page 130. [7] Page 36.

" with the experience of half a century, believes it to have been written at the latter end of the sixth century." "But the age of the illustrations probably belongs to the end of the fifth or beginning of the sixth century." [1]

Mr. B. O'Looney, an Irish scholar, attributes part of the illuminated work to the early sixth century. [2]

J. Arntz, in his essay described at pages 141-144, considers "the Psalter" not older than the seventh century." [3]

The theological controversialist, Mr. Ffoulkes, [4] is willing to admit that the Psalter was transcribed in the fifth century, but that the pieces following the Psalms must have been written during, or after, the ninth century, the period in which, as he asserts, the Athanasian Creed was concocted. [5] This statement is so manifestly unsatisfactory that it is unnecessary here to discuss it.

Dean Stanley's Collection of *Reports* recapitulates the opinions of the Reporters thus :—

Mr. Bond " concludes [6] that it is not earlier than the end of the eighth century, and is disposed to assign it to the ninth."

Mr. Thompson gathers negatively " that [7] it cannot be assigned to an earlier age than the close of the eighth century."

The Rev. H. O. Coxe sees no reason to conclude that it was written before the commencement of the ninth century. [8]

---

[1] See page 140: *Report*, page 24.   [2] See page 140.   [3] Page 143.

[4] In his letter to the *Times*, 17 Feb., 1874.   [5] Hardy, *Further Report*, p. 50.

[6] See page 148.   [7] *Report*, p. 5.   [8] See page 150.

The Rev. S. S. Lewis would not assign it to an earlier date than the ninth century.[1]

Sir M. D. Wyat ascribes it to about the middle of the eighth century.[2]

Professor Westwood modifies his opinions delivered in 1859 and 1868,[3] and refers the Manuscript to the eighth or ninth century at the earliest.[4]

The Rev. Canon Swainson gives two dates, one that " the volume cannot be much earlier than the middle of the ninth century (*i.e.*, A.D. 850), and may be considerably later ; " the other that " the contents could not have been arranged, nor could the Psalter have been written long before the year 800.[5]

M. Leopold Delisle, in his remarks upon the progress of palæographical study, in 1875, quoted in the introduction to this work,[6] incidentally records his opinion upon the age of the Utrecht Psalter as " un des plus curieux monuments de la calligraphie et du dessin au VIIIe ou au IXe siècle."

By comparing the opinions of the foregoing quotations, we may see that the author of the *Elenchus* ascribes to the Utrecht Psalter the oldest date, that of the Valentinians, or fourth and fifth century :—

Mr. Ffoulkes, the fifth century.

Sir Thomas Hardy, the fifth or sixth for the art ; the end of the sixth for the palæography.

Mr. O'Looney, the early part of the sixth century.

G. Haenel, Van Westreenen van Tiellandt, and Royaards, the sixth century.

---

[1] See page 150.   [2] See page 151.   [3] See pages 134, 136, 137.
[4] See page 151.   [5] *Report*, pages 11, 13; see page 153.   [6] Pages xi.-xiv.

Professor Westwood varies between the sixth, seventh, eighth, and ninth centuries.

Ussher and Waterland, the end of the sixth or beginning of the seventh.

Schinkel and Arntz, the seventh century.

Mr. Thompson not earlier than the eighth century.

Sir Matthew D. Wyatt, the middle of the eighth.

H. Vermuelen, the middle of the eighth to the middle of the ninth.

Mr. Bond, the end of the eighth to the beginning of the ninth.

M. Delisle, the eighth or ninth.

Mr. Coxe, the beginning of the ninth century.

Canon Swainson, not long before 800; and the middle of the ninth century.

Mr. Lewis, not earlier than the ninth century.

The only real data, whereby a correct view of the period in which the text of the Psalter was written can be acquired, are the styles of the handwritings which compose that text. And it has been shown that the Rustic character was employed solely, and to the exclusion of all others, in single entire Manuscripts, as late as the sixth century, and was in its prime at that time, as exhibited by the Manuscripts discussed in the early pages of this work; while to the seventh and eighth centuries belong the mixture of Rustics and uncials seen in several instances, where the letters are even stronger and more naturally made than those in the Utrecht Psalter. We may not, therefore, date the Manuscript older than the beginning of the eighth century, a period when, as is well known, the employment of these characters was passing through a transitional stage. In this opinion, which is upheld by five, if not six, important members out of the fourteen tabulated above, great latitude must be allowed, because of the unique nature of the book, to which there is no compeer, in the points of similar art and similar writing, to be found within the whole wide range of European libraries.

It is not an insignificant fact that this date of the early eighth century, having been arrived at on purely palæographical reasons, is corroborated, in a remarkable manner, by what has been laid down already with regard to the history of the book in connection with Canterbury and Archbishop Bercwald. We shall not be exceeding probabilities if we choose to imagine that the Manuscript was prepared, not far from England at any rate, under this prelate's direction, for a royal owner, or even for himself, by an ancient master of the penman's craft, and that it was embellished by the hands and thoughts and feelings of some one or more, who formed their ideas on what to them were ancient and classical models, and who yet at the same time breathed into their pictures, thus defined in the abstract, and thus classically conventional, details of expression which to one body of critics appear to be Byzantine, Syrian, and Alexandrian, and to another body Frankish and Anglo-Frankish, while they really are in a great measure common to the whole cycle of Western pictorial representations at this early period.

That we may observe how this so called Byzantine, or Oriental element lingered in the West, even in England, for long after the latest era to which any writer has ventured to ascribe the art-work we have analyzed in the foregoing pages, let us glance for a moment at a priceless Manuscript written and illustrated, without a shadow of doubt, by Anglo-Saxon hands in the first half of the eleventh century. The Cottonian Manuscript, Claudius B IV., in the British Museum, contains the celebrated Ælfric's Anglo-Saxon Paraphrase of the Pentateuch and Joshua. In this Manuscript, which must be dated three hundred years nearer to our own days than the Utrecht Psalter, one sees the same classical treatment of the sun, as a figure, half length, holding a flaming torch, and set in a circle or medallion (folio 3); trees with truncated branches and close cut heads (folio 8); masonry of ashlar-work with alternate joints as it is found in almost every page of the Psalter (folio 9); imbricated roofs with pavonaceous and other tilings (folios 21 b, 22, 23 b, etc.); curtains twisted in a peculiar manner round the columns of a temple (folio 138); scroll-like door-hinges (folio 36 b); concave shields with central spike (folio 142); pillars with egg and fillet carving, foliated capitals, and circular dome roofs (folio 39 b); crowns with the triple fleur-de-lys (folios 22, 35, 37 b); and tents more elaborate, certainly, but not very unlike those described above at Psalm XXVI. (folios 9 b, 17 b, 18, 21 b, 23, 24): while out of many Anglo-Saxon groups which correspond with those in the Utrecht drawings we should especially observe those of the births of Jewish personages, the reclining mothers, and the attendants washing the newly born infants in large bowls or ceramic vessels of great capacity and various outline, as seen at folios 28, 35, 36, etc., which must have been derived from an extensive acquaintance with the styles which led to the production of the corresponding drawings in the Utrecht Manuscript.

And here must be closed the present investigations into the history, the palæography, and the art of an ancient relic of our Christian faith, which reaches back considerably more than half the way towards the epoch of the establishment of that faith itself. What has been said throughout this enquiry will, it is hoped, be taken not as from a critic, but from an earnest enquirer, and from a student whose researches into the many and intricate fields that this book open to us may haply guide others, who approach it as he has done, hereafter to a more correct and complete knowledge of the true position occupied by the book in the series of palæographic vestiges to which it forms so important and so interesting an adornment.

"Our sweetest songs are those that tell of saddest thought,"

and in like manner the sweet music discoursed by the Hebrew poet to the rhythmic cadences of psaltery and harp, and lute and timbrel, in the bygone days of Jewish culture and Jewish power, strikes upon our ears to day as we read it in the light of this Manuscript, not without some still small voice of saddest thought to think that those who wrote and drew and painted the various parts that make up this enigmatic work have left no record of their being, not a single word which, as a magic spell, might guide us to uncover the mysteries which enwrap every page we have scanned. These secrets of an undetermined age and region demand patience and toleration rather than indignation, on the part of those who would successfully expound them. It is not to be doubted that sufficient means exist for this work, but they have yet to be brought to light; and an era which has been so fertile in the reading of the "records of the past," in the decipherment of dead languages, and the recovery of a clay literature corroborative of Old Testament History can hardly pass away without rendering up to us new and fresh material with which the ancient copy of the Book of Psalms in the Library of Utrecht University may hereafter be compared more closely and collated more systematically than existing Manuscript remains have hitherto allowed us to do.

By the same Author:

(UNIFORM WITH THE HISTORY OF THE UTRECHT PSALTER).

(*In progress.*)

———

ANCIENT PSALTERS

PRESERVED IN THE

BRITISH MUSEUM.

———

Being an account of the principal Manuscripts of the BOOK OF PSALMS contained in the *Harley, Cotton, Egerton, Additional,* and other Collections in the National Library. With notices of the chief points of interest connected with their pictorial and palæographic art, their history, and their importance.

SB

SAMUEL BAGSTER AND SONS,

15, PATERNOSTER ROW, LONDON.

ARCHAIC CLASSICS.

ASSYRIAN GRAMMAR.

An Elementary Grammar and Reading Book of the Assyrian Language, in the Cuneiform Character: containing the most complete Syllabary yet extant, and which will serve also as a Vocabulary of both Accadian and Assyrian. By Rev. A. H. SAYCE, M.A.

Quarto, Cloth. Price 7s. 6d.

INSCRIPTIONS OF ESARHADDON,

King of Assyria, B.C. 681-668. Translated, with Text and Commentary, for the use of Students. By W. BOSCAWEN.

In the Press.

EGYPTIAN GRAMMAR.

An Elementary Manual of the Egyptian Language: with an interlineary Reading Book: in the Hieroglyphic Character. In two Parts. Part I. Grammar. By P. LE PAGE RENOUF.

Quarto, Cloth. Price 7s. 6d.

Part II. Reading Book. *Shortly to follow.*

EXERCISE SHEETS:

Prepared to enable the Student to test his progress by translating a short passage from some well-known Text.

On Writing Paper. Price 2d. each.

SAMUEL BAGSTER AND SONS, LONDON.

RECORDS OF THE PAST.

BEING ENGLISH TRANSLATIONS OF

THE ASSYRIAN AND EGYPTIAN MONUMENTS.

Published under the sanction of the Society of Biblical Archæology.

Edited by S. BIRCH, LL.D.

Crown octavo, Cloth. Price, each Vol., 3s. 6d.

VOL. I. ASSYRIAN TEXTS, 1.

Inscription of Rimmon-Nirari; Monolith Inscription of Samas-Rimmon; Babylonian Exorcisms; Private Will of Sennacherib; Assyrian Private Contract Tablets; Assyrian Astronomical Tablets; Assyrian Calendar; Tables of Assyrian Weights and Measures. By Rev. A. H. Sayce, M.A.

Inscription of Khammurabi; Bellino's Cylinder of Sennacherib; Taylor's Cylinder of Sennacherib; Legend of the Descent of Ishtar. By H. Fox Talbot, F.R.S.

Annals of Assurbanipal (Cylinder A). By George Smith.

Behistun Inscription of Darius. By Sir Henry Rawlinson, K.C.B., D.C.L.

Lists of further Texts, Assyrian and Egyptian. Selected by George Smith and P. Le Page Renouf.

VOL. II. EGYPTIAN TEXTS, 1.

Inscription of Una; Statistical Tablet; Tablet of Thothmes III.; Battle of Megiddo; Inscription of Amen-em-heb. By S. Birch, LL.D.

Instructions of Amen-em-hat. By G. Maspero.

The Wars of Rameses II. with the Khita. By Prof. E. L. Lushington.

Inscription of Pianchi Mer-Amon. By Rev. F. C. Cook, M.A., Canon of Exeter.

Tablet of Newer-Hotep. By Paul Pierret.

Travels of an Egyptian. By François Chabas.

The Lamentations of Isis and Nephthys. By P. J. De Horrack.

Hymn to Amen Ra; The Tale of the Doomed Prince. By C. W. Goodwin, M.A.

The Tale of the Two Brothers. By P. Le Page Renouf.

Egyptian Calendar; Table of Dynasties; Egyptian Measures and Weights.

Lists of further Texts, Assyrian and Egyptian. Selected by George Smith and P. Le Page Renouf.

VOL. III. ASSYRIAN TEXTS, 2.

Early History of Babylonia. By George Smith.

Tablet of Ancient Accadian Laws; Synchronous History of Assyria and Babylonia; Kurkh Inscription of Shalmaneser; An Accadian Liturgy; Babylonian Charms. By Rev. A. H. Sayce, M.A.

Annals of Assur-nasir-pal. By Rev. J. M. Rodwell, M.A.

Inscription of Esarhaddon; Second Inscription of Esarhaddon; Sacred Assyrian Poetry. By H. F. Talbot, F.R.S.

List of further Texts.

SAMUEL BAGSTER AND SONS, LONDON.

VOL. IV. EGYPTIAN TEXTS, 2.

Inscription of Anebni; Inscription of Aahmes; Obelisk of the Lateran; Tablet of 400 years; Invasion of Egypt by the Greeks in the Reign of Menephtah; Dirge of Menephtah; Possessed Princess; Rosetta Stone. By S. Birch, LL.D.

Obelisk of Rameses II.; Hymn to Osiris. By François Chabas.

Treaty of Peace between Rameses II. and the Hittites; Neapolitan Stele; Festal Dirge of the Egyptians. By C. W. Goodwin, M.A.

Tablet of Ahmes; Inscription of Queen Madsenen. By Paul Pierret.

Stele of the Dream; Stele of the Excommunication. By G. Maspero

Hymn to the Nile. By Rev. F. C. Cook.

Book of Respirations. By P. J. De Horrack.

Tale of Setnau. By P. Le Page Renouf.

List of further Texts.

VOL. V. ASSYRIAN TEXTS, 3.

Legend of the infancy of Sargina I.; Inscription of Nabonidus; Inscription of Darius at Nakshi-Rustam; War of the Seven Evil Spirits against Heaven. By H. F. Talbot, F.R.S.

Inscription of Tiglath-Pileser I. By Sir Henry Rawlinson, K.C.B., D.C.L., etc.

Black Obelisk Inscription of Shalmaneser II.; Accadian Hymn to Istar; Tables of Omens. By Rev. A. H. Sayce, M.A.

Inscription of Tiglath-Pileser II. Inscription of Nebuchadnezzar; Inscription of Neriglissir. By Rev. J. M. Rodwell, M.A.

Early History of Babylonia, Part II. By George Smith.

List of further Texts.

VOL. VI. EGYPTIAN TEXTS, 3.

Sepulchral Inscription of Ameni; The Conquests in Asia; Egyptian Magical Text. By S. Birch, LL.D.

Great Harris Papyrus, Part I. By Professor Eisenlohr and S. Birch, LL.D.

Inscription of Aahmes, son of Abana. By P. Le Page Renouf.

Letter of Panbesa; Hymns to Amen; The Story of Saneha. By C. W. Goodwin, M.A.

Stele of the Coronation; Stele of King Horsiatef. By G. Maspero.

The Inscription of the Governor Nes-hor. By Paul Pierret.

Inscription of the Destruction of Mankind. By Edouard Naville.

The Song of the Harper. By Ludwig Stern.

The Tale of the Garden of Flowers. By François Chabas.

List of further Texts.

Succeeding Volumes, in the Press.

Multæ terricolis linguæ, cœlestibus una.

LONDON:—SAMUEL BAGSTER AND SONS,
15, PATERNOSTER ROW.

THE ASSYRIAN EPONYM CANON:

Containing Translations of the Documents, and an Account of the Evidence, on the Comparative Chronology of the Assyrian and Jewish Kingdoms, from the Death of Solomon to Nebuchadnezzar.

By the late GEORGE SMITH, of the Department of Oriental Antiquities, British Museum.

Octavo, Cloth extra. Price 9s.

WORKS BY W. R. COOPER, F.R.A.S., M.R.A.S.,
Secretary of the Society of Biblical Archæology.

AN ARCHAIC DICTIONARY,

Biographical, Historical, and Mythological; from the Egyptian, Assyrian, and Etruscan Monuments and Papyri.

Cloth extra, 15s.

THE RESURRECTION OF ASSYRIA.

A Lecture delivered in Renfield Presbyterian Church, Glasgow.

Paper Wrapper. Price 1s. 6d.

THE HEROINES OF THE PAST.

A Lecture delivered at the Working Mens' Institute, Leighton Buzzard.

Paper Wrapper. Price 1s. 6d.

EGYPT AND THE PENTATEUCH.

An Address to the Members of the Open Air Mission.

Paper Wrapper. Price 2s.

THE SERPENT MYTHS OF THE ANCIENT EGYPTIANS.

Paper Wrapper. Price 4s.

ANCIENT CHALDEAN MAGIC.

Translated from the French of M. FRANÇOIS LENORMANT, with Notes and References by the English Editor.

Nearly ready.

THE MONUMENTAL HISTORY OF EGYPT.

Rede Lecture, delivered in the Senate House of the University of Cambridge. By S. BIRCH, LL.D., etc.

Paper Wrapper. Price 1s. 6d.

PHILOLOGICAL LECTURES

On the Assyrian Language, delivered to the Students of the Archaic Classes. By Rev. A. H. SAYCE, M.A., Deputy Professor of Comparative Philology, Oxford.

In the Press.

A REVISION OF THE HEBREW TEXT OF THE OLD TESTAMENT.

Synopsis of Readings revised from critical sources; being an attempt to present a purer and more correct Text than the "Received" one of Van der Hooght, by the aid of the best existing materials: with the principal Various Readings found in MSS., ancient Versions, Jewish Books and Writers, Parallels, Quotations, etc. By SAMUEL DAVIDSON, D.D. Octavo, Cloth, price 10s. 6d.

THE HEADS OF HEBREW GRAMMAR.

Containing all the Principles needed by a Learner; with a Series of Hebrew Paradigms. By S. P. TREGELLES, LL.D. Foolscap octavo, Cloth, price 3s.

A PRACTICAL HEBREW GRAMMAR.

The Grammar with progressive constructive Exercises to every Rule; and a Reading Book. By Dr. J. ROBERT WOLFE. Post octavo, Cloth, price 6s.

A POCKET HEBREW-ENGLISH LEXICON.

The Lexicon contains all the Hebrew and Chaldee words in the Old Testament Scriptures, with their meanings in English, and combining the alphabetical with the radical arrangement of the words. Foolscap octavo, Cloth, price 4s. 6d.

THE HEXAPLAR PSALTER.

The Book of Psalms in Hebrew; the Greek of the LXX.; the Vulgate Latin; Jerome's Hebrew-Latin; the English Liturgical Version; and the English Authorised Version: in six Parallel Columns. Quarto, Cloth, price 15s.

LONDON: SAMUEL BAGSTER AND SONS.

THE HEBREW STUDENT'S MANUAL.

Containing: Recommendations to the Learner; a Hebrew Grammar; a series of Hebrew Reading Lessons, analysed; the Book of Psalms, with interlineary translation—the construction of every Hebrew word being clearly indicated, and the root of each distinguished by the use of hollow and other types; and a Hebrew and English Lexicon, containing all the Hebrew and Chaldee words in the Old Testament Scriptures. Foolscap octavo, Cloth, price 10s.

THE ANALYTICAL HEBREW LEXICON.

A Lexicon in the ordinary sense of supplying the various meanings of the various roots; a Dictionary of every derivative and modification of every root, in alphabetical order, with analysis; a storehouse of the anomalies of the language, carefully arranged and referred to from all parts of the work; and a Concordance of the least easily understood words. By Professor B. DAVIDSON. Quarto, Cloth, price £1 5s.

GESENIUS'S HEBREW GRAMMAR;

Enlarged and improved by Professor E. RODIGER. With a Hebrew Reading Book, Quarto, Cloth, price 7s. 6d.

With LLOYD'S ANALYSIS OF GENESIS I-XI., price 10s. 6d.

GESENIUS'S HEBREW LEXICON:

Comprising an Address to the Student; Table of Alphabets; the Lexicon; and English-Hebrew Index. By S. P. TREGELLES, LL.D. Quarto, Cloth, price £1 1s.

GESENIUS'S HEBREW LEXICON. ABRIDGED EDITION.
Small Quarto. (*In the Press.*)

HEBREW READING LESSONS;

With Introductory Notice. The first four chapters of the Book of Genesis, and the eighth chapter of the Proverbs, with a Grammatical Praxis, and an Interlineary Translation. By S. P. TREGELLES, LL.D. Foolscap octavo, Cloth, price 3s. 6d.

THE HEBREW BIBLE OF THE POLYGLOT SERIES.

The Hebrew Text after Van der Hooght, with the *Keri* and *Chetib*. Together with the Various Readings of the Samaritan Pentateuch. Foolscap octavo, Cloth, price 10s.

HEBREW AND ENGLISH, OLD TESTAMENT, INTERPAGED.
Foolscap octavo, Cloth, price 18s.

With GREEK and ENGLISH NEW TESTAMENT, £1 4s.

AN ANALYSIS OF THE FIRST ELEVEN CHAPTERS OF GENESIS:

With copious References to Gesenius's Hebrew Grammar. By the Rev. JOHN LLOYD, M.A. Quarto, Boards, price 3s. 6d.

With GESENIUS'S HEBREW GRAMMAR, price 10s. 6d.

AN ANALYSIS OF THE BOOK OF ECCLESIASTES:

With reference to the Hebrew Grammar of Gesenius, and with Notes critical and explanatory. To which is added the Book of Ecclesiastes, in Hebrew and English in parallel columns. By the Rev. JOHN LLOYD, M.A. Quarto, Cloth, 7s. 6d.

With GESENIUS'S HEBREW GRAMMAR, price 15s.

A NEW HEBREW CONCORDANCE.

A Concordance of the Hebrew and Chaldee Scriptures. Revised and corrected by Professor B. DAVIDSON. Royal octavo, Cloth, price £3 3s.; Turkey morocco plain, price £4 4s.

A METHODIZATION OF THE HEBREW VERBS.

This original plan includes the verbs, regular and irregular. By the Rev. TRESHAM D. GREGG, D.D. Octavo, Boards, price 2s. 6d.

LONDON: SAMUEL BAGSTER AND SONS.

AN INTERLINEARY HEBREW-ENGLISH PSALTER.

The Book of Psalms in Hebrew, printed so as to distinguish the servile letters from the radical; with a closely literal English Translation under each word. Foolscap octavo, Cloth, price 5s.

HEBREW PSALMS,

Without Points. Foolscap octavo, price 1s.

HEBREW AND ENGLISH PSALMS.

The Hebrew Text is that of Van der Hooght, carefully reprinted from the edition A.D. 1705. The English Version is the Authorised Translation according to the edition of A.D. 1611. Arranged in Parallel Columns. Foolscap octavo, Cloth, price 4s.

THE STUDY OF THE HEBREW VOWEL POINTS.

A Series of Exercises in very large Hebrew Type, printed upon writing-paper, with space between the lines for the addition in manuscript of the Vowel Points and Accents. Quarto. Nos. 1 and 2. Price 4d. each.

CHALDEE READING LESSONS.

The whole of the Biblical Chaldee, with a Grammatical Praxis, and an Interlineary Translation. A series of Chaldee Paradigms. Foolscap octavo, Cloth, price 3s. 6d.

THE HEBREW LANGUAGE.

The History and Characteristics of the Hebrew Language, including improved renderings of select passages in our Authorised Translation of the Old Testament. By HENRY CRAIK. Crown octavo, Cloth, price 3s. 6d.

PRINCIPIA HEBRAICA.

The Principles of Hebrew Grammar; an easy Introduction to the Hebrew Language, in twenty-four large folio Tables, which contain the Interpretation of all the Hebrew and Chaldee words, both Primitives and Derivatives, contained in the Old Testament Scriptures. By HENRY CRAIK. Folio, Cloth, price 10s. 6d.

THE ENGLISHMAN'S HEBREW AND CHALDEE CONCORDANCE OF THE OLD TESTAMENT:

Being an attempt at a Verbal Connection between the Original and the English Translation; with Indexes, a List of the Proper Names, and their occurrences, etc. Third Edition. Two Volumes. Royal octavo, Cloth, price £3 13s. 6d.

THE HEBRAIST'S VADE MECUM:

A first attempt at a Complete Verbal Index to the Contents of the Hebrew and Chaldee Scriptures. Arranged according to Grammar: the occurrences in full. Demy octavo, price 15s.

THE HEBREW PENTATEUCH.

The five Books of Moses in Hebrew, with Points. Foolscap octavo, Cloth, price 2s. 6d.

THE PROPHECY OF JOEL.

The Hebrew Text of Joel printed metrically, with a new English Translation and Critical Notes. By the Rev. JOSEPH HUGHES, B.A. Foolscap octavo, price 2s. 6d.

BIBLIA SACRA POLYGLOTTA.

THE MODERN POLYGLOT BIBLE IN EIGHT LANGUAGES.

TWO VOLUMES, FOLIO.

THE BIBLIA SACRA POLYGLOTTA is invaluable to the Biblical Student, who can, by its aid, compare with facility the various Texts of the Bible. Every Clergyman also, will find it a great addition to his library.

The advantages offered by this Polyglot Bible are great. Unlike the older Polyglots, it addresses itself primarily to the Interpretation of Scripture. It gives under one simultaneous view the Hebrew Text, the two ancient indispensable versions, the Septuagint and the Vulgate, and a series of the best European translations.

The older Polyglots, the Complutensian, the Antwerp, the Paris, and the London, are inaccessible to most people, and many would find a difficulty in using them; but this Modern Polyglot is at once accessible, convenient, moderate in price, and of easy practical use. The study of Hebrew is spreading every day, the Greek is familiar to most Biblical Students, while the Latin and European Versions are more or less universally understood.

Bishop Coverdale says in the prologue of his Bible, "Sure I am that there cometh more knowledge and understanding of the Scriptures by their sundry translations, than by all the glosses of our sophistical doctors."

The NEW TESTAMENT is presented on a precisely similar plan, with a Supplement containing the Peschito Syriac Version.

This Polyglot also contains Tables of the Various Readings of the Hebrew, the Septuagint, the Greek, and Syriac New Testaments.

HIC LIBER CONTINET:—Prolegomena in Biblia Polyglotta; Biblia Hebraica, ex editione celeberrima Everardi Van der Hooght, quæ A.D. 1705 lucem vidit, punctis vocalibus et accentibus instructa; Versionem Græcam Septuaginta Seniorum, juxta exemplar Vaticanum, a Cardinali Carafa in lucem emissum; Novum Testamentum Græcum juxta textum, ut aiunt, Receptum; Biblia Sacra Vulgatæ Editionis Sixti V. et Clementis VIII. jussu recognita atque edita; Versionem Anglicanam, lectionibus marginalibus, numerisque loca parallela indicantibus adornatam; Versionem Germanicam a Martino Luthero; Versionem Gallicam a Johanne Frederico Ostervald; Versionem Italianam a Giovanni Diodati; Versionem Hispanicam a Patre Scio; Novum Testamentum Hebraicum a Gulielmo Greenfield; et in Appendice, Syrorum Novi Testamenti Versionem, quam Peschito nuncupant, juxta exemplar Viennense a Johanne Alberto Widmanstadio, A. D. 1555 typis mandatum, literis Syriacis atque punctis vocalibus instructam, cumque collatione editionis quam Societas ad Biblia Sacra evulganda instituta in lucem emisit; Pentateuchum Hebræo-Samaritanum juxta Kennicotti editionem; Varias Lectiones in Versionem LXX. ex editione Grabii; Lectionis Varietates in Novum Testamentum Græcum, e notis Griesbachii ductas.

The Work is handsomely printed in Two Volumes, Crown folio, and is issued ready bound in best morocco Roxburgh, £8 8s.; or bound in Cloth, £6 6s.; also in 12 Parts, stiff wrapper, 10s. 6d. each.

Lightning Source UK Ltd.
Milton Keynes UK
26 November 2010

163500UK00006B/87/P